BIBLE CHRONOLOGY

The Two Great Divides

A DEFENSE OF THE UNBROKEN *BIBLICAL* CHRONOLOGY FROM ADAM TO CHRIST

J.A. Moorman

Copyright © 2010 by Bible For Today Press
All Rights Reserved
Printed in the United States of America

ISBN 978-1-56848-076-3

All Scripture quotes are from the King James Bible except those verses compared and then the source is identified.

No part of this work may be reproduced without the expressed consent of the publisher, except for brief quotes, whether by electronic, photocopying, recording, or information storage and retrieval systems.

Address All Inquiries To:
Bible For Today Press
900 Park Avenue
Collingswood, New Jersey, 08108
U.S.A.

Web: www.biblefortoday.org
E-mail: BFT@BibleForToday.org
Phone: 856-854-4452
Orders: 1-800-John 10:9
FAX: 856-854-2464

BIBLE FOR TODAY #2934

Formatted by **TOP**:
The Old Paths Publications, Inc.
Directors: H. D. & Patricia Williams
142 Gold Flume Way
Cleveland, GA 30528
Web: www.theoldpathspublications.com
Email: TOP@theoldpathspublications.com
Jeremiah 6:16

1.0

DEDICATION

In appreciation of two students of Bible Chronology who stood as lone voices in addressing the two great chronological divides (only Anstey addressed both), this book is gratefully dedicated. The first is Sir Edward Denny who in 1849 demonstrated the solution to the Crux Chronologorum in his work, Forgiveness Seventy and Sevenfold. Denny, who received a knighthood, was associated with the Brethren movement in Britain. In dealing with the chronology from the Exodus to the Temple, Denny set out the reality of passages like Deuteronomy 6:23, He brought us out that He might bring us in. The ultimate purpose of the Exodus was worship in the Temple; and whatever may have hindered that goal was in the final Divine reckoning ignored!

The second and better-known work is The Romance of Bible Chronology (1913) by Martin Anstey, a close friend of G. Campbell Morgan. Anstey showed convincingly from Scripture and history that the Seventy Weeks must be counted from near the time Daniel received the prophecy rather than 90 years later.

While there will be a number of disagreements with these two authors, I am thankful for the inestimable contribution they have made to the study of Bible Chronology.

"And he brought us out from thence, that he might bring us in, to give us the land which he sware unto our fathers."
(Deuteronomy 6:23)

PREFACE

The Bible's chronology as with all else in Scripture is given and preserved by the Holy Spirit. Chronology gives the Bible its form, its structure, its actuality. The Bible can be tested in all points, and so in the subject before us it can be tested as regards *time*. Our study here presents the view that the Bible (the King James Version translated from the Masoretic and Received Texts) gives a complete, unbroken chronology of the years from the creation of Adam to the Death of Christ on the Cross. There are no gaps. The Bible and the Bible alone gives the complete chronology of the years from the First Adam to the Last Adam (I Corinthians 15:45). The Bible is not dependent in any way upon secular chronology to "fill in" any supposed gaps.

The above may be taken for granted among Bible believers, but the actual case is in fact substantially different. The standard Bible chronology followed for many generations presupposes a gap in the Biblical Record of about 90 years and seeks to fill that gap by resorting to secular history. This supposed gap lies at the beginning of the famous *Seventy Weeks of Daniel*. By following the "conventional wisdom" of standard chronology this great portion in the Book of Daniel is dislodged from its place as the primary cornerstone of history, chronology and prophecy.

Another chronological problem of an entirely different nature, and indeed one that has been called the Bible's *Crux Chronologorum* is also dealt with in this book. The period concerned is that from the Exodus to the building of the Temple and involves some 130 years.

I would like to express special thanks to Clive Spencer-Bentley, whose studies in chronology provided part of the incentive to undertake this project, and who also typed the initial manuscript. Inestimable help was received through access to the British Museum and British Library here in London. The book was written over a seven-year period from 1993-1999, and amidst a busy schedule of tract evangelism, pastoring and missionary work in London.

The Authorized Version is the basis of this chronological study and is followed and upheld at every point.

In these days when it is common to chip away at the Bible, and no less at its chronological framework, it is the author's desire that *Bible Chronology: The Two Great Divides* will provide help in the *Defense of the Unbroken <u>Biblical</u> Chronology from Adam to Christ.*

J. A. Moorman London, England 2010

TABLE OF CONTENTS

TITLE	PAGE
DEDICATION	3
PREFACE	5
TABLE OF CONTENTS	7
INTRODUCTION	13

CHAPTER I: SEVEN CHRONOLOGIES COMPARED — 15
Ptolemy and the Canon — 15
1. James Ussher — 17
2. Floyd Jones — 17
3. Edwin Theile — 19
4. Edward Denny — 20
5. The Seder Olam Rabbah — 24
6. Ethelbert Bullinger — 32
7. Martin Anstey — 35

Table of the Seven Chronologies — 39
Notes: Chapter 1 — 42

CHAPTER II: FIRST DIVIDE: THE EXODUS TO THE TEMPLE — 47
1. No Obvious Overlapping in Judges — 48
2. The Genealogy of David — 51
3. Six Disputed Time Periods: — 54
   (1) From the Division of Canaan to the First Oppression—20 years — 55
   (2) The Three Hundred Years — 57
   (3) The Ages of Joshua, Caleb and Othniel — 59
   (4) From Samuel's Victory at Mizpeh to the Beginning of Saul's Reign—Ten years — 60
   (5) From the Completion of the Temple to its Dedication—3 years — 61
   (6) Absalom's Forty Years — 62
4. Fitting 611 years into 480 years! — 63

(1) Straining the Text	63
(2) Denying the Text	64
(3) Conjectural Overlaps	64
Conclusion	65
Notes: Chapter 2	67

CHAPTER III: SECOND DIVIDE: CYRUS TO ALEXANDER — 69
Introduction
1. The Seventy Weeks Seem Certain to Begin With the Cyrus Decree — 71
    (1) It was prophesied that Cyrus would indeed *build* Jerusalem — 71
    (2) It is likely that God "stirred" the heart of Cyrus by acquainting him with the prophecy of Isa. 44:28-45:13 — 72
    (3) Even allowing for exaggeration, the Jews' enemies are adamant that the early returnees had begun to rebuild the city — 72
    (4) The repetition of *the commandment going forth* in 9:23, 25 indicates that they are one and the same, thus showing that the weeks are in the process of beginning — 73
    (5) The decree of Cyrus was the basis and precedent for actions of subsequent Persian kings — 74
    (6) The revelation of the Seventy *Weeks* was the Lord's answer to Daniel's prayer concerning the seventy *years* (Daniel 9:2), and are therefore linked — 74
    (7) The start of the Seventy Weeks was something Daniel could *know* — 74
    (8) Only the Cyrus decree would alert the Jews to begin a count to the Messiah — 75
    (9) Only the Cyrus decree would be a basis for the calculation of the Wise Men — 75
    (10) Jerusalem's desolation was to be *limited* to seventy years and its rebuilding would span forty-nine years — 76
    (11) How could Nehemiah be shocked over the report of Jerusalem's broken walls if ninety-one years had passed since the return from Babylon? — 78
    (12) Josephus says that Cyrus' decree applied to the city — 80
2. The Scripture lists show that the 586/536/445 chronology is untenable — 81

TABLE OF CONTENTS

(1) Seventeen priests and Levites	81
(2) Sixteen wall-builders	84
(3) Fifteen chiefs of the people	85
(4) Thirteen "first inhabitants" of Jerusalem	86
(5) Jeshua and Kadmiel	87
3. Mordecai and Ezra were living at the time of Jerusalem's fall	88
(1) Ezra's genealogy	89
(2) Mordecai's genealogy	91
4. Ezra, Nehemiah and Mordecai are listed among the returnees from Babylon	93
5. There does not appear to be a long interval between the governorships of Zerubbabel and Nehemiah	95
6. The line of the High Priests shows that the Ptolemaic Chronology from Cyrus to Alexander is too long	96
(1) Jeshua	97
(2) Joiakim	98
(3) Eliashib	100
(4) Joiada	103
(5) Johnathan (Johanan)	104
(6) Jaddua	106
7. Daniel 10:21-11:4 limits the times and numbers of the Persian Kings	112
(1) Xerxes rather than Artaxerxes Longimanus appears to be the last Persian king mentioned in Scripture	114
(2) The prominent king in Ezra, Nehemiah and Esther is the same, and is Darius rather than Xerxes	116
(a) Xerxes is not the Artaxerxes that Ezra and Nehemiah dealt with	117
(b) Darius and not Xerxes is the is the Ahasuerus of Esther	118
(c) Darius Hystaspes is probably the Artaxerxes of Ezra and Nehemiah	121
(d) The regnal years in Ezra, Nehemiah and Esther are those of one king—Darius Hystaspes	125
(e) The reign of Darius completes the first seven of the Seventy Weeks	128
(f) A 120 year harmony can be demonstrated between the kings and priests of Ezra and Nehemiah	129

Notes: Chapter 3 ... 132

CHAPTER IV: FAULTLINES IN THE PERSIAN EVIDENCE ... 137
1. The Early Histories ... 138
   (1) Diodorus of Sicily 50 BC ... 138
   (2) Berossus 281 BC ... 143
   (3) Manetho 258 BC ... 144
   (4) Josephus 93 AD ... 144
   (5) The Sedar Olam Rabbah 150 AD ... 145
   (6) Firduse 1000 AD ... 146
   (7) The Marmor Parium 263 BC ... 146
   (8) Thucydides, Xenophon and Ctesias ... 147
2. Inscriptions from the Palaces of Persia ... 148
   (1) Artaxerxes I (464-423 BC) ... 149
   (2) Darius II (423-404 BC) ... 149
   (3) Artaxerxes II (404-359 BC) ... 150
   (4) Artaxerxes III (359-358 BC) ... 150
   (5) Arses (338-336 BC), ... 150
   (6) Darius III (336-330 BC) ... 150
   (7) Tombs of the Kings ... 151
3. The Tablets ... 152
   (1) The Persepolis Tablets ... 152
   (2) The Babylonian Tablets ... 152
      (a) Chronicles ... 153
      (b) Astronomical Tablets ... 153
         Consecutive Eclipse Cycles ... 153
         Planetary and Lunar Observations ... 155
         Astronomical Diaries ... 156
         The Use of Intercalary Months ... 158
      (c) Economic Tablets ... 161
         The Murashu Archive ... 161
         Tablets Compiled by H. Figulla ... 162
4. Two Further Areas of Evidence ... 166
   (1) Egyptian Hieroglyphic Inscriptions ... 166

(2) Persian Coins	166
Conclusion	166
Acknowledgments of Sparse Evidence	167
The Argument Thus Far	168
Notes: Chapter 4	169

CHAPTER V: FAULTLINES IN THE GREEK EVIDENCE — 175

The Inherent Weakness in Greek Chronology	175
1. Diodorus of Sicily	176
(1) The Sources Diodorus Used	176
(2) A Chronological Table (Mainly of Athens)	182
2. Key Architects of Greek Chronology	200
(1) Ephorus	201
(2) Eratosthenes	202
(3) Apollodorus	204
3. The Primary Timescales	207
(1) The Spartan King Lists	207
(2) The Olympiads	209
(3) The Archons of Athens	210
(4) The Marmor Parium	213
4. Three Notable Faultlines	216
(1) Men Who Were Too Long in the "Limelight"	216
(2) An Artifact Gap in the British Museum	218
(3) Judea—A One Hundred Year Blank	224
Conclusion	227
Notes: Chapter 5 and Conclusion	232
Index	235
Bibliographical Sources	243
About The Author	249

"And it came to pass in the four hundred and eightieth year after the children of Israel were come out of the land of Egypt, in the fourth year of Solomon's reign over Israel, in the month Zif, which is the second month, that he began to build the house of the LORD."

(I Kings 6:1)

INTRODUCTION

Back in 1995/96 Jerusalem celebrated the 3000th anniversary of its founding by King David, and it did so on the basis of Edwin Thiele's chronology which has been in popular use since the 1950s. But the date 1005 BC for that event is in contrast to the traditional Ussher date of about 1048 BC, when David captured Jerusalem and two or three years later when he brought the ark into the city. Which is right? Further, orthodox rabbis say that the anniversary was being observed *136 years too early* (*London Times*, 9 March 1995). When we go to the Bible itself (the Authorized Version), does it confirm that David established Jerusalem as Israel's capital in 1048, 1005, 869, or another date?

Before *other factors* are considered it is likely that Ussher's date would be the correct one. Thiele to a certain extent manipulates the Scripture chronology. And, for some truly astounding reasons the orthodox Jewish date is *miles off*.

The purpose for writing this book is to demonstrate the extent to which the *other factors* mentioned above affect the dating of events in Scripture. There are several places of marginal disagreement, but two areas are so fundamental in nature that they are here presented as <u>The Two Great Divides</u>. And before accepting a chronologist's Old Testament dates it is important to enquire as to how he approached these *Two Divides*.

The second of these *Divides* affects the timing of Jerusalem's 3000th anniversary (and a lot more!). It concerns the question of *how long* the Kingdom of Persia lasted, and *when* Daniel's Seventy Week prophecy actually commenced. If the traditional dates are accepted - that Babylon fell to Persia in 539 BC, that Daniel was given the Seventy Week prophecy in 538 BC, that Cyrus allowed the Jews to return in 536 BC, that Ezra returned to Jerusalem in 458 BC, and that Nehemiah returned in 445 BC at which time the Seventy Weeks begin - then a number of questions need to be answered.

- How old is Ezra as a co-reformer with Nehemiah in 445 if his father Seraiah was slain by Nebuchadnezzar in 586 BC?

- How old are sixteen to twenty leaders who returned with Zerubbabel in 536 BC if they also lived to seal the covenant with Nehemiah in 445 BC?

- Why was Nehemiah so distressed to hear about the destruction of Jerusalem's walls and gates if it happened 141 years before (586-445 BC)?

- Why do 483 years (69 weeks) from 445 BC extend well beyond 33 AD? Is Sir Robert Anderson's solution valid? Are there *Biblical* reasons for *not* dating the Seventy Weeks from Cyrus' decree?

- And, the question with the most tragic answer of all - Why do the Jewish people say the current year (2010) is 5771? And why does their traditional chronology, the Sedar Olam, reckon only 53 years from Cyrus to Alexander?

The other *Divide* we are examining occurs before Jerusalem's capture by David. It concerns the length of time from the Exodus to the building of Solomon's Temple. According to I Kings 6:1 it is 480 years. But if the time periods are added up in Exodus to I Kings, and also in Acts 13:18-21, they are shown to be over 600 years. This has been called the *Crux Chronologorum*. But as we will show, this seeming contradiction opens up some wonderful truths about the Lord's forgiveness that could not otherwise be known.

Apart from marginal disagreements (except in the case of Thiele) as to how long the divided monarchy lasted, there is little in the other periods of Old Testament chronology that is not straightforward for the Bible believer. The *Two Divides*, however, are different, and cannot be approached without a good deal of prayerful and diligent study.

We begin by showing how seven generally conservative[1] and representative chronologists approach the TWO GREAT DIVIDES.

CHAPTER ONE

SEVEN CHRONOLOGIES COMPARED

The chronologies we are about to look at show an unbroken linkage from Adam to the end of the seventy-year captivity. Such a linkage is perfectly evident in God's Word. But the question arises as to whether there is a clearly defined Biblical link after the captivities. If the Seventy Weeks of Daniel do not directly connect with the captivities and span the period down to the time of Christ, then there is in fact no Biblical link to rely upon and extra-Biblical sources must be used. Most today believe that this latter is the case, and though Daniel received the Seventy Week prophecy in 538 BC, it did not commence for another 93 years until 445 BC when Nehemiah in Artaxerxes' 20th year was given permission to build the walls of Jerusalem.

The fact that most accept that such a gap exists is not really due to a search of Scriptures which may be relative to this question, but rather, *and this is crucial*, to the calculations and influence of a famous 2nd century AD astronomer, astrologer and geographer. Before we look at our seven chronologers, we must first introduce

PTOLEMY AND THE CANON

Based on historical sources and astronomical calculations made at Alexandria, Egypt, from 127 to 151 AD, Claudius Ptolemaeus composed a list of rulers (Babylonian, Egyptian, Persian, Grecian, Roman and others) for some nine centuries down to his day. The list gives the number of years a king reigned, and some of the kings are linked to lunar eclipse data which Ptolemy gleaned from historical records. Apart from this there is no explanatory detail in the list. The Canon begins with the first year of the Babylonian King Nabonassar, and all other reigns are dated from his first year. According to Ptolemy's figures, Anno Nabonassar 1 would equal 747 BC. There are other secular records and inscriptions that give chronological details for parts of this period, but Ptolemy's Canon is the only extra-Biblical authority that claims to bridge the *entire* span from 747 BC to the Christian era.

In a number of instances the Canon appears to conflict with Scripture. The notable example: if 536 BC is the date for Zerubbabel's return and 445 BC for Nehemiah's return (both based on Ptolemy's data), how is it possible that sixteen and more priests and Levites who returned with Zerubbabel (Neh. 12:1-9) could also sign the covenant with Nehemiah after the wall building (Neh. 10:1-10), 91 years later?

BIBLE CHRONOLOGY: THE TWO GREAT DIVIDES

In the crucial Persian period, Ptolemy lists ten kings from Cyrus to the last Persian king before Alexander the Great, whereas their epic poet Firdusi (931-1020 AD) in his versification of Persian history names six monarchs, as does also Josephus (37-103 AD). The *Sedar Olam* (2nd century AD), the standard Jewish chronology, gives only three kings and has the Persian Empire lasting but 53 years. Certainly greater attention needs to be given to the wording in Dan. 10:19-11:4, which seems clearly to point to a shorter time frame than that given by Ptolemy.

Regarding Ptolemy's eclipse data it should be pointed out that in each year there are at least two solar eclipses, and as many as three lunar eclipses, with the total sometimes as many as seven. Therefore it is not unusual to have eclipses occurring during or near a number of important events each year. If there were only several eclipses each century this would be a valuable pointer for dating events in the ancient world. But as there are several each year, it is about as tenuous as attempting to date events in "ancient Florida" by the occurrence of hurricanes! Further, do we know that the observations were accurate and accurately preserved, and does it clearly indicate the location of the observation, and whether the eclipse was solar, lunar, total, partial or annular? Apart from three eclipses said to occur in 381 and 380 BC,[2] there are no further eclipses mentioned from the 31st year of Darius Hystaspes (the Persian king who allowed the Jews to resume building the Temple) down to Alexander the Great - the period of time most in dispute!

Despite these and other objections, Ptolemy's Canon has been universally accepted and few Bible chronologists are prepared to suggest any major departure. They merely *slide* the long span from Adam to the captivities into alignment with the Canon's dating of the Persian Kingdom. Thus the Canon rather than the Seventy Weeks has become the primary basestone for the Inter-Testamental Period.

With these factors in mind, and realizing that Bible Chronology is a subject of ongoing study with perhaps some aspects not to be understood before the Lord returns, it will help us put things into perspective by comparing seven important and representative works.

First among the mighty, and the standard against which all others are measured, we mention briefly the work of –

CHAPTER 1: SEVEN CHRONOLOGIES COMPARED

1. JAMES USSHER

The learned Archbishop of Armagh in Ireland and opponent of Romanism produced his great chronological work the *Annals of the World* in 1658. His dates were slightly revised by William Lloyd in 1701 and thereafter appeared in the margins of many printings of the Authorized Version. With one or two exceptions (see Anstey p.48) he adhered firmly to the text of Scripture, and took none of the liberties that some later chronologists have.

Ussher believed the 480 years of I Kings 6:1 to be an absolute figure and that the reigns of some of the judges overlapped. For the most part, he accepted Ptolemy's Canon for the captivities to Christ, but did not address the Scriptural problems that this entails. He is apparently the first to calculate that Terah was 130 rather than 70 at the birth of Abraham. These principal considerations resulted in the famous 4004 BC date for Creation.

Unless compelled by alternative evidence - and some of the evidence appears to be compelling - it is always best to stay with Ussher.

A modern counterpart who comes independently to most of Ussher's conclusions and to whom we will refer frequently is -

2. FLOYD JONES

Floyd Jones is a fervent Biblicist. His huge work with elaborate charts is one of the very best chronological sources we have today. [3] It is a rare combination of fidelity to the Authorized Version and scholarly attention to historical detail. Yet in accepting the 480 years of I Kings 6:1 as an absolute figure, even he has to take some measures that I doubt he is comfortable with. When over 600 years of data are squeezed into 480 years, *something has to give* ! Jones is forced to place an unnatural strain and interpretation on the AV wording in Judges 3:30 and Acts 13:17-22, and proposes a number of overlaps to reduce the 450 years (Acts 13:20) to 299 years.[4]

Regarding the second major divide, Floyd Jones basically accepts Ptolemy's chronology for the period from Cyrus to Christ, and argues against the opposing views of Anstey and Bullinger. In contrast to many others, he addresses at length the question of how Neh. 10 and 12 can be reconciled to Ptolemy's dates. That is, how could Nehemiah in Artaxerxes' 20th year (445 BC) build the walls and seal the covenant with at least 16 priests and Levites who returned from the captivity in 536 BC?

In the first edition of his work, Jones suggested that rather than the Artaxerxes of Neh.2:1 being Artaxerxes Longimanus (reigned 464-423 BC), he should instead be identified with Xerxes (486-465 BC). He then proposed that Xerxes was co-regent with his father Darius Hystaspes (522-486 BC) from the year 505 BC to the beginning of his sole reign in 486 BC. Thus in this sense 486 BC would be his 20th year, and the time of Nehemiah's commission, and also the beginning of the 69 weeks (483 years) to Messiah, which in this scenario would culminate with Christ's birth in 4 BC. [5] This proposal reduces the minimum age of the covenant signers from 120 years down to their eighties. But without any clear historical evidence this proposal can only be considered a possibility.

On the basis of further evidence which came to hand, Jones in his second edition favours a return to, but revision of the traditional view. Ussher in his *Annals* had pointed to material which indicated that Artaxerxes Longimanus came to the throne nine years earlier than the 464 BC given by Ptolemy. [6] And now having seen reference to an Egyptian inscription stating that Artaxerxes was associated with his father on the throne in the 12th year of Xerxes' reign (474 BC), Jones feels confident in concluding that Artaxerxes' 20th year is 454 BC. Taking the 69 weeks from this point brings us to one of the commonly accepted years for Christ's death - 30 AD. [7]

Jones believes this is preferable to the widely accepted proposal of Sir Robert Anderson, that the 483 years are prophetic years of 360 days, thus reducing them to 476 solar years which from 445 BC comes to 32 AD.[8] But in opting for 454 BC we are back to where we started with the huge ages of those who sign the covenant with Nehemiah. To meet this, Jones appeals to the theory of Sir Isaac Newton.[9]

It may come as a surprise to many that the famous Isaac Newton was a careful student of Bible Chronology and at least as far back as 1728 AD recognized the great dilemma in reconciling Nehemiah 10 and 12 with the Ptolemaic dating.

After the description of Nehemiah's return to build the walls in Neh. 1:1-7:4 (in the 20th year of Artaxerxes), Newton proposed that Neh.7:5-12:26 was a "flashback" to the time of the captives' original return under Zerubbabel in 536 BC at which time both Ezra and Nehemiah (Neh.8:9) take part in the Temple ground-laying services. After this Ezra and Nehemiah returned to their duties in Persia. With the passing of at least 69 years Ezra comes again to Jerusalem in the 7th year of Artaxerxes and challenges the nation to revival and reform (Ezra 7-10). Nehemiah follows 13 years later, builds the wall (Neh. 1:1-7:4), and after the flashback is described, dedicates the wall (Neh.12:27-43), and institutes further reforms (12:44-13:31).

CHAPTER 1: SEVEN CHRONOLOGIES COMPARED

Thus, according to Newton and Jones, with the sealing of Neh.10 taking place in 536 BC, the question of excessive age applies only to Ezra and Nehemiah.

Few have followed Newton's attempt at a solution. A natural reading of Nehemiah seems clearly to convey that chapters 10-12 follow rather than precede the building of the wall. And as the reforms of Neh.13 take place in the 32nd year[10] of Artaxerxes (13:6), Nehemiah would be at least 130 years old! [11] This is quite an age for a man who threatened to lay hands on the sabbath breakers (13:21), who smote and plucked off the hair of men who married heathen wives (13:23-27), and who chased away a son of the High Priest (13:28).

Yet this seems to be the best possible solution if both the Scripture and the dates of Ptolemy are upheld. It is no wonder that many when dating this period have opted for ignoring the matter altogether.

Regarding the times of the kings, Jones takes to task the chronology of Edwin Thiele. He demonstrates a number of instances where Thiele contorts the text in order to make the parallel reigns of Judah and Israel "fit". This results in Thiele removing 45 years from the divided monarchy. [12]

Whether or not we follow Floyd Jones on the two *Great Divides*, his work as a modern refinement of Ussher is a standard in which the Bible believer can learn a great deal and also test any alternative proposals.

Having mentioned Thiele a number of times, we now look briefly at his work.

3. EDWIN THIELE

Until the middle of the twentieth century, Ussher's dates generally remained the standard for conservative students of the Bible. With the publication in 1951 of *The Mysterious Numbers of the Hebrew Kings* by the Seventh Day Adventist scholar Edwin R. Thiele, a substantially different chronological standard soon became accepted. Dealing with the period of the monarchy, the new work seems to resolve problems experienced at different points by previous chronologists in linking the reigns of the Northern and Southern kings.

The result was said to be:

> ... the combination of interlocking synchronisms and lengths of reign, [which] ties the years of Israel and Judah so tightly together as to make impossible any arbitrary adjustment of as much as a single year ... [13]

Further, Thiele's system was claimed to harmonize with the six "absolute" dates of extra-Biblical chronology.[14] Such a workable system met with almost immediate acceptance and was hailed widely as a breakthrough.[15] But a price was to be paid! Despite his claims to be a champion of the Hebrew Scriptures, "Thiele did not hold to an accurate transmission of the original autographs of Kings and Chronicles in every detail. Indeed, he argued that errors were made in the original composition of those autographs."[16] "When the Hebrew text did not directly fit into the Assyrian chronological scheme, it was contorted and disfigured until it apparently conformed." [17] He postulated an Autumn rather than Spring (Ex.12:2) accession year for Judah. And in addition to Judah and Israel in the divided monarchy *created a third Hebrew Kingdom* which he called "Ephraim".

Despite this, Thiele's system, grafted into Ptolemy's Canon and other secular chronologies, is the unrivalled standard in use today. And as it reduces Ussher's and Jones' 389/90 years for the divided monarchy down to 345 years, anyone still wanting to use Ussher for the earlier period combined with Thiele for the monarchy would have a creation date of 3960 BC. However, many now take a far less literal view than Ussher of the Bible's early chronology and *lengthen* the period from Creation to Abraham.

As we have shown, even the Jews departed from their own system (see below) to follow Thiele's date (1005 BC) in calculating the September 1995 commemoration of Jerusalem's 3000th anniversary. Such is the current tenuous state of Bible Chronology.

We now look at several authors who have taken an alternative approach in the two great divides of Bible Chronology.

4. EDWARD DENNY

Unhappy with previous attempts to resolve the seeming contradiction for the years from the Exodus to the Temple, the British Brethren author Sir Edward Denny published in 1849 *Forgiveness Seventy and Sevenfold*. A godly Bible believer, Denny knew that each set of chronological statements was true, and each was to be upheld in its full verity. After considerable prayer and searching he pointed to a very simple fact: if the years recorded in Judges when Israel because of apostasy was under foreign domination are subtracted from the total, the result will equal the 480 years of I Kings 6:1. Therefore, years of broken fellowship are

CHAPTER 1: SEVEN CHRONOLOGIES COMPARED

not counted! "He brought us out that He might bring us in." (Deut.6:23). The purpose of the Exodus was fellowship in the Temple - from redemption to glory with no mention of sin in between! This to Denny was the great truth of I Kings 6:1, and the key to the baffling *Crux Chronologorum*.

Denny further proposed that I Kings 6:1 was the key to opening up the truth that *two* chronological systems run parallel through Scripture. The first is the ACTUAL TIME recorded in the Bible's many chronological references. Here, most but not all of the years of actual time are recorded. For when the years are added several notable gaps are shown to exist. The second is REDEMPTION TIME, which though coming to light in I Kings 6:1, is generally to be found beneath the surface of Scripture. Its principles are based on the Jubilee Cycles of Leviticus 25 and our Lord's words concerning seventy times seven forgiveness in Matt.18:22.

> *I say not unto thee, Until seven times; but, Until seventy times seven.*

To find the true length of Old Testament time, and to fill in the several unstated periods of actual time,[18] Denny taught that both systems must be used.

At the heart of Redemption Time is the Jubilee Cycle (7x7 Sabbatic years) recorded in Leviticus 25. Here there is a further truth, for though the year of Jubilee is regarded as the 50th year (25:10), there are only 49 years from one Jubilee to the next. Lev.25:8-10 shows that rather than the 50th year beginning at the end of the 49th, it begins midway through the 49th on the Day of Atonement and extends midway into the first year of the next cycle, thus overlapping the two years. Therefore, though man reckons it to be 49 years, God calls it the 50th year! And in so doing, God declares that through redemption all has now been brought to *divine completion*.

This remarkable 50th year according to Denny does not add to time. It is only reckoned by God, and does not figure into the actual count of years in the Bible's chronology. As it is integrated into the 49th year of the old cycle and the 1st year of the new cycle, attempts to determine the Jubilee year from Jewish sources (where the principle is apparently not recognized) would be fruitless.

Denny further proposed that in Redemption Chronology ten Jubilee Cycles equalling 490 years[19] will span the major epochs of the Bible. The basic demonstration of this is to be seen in the period from the Exodus to the dedication of the Temple.[20] A chart demonstrating this is entitled *Actual and Redemption Chronology Illustrated*.[21]

BIBLE CHRONOLOGY: THE TWO GREAT DIVIDES

This appears to give a clear example of this remarkable phenomenon where two chronological systems run parallel. The actual years are 621. The Redemption Years are 490. The difference, the 131 years when Israel was under judgement, is no longer mentioned when the final count is made in I Kings 6:1. There are three periods (*) in this section where the number of actual years according to Denny can be determined only by combining and comparing the two systems.

With this Scriptural precedent, Denny applied the 490-year cycles and unreckoned periods of judgement to each of the other eras of the Old Testament chronology.

From the Creation of Adam to the Birth of Abraham

    2008 Actual Years
- 1960 Redemption Years (4x490)
      48 Unreckoned Years: postulated as the years when the Messianic Line
        was broken from the murder of Abel to the birth of Seth.

From the Birth of Abraham to the Exodus

    505 Actual Years
- 490 Redemption Years
      15 Unreckoned Years: Abraham seeks the promised seed through Hagar;
        15 years elapse unto the birth of Isaac (Gen.16:16; 21:5).

From the Exodus to the Dedication of the Temple

    621 Actual Years
- 490 Redemption Years
      131 Unreckoned Years: The years recorded in Judges when Israel was under foreign
        overlords because of her idolatry.

From the Dedication of the Temple to Nehemiah's Commission [22]

    560 Actual Years
- 490 Redemption Years
      70 Unreckoned Years: The 70-year captivity in Babylon.

To arrive at the figures for this period, 405 years are reckoned for the divided monarchy. This compares with 389/390 for Ussher and Jones, Thiele 345, the Sedar Olam 374, Anstey 396 and Bullinger 403. The Ptolemaic dating was generally followed by Denny, but Nehemiah's commission (20th year of Artaxerxes, Neh.1:1) and the start of the Seventy Weeks is set at 458 BC rather than the usual 445 BC.

CHAPTER 1: SEVEN CHRONOLOGIES COMPARED

Again, Denny arrived at this date by combining the 490-year cycle with what he calculated as the actual time. From 536 BC, 78 years were subtracted to arrive at 458 BC. How the 78 years were calculated is as follows:

As by actual count the years from the Temple
dedication to the beginning of the captivity are: 412 years

And as the years of captivity are not counted: 0 years

Therefore in order to complete the 490 years,
the time from the end of the captivity
to Nehemiah's commission must be: <u>78 years</u>
   490 years

There is, however, no explanation as to how Nehemiah in 458 BC could seal a covenant with the *leaders* who returned with Zerubbabel in 536 (Neh.10:1-10; 12:1-9). Nor is any additional evidence given to support the change of Artaxerxes' 20th year from 445 to 458 BC.

<u>From Nehemiah's Commission (458 BC) to the Cross (33 AD)</u>

   490 Actual Years
- <u>490</u> Redemption Years
   0 Unreckoned Years

Those who follow Denny are usually Pre-Millennial and Pre-Tribulational. However, they propose a *two-phase* view of Daniel's 70th week that is completely unique (and almost certainly wrong). [23] The first seven-year phase is the ministry of John the Baptist followed by the ministry of Christ, with each lasting 3½ years. But, as Israel rejected the *seven plenteous years* (cf. Gen.41:47) and the offers of the Kingdom, the week was cancelled and there must now come the *seven years of dearth* (Gen. 41:53), the Tribulation Period, after the close of the Church Age.

They say that the words of Dan.9:25, *"unto the Messiah the Prince shall be (69) weeks"* can only refer to the *beginning* of John the Baptist's proclamation of Christ, an event that is dated with greater emphasis than any other in the New Testament (Luke 3:1,2).

The view is interesting, but a reading of the four Gospels does not give the impression that John had been preaching 3½ years before the baptism of Christ. John's proclamation spread rapidly and Christ was baptized shortly after. Mark 1:9 says it was *in those days*, and Matt.3:13 *then cometh Jesus*. John 1:15-29 shows that Christ was baptized the day after a delegation of religious leaders came to question John. Certainly they would not have waited 3½ years to ask *Who art thou?*

Though Denny's school refers Dan.9:24 to Christ's death, the language points far more naturally to the Second Coming. And of course verse 27 limits the 70th week to the time of antichrist and Christ's return.

At a number of places in their chronological systems, Denny along with others, most notably Sir Robert Anderson, converts back and forth from solar to lunar years. Whether there is ever any justification for measuring an extended period of time in terms of lunar years is to be doubted. See endnote 73.

Denny's book *Forgiveness Seventy and Sevenfold* is very difficult to find today and his views must be studied in the works of other authors. His work opens up some remarkable possibilities, and to my mind presents a convincing case for the longer period of the Judges. This, however, would move the date of Creation back considerably from the 4004 BC date determined by Ussher and Jones. 24

Before considering two chronologies which depart from Ussher/Jones in both of the great divides we must look at the very old system the Jews have followed.

5. THE SEDAR OLAM RABBAH

The Sedar Olam Rabbah or the "Book of the Order of the World" was compiled by Rabbi Yose ben Halafta (died 160 AD) and is to this day the traditional Jewish chronology. It is the reason why the Jewish people reckon the current year (2010) to be 5770 - that is, the 5770th year from the creation of Adam.

The Sedar Olam is divided into three parts, each consisting of ten chapters. Part One enumerates the dates of major events from the Creation to the crossing of Jordan by Joshua. Part Two extends from the Jordan crossing to the murder of Zechariah King of Israel (II Kings 15:10). Chapters 21-27 in Part Three extend to the destruction of the Temple by Nebuchadnezzar, and chapter 28 to the conquest of Babylon by Cyrus. Chapter 29 and the first part of chapter 30 cover the Persian period, and the remainder of chapter 30 contains a summary of events from the conquest of Persia by Alexander to the Bar Kokhba revolt.

CHAPTER 1: SEVEN CHRONOLOGIES COMPARED

At the time of its composition, the Jews generally dated their years from the beginning of the Seleucid era in 312 BC, and for the next centuries the Sedar Olam was of interest only to students of the Talmud.

Only when the center of Jewish life moved to Europe and the calculation according to the Seleucid era became meaningless was it replaced by the anno mundi or "from the creation of the world" reckoning of the Sedar Olam. It began to appear in the 8th and 9th centuries, and from the 11th century became dominant in most of the world's Jewish communities. [25]

We would expect the Jewish chronology to be similar to that of Ussher, with creation taking place about 6000 years ago. But rather than 4000 BC, the Sedar Olam places creation in 3761! What is the reason for this? On what basis do the Jews count their years according to a system which appears to be some 240 years short? The answer seems clearly to involve something more than a mere disagreement over computation. Before examining this, the following shows where the shortfall lies.

The Missing Years

1. From the Creation of Adam to the Birth of Abraham

   Ussher   2008 years 4004-1996 BC
   Sedar Olam <u>1948 years</u> 3761-1811 BC (exclusive reckoning)
         60 years

Most today have accepted that Terah was 130 years old [26] rather than 70 years when Abraham was born (Gen 11:26). Thus the first shortfall is 60 years.

2. From the Birth of Abraham to the Exodus

   Ussher   505 years 1996-1491 BC
   Sedar Olam <u>500 years</u>1 811-1311 BC
         5 years

Abraham was 75 years old when the covenant was made (Gen.12:4), the Exodus was 430 years later (Gal.3:17; Ex.12:40,41). The Sedar Olam without the New Testament revelation reckons five fewer years. The shortfall is now 65 years.

BIBLE CHRONOLOGY: THE TWO GREAT DIVIDES

3. From the Exodus to the Temple Foundation (I Kings 6:1)

    Ussher   480 years   1491-1012 BC
    Sedar Olam 480 years   1311-831 BC

The shortfall remains at 65 years.

4. From the Foundation of the First Temple to the Consecration of the Second Temple

    Ussher   497 years   1012-515 BC
    Sedar Olam <u>480 years</u>   831-351 BC
                 17 years

Differences in computing the divided monarchy would be the reason for these 17 years. Thus the Sedar Olam reckons 82 fewer years from the Creation to the consecration of the Second Temple, of which the major part concerns the age of Terah at Abraham's birth. Now, however, the difference between the two chronological systems becomes radical.

5. From the Consecration of the Second Temple to its destruction by the Romans

    Ussher   584 years   515 BC - 70 AD
    Sedar Olam <u>420 years</u>   351 BC - 70 AD
                164 years

Here we have the primary source of the much shorter chronology in the Sedar Olam. And as these 420 years are divided into periods of 34, 180, 103 and 103 years of successive rule in Israel, it is remarkable to note that the 164-year difference is virtually entirely in the *first Persian period*. The remaining three periods are reasonably close to the standard chronology.

<u>34 years</u> (351-317 BC) for the remainder of the Persian rule in the land: from the dedication of the Temple to Ptolemy's invasion of Jerusalem.

<u>180 years</u> (317-137 BC) for the Grecian rule: from Ptolemy's invasion to the times when Simon the Maccabean became ruler in Israel and Rome recognized the independence of the Jewish state.

<u>103 years</u> (137-34 BC) for the rule of the Hasmonean (Maccabean) family in Israel: from Simon to the beginning of Herod's reign.

<u>103 years</u> (34 BC - 70 AD) for the Herodian rule until the time of the Temple's destruction.

CHAPTER 1: SEVEN CHRONOLOGIES COMPARED

In the later three periods there is some discrepancy with the standard dates. Alexander defeated Darius in 331 rather than 321, Simon's rule is accepted to have begun in 142 BC, and Herod's in 38 BC. But what are we to make of only 34 years for the remainder of the Persian period? In fact, by the Sedar Olam reckoning, it is only 30 years from the Temple dedication to Darius' defeat at the hands of Alexander in 321 BC and four further years to Jerusalem's capture by Ptolemy after Alexander's death.

It is striking to note that the Ptolemaic chronology lists eight Persian kings from Darius Hystaspes to Darius III, the king defeated by Alexander. But according to the Sedar Olam, the Darius during whose reign the Temple was dedicated and the Darius defeated by Alexander are one and the same.

Based on the Sedar Olam we have the following construction for the 52/53 years of the Persian Kingdom. [27]

- Darius the Mede reigns 1 year   3389-3390 AM (374-373 BC)
    Babylon conquered
    Daniel in the lions' den

- Cyrus reigns 3 years   3390-3392 AM (373-371 BC)
    The Jews return
    Temple construction begins

- Artaxerxes (Cambyses) reigns one half year   3393 AM (370 BC)
    Temple construction halted

- Ahasuerus reigns 14 years   3393-3407 AM (370-356 BC)
    Esther chosen Queen; bears Darius the Persian

- Darius the Persian reigns 35 years   3407-3442 AM (356-321 BC)
    Temple construction resumes   3408 (355 BC)
    Temple dedicated   3412 (351 BC)
    Ezra settles in Jerusalem   3413 (350 BC)
    Nehemiah settles in Jerusalem   3426 (337 BC)
    Defeated by Alexander   3442 (321 BC)

Thus the kingdom of Persia lasts only 53 years, from 374 to 321 BC.

Through the centuries orthodox rabbis have differed somewhat in their listing of the Persian kings, [28] but they generally have not departed from the 52/3-year parameter laid down for the Persian period in the Sedar Olam.

Humphrey Prideaux gives an interesting summary of this traditional Jewish position:

> ... In the last year of Darius Hystaspes, the prophets Haggai, Zechariah and Malachi died, that thereon the spirit of prophecy ceased from among the children of Israel, and that this was the obsignation or sealing up of the vision and prophecy spoken of by the prophet Daniel (Dan. 9:24). The same tradition tells us that the kingdom of the Persians ceased also the same year, for they will have it that this was the Darius whom Alexander the Great conquered, and that the whole continuance was only 52 years.[29]

Therefore, rather than an extended gap between Zerubbabel and Ezra, Nehemiah and Malachi, rabbinic scholars believed, or at least said they believed, that these men were of the same generation, and that this generation spanned the Persian period to Alexander.

He Shall Think to Change Times !

These words are from Daniel 7:25 and refer to the Antichrist's time-changing activities during the coming Tribulation Period. There are reasons to believe that a major precedent for time-changing has already taken place in both the Gentile and Jewish worlds. Evidence will be shown that the chronologists who influenced Ptolemy may have lengthened the Persian era and the Sedar Olam *most certainly* shortened it. The result is that the primary prophecy and foundation block of chronology - The Seventy Weeks of Daniel - has become dislodged.

If indeed some adjustments occurred leading up to Ptolemy and whether it was an accident or plan are matters we will look at later. With the Sedar Olam the plan was deliberate! And while not openly admitting this, Jewish scholars of the present day acknowledge that there is something enigmatic about the Sedar Olam dating.

Rabbi Simon Schwab, after enumerating the Ptolemaic and Sedar Olam systems from Cyrus onward, and agreeing that the commonly received dates "can hardly be doubted", yet at the same time upholding his own tradition, writes:

> ...The gravity of this intellectual dilemma posed by such enormous discrepancies must not be underestimated. The unsuspecting students - including the pupils of our own yeshivoth and Beth Jacob High Schools - are faced with a puzzle that appears insoluble. How could it have been that our forebears had no knowledge of a period in history, otherwise widely known and amply documented, which lasted over a span of 165 years and which was less than 600 years removed in time from the days of the Sages who recorded our traditional chronology in Sedar Olam? Is it really possible to assume that some form of historical amnesia had been allowed to take possession of the collective memory of an entire people? This should be quite like assuming that some group of recognized historians of today would publish a textbook on mediaeval history, ignoring all the records of, say, the thirteenth and fourteenth centuries.[30]

CHAPTER 1: SEVEN CHRONOLOGIES COMPARED

Rabbi Schwab lists a number of clearly unsatisfactory attempts at a solution by recent orthodox writers and then puts forward his own view:

> There seems to be left, as yet unexplored, only *one* avenue of approach to the vexing problem confronting us. It should have been possible that our Sages - for some unknown reason - had "covered up" a certain historic period and *purposely eliminated and suppressed all records and other material pertaining thereto.* If so, what might have been their compelling reason for so unusual a procedure? Nothing short of a *Divine command* could have prompted ... those saintly "men of truth" to leave out completely from our annals a period of 165 years and to correct all data and historic tables in such a fashion that the subsequent chronological gap could escape being noticed by countless generations, known to a few initiates only who were duty-bound to keep the secret to themselves.[31]

This is an astonishing proposal! And yet apart from his appeal to Divine direction in such a cover-up, the possibility that Talmudic rabbis of the 2nd century AD became involved in a "time-changing" exercise becomes, upon investigation, increasingly likely.

The reason why God would have so directed them to hide these years was, as Schwab goes on to explain, to prevent past generations from using the prophecies of Daniel to determine the time of the Messiah's coming. He then adds that if the 165 years are added in, it demonstrates "we are much closer to the end of the 6th Millennium than we had surmised."[32]

But as the facts unfold, I think it will become clear that Rabbi Schwab is avoiding some matters here. It will become difficult to escape the conclusion that in the Sedar Olam there *is* the deliberate hiding of Messiah's coming according to Daniel's prophecies, but not after 6000 years, but rather at that time when *He came unto his own and His own received Him not*. A matter of simple arithmetic will show that the 2nd century rabbis made major alterations to their own national chronology in order to point the Seventy Week prophecy not to Christ but to Bar Kokhba!

Rabbis in the century immediately after Christ had a tremendous problem with so direct a prophecy as Daniel 9, i.e. that the Messiah would be cut off 69 weeks or 483 years after the *going forth of a commandment to restore and to build Jerusalem*. Any thought of this decree being proclaimed in the mid-fifth century BC would of course point to Jesus Christ and His crucifixion. Such a prospect must be completely erased from the Jewish consciousness. If, however, the 69 or 70 weeks could begin a century later, then it will be possible for them to point to *another messiah* who, as circumstances would have it, was cut off in death some 100 years after the crucifixion of Christ.

BIBLE CHRONOLOGY: THE TWO GREAT DIVIDES

The 9th day of the Jewish month Av (around mid-July) is to Israel the great day of sorrow. On this day Solomon's Temple was destroyed by the Babylonians and the second Temple was destroyed by the Romans in 70 AD. *And* on this same day in 135 AD, after a 3½ year revolt, the army of the "messianic" Simon Bar Kokhba was crushed by the Romans.

Bar Kokhba had been declared the long-awaited Messiah by the foremost scholar of the time, the much venerated Rabbi Akiva. To Akiva, he was the *star out of Jacob,* and the *sceptre out of Israel* (Num. 24:17).[33] And, for his part in the rebellion, Akiva was also to die at the hands of the Romans in 135 AD.

Among the many accolades heaped upon Akiva and that which gave him such pre-eminent authority was the acknowledgement that he was "the father of the Mishnah."[34] He made a preliminary gathering and formulation of the material for the six orders (containing 63 chapters or tractates) of that religious code which was the heart of the Talmud. Near the end of the 2nd century, Judah ha-Nasi completed the work. Thus, with such prominence, Akiva gave great weight to the messianic expectancy upon Bar Kokhba.

Akiva's students became some of the most prominent sages of the following generation. Among these was Yose (Josi) ben Halafta. The influence of Akiva was so strong upon him that when the matter of Yose's education was discussed, it was merely said, "Rabbi Akiva his teacher."[35] And as such, Yose would have been thoroughly imbued with Akiva's views on Bar Kokhba.

Yose's own influence is demonstrated by the fact that some of his writings were included in Judah ha-Nasi's final editing of the Mishnah, and his name is mentioned in 59 of its 63 tractates.[36] His Sedar Olam, though referred to in the Mishnah and Talmud, is not a formal part of that work. It is what the Jews call a *baraita*, meaning an "outside" Mishnah. That is, it was not included in Judah ha-Nasi's final edition of the Mishnah. It is, though, a work of Talmudic authority, and openly to contradict it is unthinkable to orthodox Jews.

As Rabbi Schwab stresses,

> However, our traditional chronology is based on Sedar Olam because of the authority of its author. It is therefore quite inconceivable that any post-Talmudic teacher could possibly "reject" those chronological calculations which have been the subject of many a Talmudic discussion.[37]

And Judah ha-Nisi, who because of his own esteem was know simply as "Rabbi", writes at the end of the Mishnah tractate *Gittin*:

CHAPTER 1: SEVEN CHRONOLOGIES COMPARED

> *How can we humble disciples question the words of Rabbi Josi since the difference between our generation and that of Rabbi Josi is comparable to the difference between the most holy and the most profane...* [38]

In all this we can see why the Sedar Olam holds such sway and why Jews to this day use it for their national dating. But despite the heaping of laurels the fact remains that it is an attempt to hide the true end and goal of the Seventy Weeks of Daniel.

A Demonstration

By Sedar Olam reckoning, the decree of Cyrus and the commencing of the Seventy Weeks would be about 372 BC.[39]

372 BC + 490 years = 119 AD
372 BC + 483 years = 112 AD

This would indicate a termination for the 69 or 70 weeks some 13 to 20 years before the revolt began in 132 AD. Thus, this is reasonably close to the years in which Bar Kokhba rose to prominence as Israel's military and economic leader [40] – And, when Akiva proclaimed, "This is the King Messiah"[41] – And, "all the contemporary sages regarded him as the King Messiah"[42] - And, "even in later generations, despite the disappointment engendered by his defeat, his image persisted as the embodiment of messianic hopes." [43] – And, the consistent verdict of Jewish historians: "The most important historical messianic figure was surely Bar Kokhba."[44]

Yose and his fellow compilers of the Sedar Olam would have sought to terminate the 69/70 weeks as close to the 132 AD revolt as possible. But they were limited as to where the "cuts" could be made. Years could not be pared from their history after 312 BC, for as we have seen, the chronology of the Seleucid era and onward was firmly fixed among the Jews. This left only the Persian period, and this they cut down radically. But here the point needs to be made that in order for them to get away with such a wholesale reduction there must have been room for considerable doubt in those days as to how long the Persian period actually lasted!

I have not seen, and one would have to search very hard indeed to find any trace of a Jewish admission that they so altered their chronology to make the 69/70 weeks point to Bar Kokhba rather than Jesus Christ. Apart from faith in Christ it would be virtually impossible for a Jew to bring himself to such an admission. Yet this appears to be the only reasonable conclusion that can be drawn from the facts as they now appear.

We now return to two chronologies which depart from Ussher in both divides.

In 1867 at the age of only twenty-nine a new secretary was to take the helm of the faltering Trinitarian Bible Society in London. For forty-six years this man's vigorous leadership saw the Society confirmed as one of the world's leading bulwarks against the ravages of the Westcott and Hort text. He is best known, though, as the author of the Companion Bible, a work which while having some serious errors is quite remarkable in many respects, one being its full chronology and break from Ussher in both of the great divides. The man is -

6. ETHELBERT BULLINGER[45]

Considering that Bullinger adds to the years Ussher and Jones give for the period of the Judges and reduces the time they give for Cyrus to Christ, it is remarkable that he arrives at their same date for Creation - 4004 BC!

Bullinger follows Denny's basic principles for the Exodus to the Temple span. But while Denny computes 611 years to the start of construction, Bullinger gives 573 years. This is because 13 rather than 20 years are allotted from the division of Canaan to the first oppression in the book of Judges, and the period of Samuel's rule is reckoned within rather than outside the 450 years of Acts 13:20. But as these factors add up to more than 450 years he reduces the judgeship of Jair from the stated 22 years to 4 (Judges 10:3). I think Denny is a sounder guide on this period of the chronology.

It is in his handling of the second divide that Bullinger presents the most radical of departures from the traditional view. Rather than having Nehemiah return to build the walls after Cyrus, he sees this as occurring *before* Cyrus released the Jews. And, the Artaxerxes during whose 20th year Nehemiah was permitted to return is the *father* of Cyrus and married to *Esther*. Thus, according to Bullinger, the Book of Esther and much of Ezra and Nehemiah take place in the *Persian provinces* of Babylon, *before* Babylon fell to Persia.[46] And, four weeks (28 years) of the Seventy Weeks prophecy are shown to transpire *before*[47] Daniel actually receives the prophecy (Dan.9).

Bullinger's Construction of the Babylonian and Persian Period

BC
496   Nebuchadnezzar's 1st siege of Jerusalem in Jehoiakim's 4th year; Daniel taken; the 70-year *servitude*[48] begins.

CHAPTER 1: SEVEN CHRONOLOGIES COMPARED

489   Nebuchadnezzar's 2nd siege of Jerusalem; Ezekiel taken; the 70 year *captivity* begins, and is dated by Ezekiel's captivity.

479   Nebuchadnezzar's 3rd siege of Jerusalem; the 70-year *desolations* begin; the city falls two years later.

467   Esther marries Astyages [49] (= Ahasuerus, Artaxerxes, Darius the Median) in his 7th year. [50] Their son Cyrus is born shortly after. Astyages is the brother-in-law of Nebuchadnezzar [51] and is ruler over the Persian realms of the Babylonian Empire.[52]

461   Nebuchadnezzar's seven years of madness begin. Astyages takes over the reins of government.

454   Nebuchadnezzar's madness ends. Astyages in his 20th year gives Nehemiah temporary leave to rebuild the walls of Jerusalem (Neh.2:1-9). The first seven-week period (49 years) of the seventy-week prophecy begins (Dan. 9:24-27). The 69 sevens (483 years) end in 29 AD with the "cutting off of the Messiah."

426   Babylon falls to Persia. Astyages (= Darius the Median, [53] Dan.5:31) takes the kingdom. His son Cyrus allows the Jews to return and build the Temple, thus ending the seventy-year servitude. Daniel is given the prophecy of the Seventy Weeks. [54] Among the returnees with Zerubbabel are Mordecai (Est.2:5,6) and Nehemiah (Ezra 2:2, Neh. 7:7), with Nehemiah returning to Persia after the laying of the Temple foundation.

421   Cyrus dies (aged 45); Cambyses [55] his elder son begins to reign. Some time later work on the Temple is forced to cease.

419 [56]   The 70-year *captivity* ends with the appointment of Nehemiah as governor over Judah – from the 20th to 32nd year of Artaxerxes (Neh.5:14). [57] He was, however, not in Jerusalem for the entire period (Neh.13:6). [58]

411   Darius Hystaspes becomes King of Persia.

409   The 70-year *desolations* end; Darius Hystaspes in the 2nd year of his reign re-enacts the decree of Cyrus; work on the Temple is resumed, encouraged by Haggai and Zechariah.

407   Nehemiah completes his twelve-year term as governor of Judah in the 32nd year of the *life* of Darius (= Artaxerxes, Neh. 5:14; 13:6). This is the 4th year of his *reign* (!).

405   The Temple is finished and dedicated in the 6th year of Darius (Ezra 6:15). Nehemiah is present. [59] The seven weeks are finished, the 62 weeks begin.

404   Ezra comes to Jerusalem to "beautify" the Temple (Ezra 7:27) in the 7th year of Artaxerxes (Darius Hystaspes). He leads in a reformation and revival (Ezra 7-10) which extends into the 8th year of the king's reign (10:17). [60]

403   Nehemiah leads in the dedication of the wall (Neh. 12:27-47). [61]

Bullinger's reconstruction is a bold and carefully thought out alternative to the traditional reckoning. He contradicts himself in one or two places, and seems to rely on expediency in stating that the Artaxerxes of Neh.2:1 is Astyages, while that of Neh.5:14 and 13:6 is Darius Hystaspes (see note 57). This is nevertheless a scrupulous study of Ezra and Nehemiah, and a demonstration of the correlation with Herodotus, the Behistun Rock, the Cyrus Cylinder and other material. His system appears to resolve a number of problems associated with the traditional view:

1. The extreme ages are reduced considerably. Though Ezra and Nehemiah would be in their eighties, the returnees with Zerubbabel (Neh.12) would have to wait only 23 years for the covenant to be sealed and the wall dedicated.

2. Nehemiah's sorrow over the burnt state of Jerusalem (Neh.1:3; 2:3,17) is certainly more understandable 23 years after Nebuchadnezzar destroyed the city than the *141 years* (586-445 BC) reckoned by the traditional approach. It is reasonable to ask whether Nehemiah's question concerning the "Jews that had escaped, which were left of the captivity" (1:2) can really describe the 42,000 and their descendants who returned with Zerubbabel. On the face of it Neh.1:2 might more naturally refer to the "poor of the land" (Jer.52:16) left by the Babylonians.

3. Unless Ezra 4:12,13 is an exaggeration by those accusing the Jews (note the "if" in v.13), it supports Bullinger's contention that the wall was set up before the Temple was built.

> *Be it known unto the king, that the Jews which came up from thee to us are come unto Jerusalem, building the rebellious and the bad city, and have set up the walls thereof, and joined the foundations. Be it known now unto the king, that, if this city be builded, and the walls set up again, then will they not pay toll ...*

But notwithstanding the above and in addition to what I have shown in the notes, there are fundamental flaws in Bullinger's construction.

1. The Temple *did* exist during the time Nehemiah was building the wall.

> *Let us meet together in the house of God, within the temple, and let us shut the doors of the temple. (Neh.6:10; and see 6:15)*

Bullinger's explanation that "...this must have been a temporary structure. Nehemiah would not be without some place wherein to worship" is not convincing.

2. How could the walls of Jerusalem be built before there were sufficient people to build and inhabit the city, i.e. before Cyrus released the Jews? And if the Babylonians only "left certain poor of the land for vinedressers and for husbandmen" (Jer. 52:16), how is it that so many influential men were present to help Nehemiah complete the construction in such a short time (Neh.3)?

3. Would not this rebuilding be premature and a breach upon the Lord's declaration that the land would be "desolate to keep sabbath for 70 years" (II Chr.36:21)?

4. After finishing the work in only 52 days (Neh.6:15), it would be strange in the extreme to wait 51 years to dedicate the wall (Neh.12:27-47).

5. Even given Nebuchadnezzar's madness, how could there be a *king* (a co-regent) who reigned over 127 provinces from India to Ethiopia *while Nebuchadnezzar was still king?* How could this king approve the rebuilding of the walls his master destroyed only 23 years before? Why do we not read elsewhere about such a co-regency?

Enormous difficulties stand in the way of placing Nehemiah's wall-building in the Babylonian rather than in the Persian period, and I am not aware of any serious attempt to develop this theory further. It is not workable.

A second chronologist who departs from the traditional in both divides but not in the radical way of Bullinger and has produced a work of vast research very popular during the earlier part of the 20th century is -

7. MARTIN ANSTEY

The Romance of Bible Chronology was published in 1923 and dedicated to his close friend, the famous G. Campbell Morgan.

A number of the pre-millennial Bible teachers of that generation were influenced by Anstey. Shortly after C. I.Scofield's 1917 study Bible was published he wrote very favorably of Anstey's views. However, this approval did not affect the dates in later printings and editions of the Scofield Bible and Ussher's dates continued to be used. [62]

Whether or not one is persuaded by the case Anstey builds for a longer period for the Judges and a shorter for the Persian Kingdom, his devotion to Scripture and ready access to the British Museum items make this work one of the most valuable on the subject. When Britain and London ruled the world, the archaeological treasures of ancient Egypt, Assyria, Babylon, Persia, Greece and Rome were brought into her museums. The British Museum in London is by far the world's greatest repository of these treasures. Anstey, from a Bible-believing standpoint, made full use of this.

Anstey followed Denny's approach to the first divide. He commends Ussher highly but speaks of the "misinterpretation of the 480 years" as one of Ussher's "principal errors".[63]

With two exceptions, Anstey gives the same figures as Denny for the era from the Exodus to the Temple. Denny reckons 611 years to the beginning of construction. Anstey by giving 13 rather than 20 years for the time between Joshua and Judges and 20 rather than 30 years for Samuel's rule comes to 594 years for the period. He places an unnatural construction upon Judges 10:3-9, though it does not affect the sum of the years of oppression and rest. He is very forthright with chronologists who "have not only ... bent the chronology of the Old Testament to make it fit with this figure, but they have even ventured upon the task of correcting St Paul, and emended the text of the New Testament in Acts 13:17-20 in order to bring it into accord with the 480 years of I Kings 6:1."[64]

Anstey, as he brings a huge amount of material to bear upon the question of the Persian Kingdom, acknowledges the work of Bullinger in setting forth an alternative view.

> The conjectural results suggested in part by Lumen, the author of the Prince of the House of Judah, and adopted by the author of the Companion Bible for the period of Ezra, Nehemiah and Esther, are probably erroneous, but his bold attempt to free the Chronology of the Bible from the tyranny of the Ptolemaic system is one of the many illustrations of the originality of the author's genius, and keenness of his insight into the meaning of Scripture.[65]

In contrast to Bullinger who proposed that the Seventy Weeks began before Cyrus' decree, and the Ptolemaic view that they begin some 90 years after that decree, Anstey believes that the Weeks begin with Cyrus' decree and complete the Bible's unbroken chronology from Adam to the Cross.

Anstey's Construction of the Babylonian and Persian Period[66]

BC
- 520 Nebuchadnezzar's 1st Invasion; Daniel taken; Times of the Gentiles begin.
- 512 2nd Invasion; Ezekiel taken.
- 501 3rd Invasion; Temple and City destroyed.
- 453 Babylon falls to Persia; Darius the Mede begins to reign; Daniel receives the prophecy of the Seventy Weeks.
- 451 Cyrus in his 1st year issues decree allowing Jews to return, and City and Temple to be built (Isa. 45:13); 69 weeks (483 years) to Death of Christ.

CHAPTER 1: SEVEN CHRONOLOGIES COMPARED

444 Cambyses begins to reign; the Samaritans petition him against Jerusalem (Ezra 4:6).
437 Smerdis begins to reign (Ezra 4:7).
436 Darius Hystaspes begins to reign; in 2nd year work on Temple is resumed.
430 Darius, 6th year, Temple completed (Ezra 6:15).
429 Darius (= Ahasuerus), 7th year, Esther is made Queen (Est. 2:16).
429 Darius (= Artaxerxes), 7th year, Ezra goes up to Jerusalem (Ezra 7:7).
417 Darius (= Artaxerxes), 20th year, Nehemiah goes up to Jerusalem (Neh.2:1).
405 Darius (= Artaxerxes) 32nd year, Nehemiah's 12th year as governor (Neh.13:6). The Battle of Marathon (contrast the 490 BC Ptolemaic date).
331 Persia falls to Alexander.

As we are rightly or wrongly so conditioned by the Ptolemaic reckonings, i.e. 605, 536, 445 BC etc., the above seems quite foreign to say the least! It is, however, based on the simple premise that from Adam to Christ there are no gaps in the Old Testament chronology. The Sixty-Nine Weeks follow directly on from the 70-year captivity. And just as we have an unbroken list of the generations of this final period in Luke chapter 3, so in these "weeks" the time span is also unbroken and we are not left to fill the gap by attempting to compute the uncertain reigns of heathen kings.

The demonstration is plain. If our Lord was crucified in 33 AD, then counting backwards 483 years brings us to 451 BC for the decree of Cyrus, and a further 70 years to 520 BC for Nebuchadnezzar's first invasion, and the beginning of the Times of the Gentiles.

But does Scripture really point to such a view? And are not the facts of secular history so overwhelming that anything other than a marginal revision of Ptolemy is completely untenable? And, why do so few today side with Anstey in his assessment of the evidence purporting to support Ptolemy's Canon?

The following gives some of the essence of Anstey's argument:

> We now reach the most difficult period in the whole realm of Bible Chronology, the period of Ezra, Nehemiah and Esther.
>
> Our sole authority for this period is the Books of Ezra, Nehemiah and Esther. There are cuneiform Inscriptions by Cyrus, by Darius Hystaspes, and by each of the succeeding Persian monarchs down to the last King of Persia, who was slain by Alexander the Great, and the Behistun Inscription by Darius Hystaspes contains some very valuable information, but none of these Inscriptions give us any help in fixing the Chronology of the period.

BIBLE CHRONOLOGY: THE TWO GREAT DIVIDES

Neither do we obtain any help in this direction from Jewish, Persian or Greek literature. The Jewish and the Persian traditions make the period of the Persian Empire a period of about 52 years. There are no contemporary chronological records whatever to fix the dates of any of the Persian Monarchs after Darius Hystaspes. The clay tablets of Babylon fix the Chronology for the reigns of Cyrus, Cambyses, Pseudo-Smerdis and Darius Hystaspes, but they do not determine the date of any subsequent Persian King.

The dates that have reached us, and which are now generally received as historical, are a late compilation made in the 2nd century A.D., and found in Ptolemy's Canon. They rest upon the calculations or guesses made by Eratosthenes and certain vague, floating traditions, in accordance with which the period of the Persian Empire was mapped out as a period of 205 years.

The count of the years is now lost, but if we may assume the correctness of the Greek Chronology from the period of Alexander the Great (B.C. 331) onward, this would leave a period of 123 years for the duration of the Persian Empire according to the prophecy of Daniel. [67]

It has always been held to be unsafe to differ from Ptolemy, and for this reason. His Canon, or List of Reigns, is the only thread by which the last year of Darius Hystaspes, B.C. 485, is connected with the first year of Alexander the Great.[68]

Had Ptolemy never written, profane Chronology must have remained to this day in a state of ambiguity and confusion, utterly unintelligible and useless, nor would it have been possible to have ascertained from the writings of the Greeks or from any other source, except from Scripture itself, the true connection between sacred Chronology and profane, in any one single instance, before the dissolution of the Persian Empire in the 1st year of Alexander the Great. Ptolemy had no means of accurately determining the Chronology of this period ... so he had to resort to the calculation of eclipses. In this way then, not by historical evidence or testimony, but by the method of astronomical calculation, and the conjectural identification of recorded with calculated eclipses, the Chronology of this period of the world's history has been fixed by Ptolemy, since when, through Eusebius and Jerome, it has won its way to universal acceptance. It is contradicted (1) by the national traditions of Persia, (2) by the national traditions of the Jews, (3) by the testimony of Josephus, and (4) by the conflicting evidence of such well-authenticated events as the Conference of Solon with Croesus, and the flight of Themistocles to the court of Artaxerxes Longimanus, which make the accepted Chronology impossible. But the human mind cannot rest in a state of perpetual doubt. There was this one system elaborated by Ptolemy. There was no other except that given in the prophecies of Daniel. Hence, while the Ptolemaic astronomy was overthrown by Copernicus in the 16th Century, the reign of the Ptolemaic Chronology remains to this day. There is one, and only one alternative. The prophecy of Daniel 9^{24-27} ... We have to choose between the Heathen Astrologer and the Hebrew Prophet.[69]

It may be objected that in the Battle of Marathon, which was fought B.C. 490, Darius Hystaspes was defeated by the Greeks, and that the Greek Chronology, which was reckoned by Olympiads from B.C. 776 onward, cannot be at fault to the extent of 82 years. But that is just the very point in dispute. The Greeks did not make a single

CHAPTER 1: SEVEN CHRONOLOGIES COMPARED

> calculation in Olympiads; nor had they any accurate chronological records till sixty years after the death of Alexander the Great. All that goes before that is guess work, and computation by generations, and other contrivances, not the testimony of contemporary records. [70]
>
> It is through the Greeks that we have received our knowledge of the history of the great Empires and civilizations of the East. Even Sanchoniathon and Berosus and Manetho, have all come to us through the Greeks. It was the Greeks who created the framework of the Chronology of the civilized ages of the past, and fitted into it all the facts of history, which have reached us through them. Apart from the Bible, the vague floating national traditions of the Persians and the later Jews, and the direct results of modern exploration, all our chronological knowledge reaches us through Greek spectacles. Here as everywhere else it is "thy sons O Zion against thy sons, O Greece" (Zech. 9[13]). It is Nehemiah and Daniel against Ptolemy and Eratosthenes. It is Hebraic Chronology against Hellenic Chronology. And here the Greek has stolen a march upon the Hebrew, for he has stolen his Old Testament and forced his own Greek Chronology into the Hebrew record, Hellenizing the ages of the Hebrew Patriarchs in the Greek LXX. [71]

Anstey presents a compelling case for a shorter Persian period. However at Ezra 6:14 and Neh. 13:4 he seeks to fortify his argument by altering the Authorized Version reading.[72] Also, in addition to the material that has become available since Anstey wrote, more needs to be said about the implications of the Greek and Persian evidence. And, as we will see, there is considerably more that can be said about the Biblical evidence.

We owe a great debt to Anstey's research, and his *Romance of Bible Chronology* will remain a, in fact *the* major resource for Bible believers.

TABLE OF THE SEVEN CHRONOLOGIES

Here, the seven representative chronologies are compared according to a five-fold division of Old Testament history. At the head of each division is the example of a chronology that accepts 621 years for the *first divide* (the Exodus to the Temple), and 120 years for the *second divide* (Cyrus to the fall of Persia). The headings also show how this relates to Denny's theory of 490-year cycles.

The figures in the table may show some slight variation when added or subtracted. In the case of Denny, the figures are from the men who later developed his work. His figures are as stated, i.e. they are not converted from lunar to solar. [73]

1. Adam to Birth of Abraham - **2008 years** (4 x 490 + 48 years out of fellowship)

                                                                                                               4050-2042 BC

   Ussher   2008 years   4004-1997 BC

BIBLE CHRONOLOGY: THE TWO GREAT DIVIDES

Ussher/Thiele	2008 years	3960-1953 BC
Jones	2008 years	4004-1997 BC
Denny	2008 years (lunar)	4152-2144 BC
Bullinger	2008 years	4004-1996 BC
Anstey	2008 years	4042-2034 BC
Sedar Olam	1948 years	1 AM (3761 BC) -1948 AM

2. Birth of Abraham to Exodus - **505 years** (490 + 15 years out of fellowship)

    2042-1537 BC

Ussher	506 years	1997-1491 BC
Ussher/Thiele	506 years	1953-1447 BC
Jones	506 years	1997-1491 BC
Denny	505 years (lunar)	2144-1639 BC
Bullinger	505 years	1996-1491 BC
Anstey	505 years	2034-1529 BC
Sedar Olam	500 years	1945-2448 AM

3. Exodus to Probable Date of Temple Dedication in Solomon's 14th year - **621 years** (490 + 131 years out of fellowship)

    1537-916 BC

Ussher	489 years	1491-1002 BC
Ussher/Thiele	490 years	1447-957 BC
Jones	489 years	1491-1002 BC
Denny	621 years (solar)	1639-1019
Bullinger	584 years	1491-907 BC
Anstey	604 years	1529-925 BC
Sedar Olam	490 years	2448-2938 AM

4. Dedication of Temple to End of Captivity - **466 years** (490 - 24)   916-450 BC

Ussher	466 years	1002-536 BC
Thiele	421 years	957-536 BC
Jones	466 years	1002-536 BC
Denny	483 years (solar)	1019-536 BC
Bullinger	481 years	907-426 BC
Anstey	472 years	925-453 BC
Sedar Olam	450 years	2938-3388 AM

5. End of Captivity to the Cross – **483 years** (490 - 7)   450 BC-33 AD

Ussher	569 years	536 BC-33 AD
Thiele	569 years	536 BC-33 AD
Jones	569 years	536 BC-30 AD
Denny	569 years (solar)	536 BC-33 AD
Bullinger	455 years	426 BC-29 AD

CHAPTER 1: SEVEN CHRONOLOGIES COMPARED

    Anstey   483 years   453 BC-30 AD
    Sedar Olam 406 years   3388-3794 AM (33 AD)

From this it will be noted that if the proposed chronology in the headings is followed -

1. Creation would be 4050 BC rather than 4004 BC. If the pre-Ussher means of dating the birth of Abraham were followed, Creation would then be sixty years later (3990 BC). Further consideration needs also to be given to the timing of the divided monarchy. As it is likely that Creation took place at about 4000 BC, several factors could be shown that would result in this date. These, however, are matters for study beyond the scope of this book.

2. The Times of the Gentiles, when Nebuchadnezzar first invaded Jerusalem, will have begun in 520 BC (70+450) rather than 605 BC.

NOTES: CHAPTER ONE

1. Thus omitting those who use the Septuagint or postulate gaps in the genealogies of Genesis 5 and 11.
2. None of which is linked to Persia. See Martin Anstey, *The Romance of Bible Chronology*, (London: Marshall Brothers, 1913), p.285.
3. Floyd Jones, *Chronology of the Old Testament,* 2nd edition. Houston: F.J.Ministries, 1993.
4. *Ibid.* pp. 73-77.
5. See pages 240-244 of his 2nd edition. But as the Seventy Weeks are God's clock for Israel (Dan.9:24), why should the 69 weeks end at Christ's birth? They must certainly end after Israel rejected Christ as their Messiah.
6. *Ibid.* pp.221-223.
7. *Ibid.* pp.246-249.
8. 483 solar years from 445 BC would be 39 AD.
9. *Ibid.* pp.258 and 235-239.
10. 442 BC according to Jones' revised reckoning.
11. Ezra would be even older, for his father Seraiah was slain by Nebuchadnezzar at the time of Jerusalem's fall in 586 BC. (Ezra 7:1; II Kings 25:18-21; Jer.52:24-27).
12. *Ibid.* pp.118ff.
13. Leslie McFall, "A Translation Guide to the Chronological Data in Kings and Chronicles", *Bibliotheca Sacra,* (Jan-Mch 1991) p.4.
14. *Ibid.* pp.4,9-11.
15. *Ibid.* p.3.
16. *Ibid.* p.4.
17. Jones, p.174.
18. For example, the number of years from Samuel's victory at Mizpeh to the beginning of Saul's reign is not stated.
19. That is, after the years of apostasy are removed, the time will equal 490 years.
20. Figured: 480 years to the beginning of construction, I Kings 6:1; 7 years to completion, 6:38; and an assumed 3 years for its furnishing, 7:13-51.
21. From an unpublished booklet entitled *Chronology* by G.Ewan.
22. Figures in these final two sections are those by 20th century exponents of Denny's theory. See for example: A.E.Ware, *The World in Liquidation.* London: Simpkin Marshall Ltd., 1953, Frank L.Paine, *The Miracle of Time.* Somerset, England, Shiloah Ministries, 1994.
23. The view, though practically unknown in America, has had a following among those holding to pre- millennial teaching in Britain.
24. In fact, charts which utilize Denny show 4152 years from Creation to the Birth of Christ. But as the years before the Exodus are considered to be lunar years, the actual solar reckoning would be 4075 BC. See note 72.
25. "Sedar Olam", *Encyclopedia Judaica,* (Jerusalem, Keter Publ. House Ltd., 1972).
26. Terah died at 205, when Abraham was 75 (Gen.11:32; 12:4; Acts 7:4). Hence Terah was 130 when Abraham was born. This seems obvious. Nevertheless, Jews based on their Book of Jasher (22:33-34 p.57) believe Terah was 70 when Abraham was born. Perhaps the matter needs to be looked at further.

CHAPTER 1: SEVEN CHRONOLOGIES COMPARED

27. See Zechariah Fendel, *Charting the Mesorah: Creation through Geonim*, (New York: Haskafah Publ.,1994), p.45.
28. For a list of various views see Simon Schwab, "Comparative Jewish Chronology", *Dr Joseph Breuer Jubilee Volume*, (New York, Rabbi Samson Raphael Hirsch Publications Society, Philipp Felheim Inc., 1962), p.187.
29. *The Old and New Testaments connected to the History of the Jews*, (Oxford: Oxford Univ. Press, 1851), p.235.
30. Simon Schwab, p.182.
31. *Ibid.* p.188. Emphasis *his!*
32. *Ibid.* pp.190,191.
33. "Akiva", *Encyclopedia Judaica*, pp.488-492.
34. "Mishna", *Encyclopedia Judaica*, p.102.
35. "Yose ben Halafta", *Encyclopedia Judaica*, p.852.
36. *Ibid.* p.853.
37. Schwab, p.186.
38. *Ibid.* p.186.
39. Fendel, *Charting the Mesorah*, p.45.
40. "Bar Kokhba", *Encyclopedia Judaica*, p.230.
41. *Ibid.* p.230.
42. *Ibid.* p.231.
43. *Ibid.* p.231.
44. "Messiah", *Encyclopedia Judaica*, p.1410.
45. E.W.Bullinger *The Companion Bible*. Grand Rapids: Zondervan Bible Publishers, 1979.
46. Anstey, p.139, indicates Bullinger was influenced toward this view by a certain Lumen in his book *The Prince of the House of Judah*.
47. Appendix 50 VII(12) in the *Companion Bible* clearly states this, but is contradicted in the *Summary* which follows. This latter is certainly a typographical error.
48. Bullinger distinguishes between three overlapping seventy-year periods: the Servitude, the Captivity, the Desolations. Each begins with a siege of Jerusalem.
49. The name given by Herodotus to the Persian king whom Bullinger believes to be the same as Ahasuerus (The Mighty, Est.1:1), Artaxerxes (The Great King, Neh. 2:1), and Darius the Median (the Restrainer, Dan.5:31).
50. By this reckoning, if Astyages is Darius the Median then he is only 21 years old at his marriage to Esther, for he was 62 years old in 426 BC when Babylon fell to Persia (Dan.5:31). And if in the 20th year of his reign (454) he permits Nehemiah to return, then he would only be 14 years old in the first year of his reign when he married Vashti (Appendix p.67). Herodotus says that Cyrus was 40 at the fall of Babylon, a factor which agrees with Bullinger's count.
51. Appendix 57, p.80 states: "At the close of the Lydio-Median war 'Syannesis the Cilician and Labynetus (or Nabonnedus) the Babylonian (identified by Humphry Prideaux - *The Old and New Testament Connected in the History of the Jews*, 19th edn. Vol.I, p.82 note, and pp.135,136 - with Nebuchadnezzar) persuaded Alyattes to give his daughter Aryenis in marriage to Astyages, son of Kyaxares' (Herodotus I:74)." Bullinger identifies Aryenis with Vashti, p.81.

52. Yet, how could it be said that "he reigned from India even unto Ethiopia, over an hundred and seven and twenty provinces", and that as *the king* "he sat on the throne of his kingdom" (Est.1:1,2) at the same time Nebuchadnezzar was king? The rulers of the provinces under Nebuchadnezzar are not called "kings" (Dan.3:2-4).
53. While the Darius of Dan.5:31-6:28 is identified as Astyages the father of Cyrus, in Dan.9:1 "Darius the son of Ahasuerus of the seed of the Medes" is said to be Cyrus. According to Bullinger we have here an "old Darius and a young Darius", the name being an appellative or title (p.1191). Later Xerxes in a Persepolis inscription was to call himself "Darius" (Appendix, p.80).
54. 28 years after the Seventy Week period begins, thus completing the first four weeks.
55. On page 67 of the Appendix, Bullinger says that Cambyses is the Artaxerxes of Neh.5:14. This is clearly an error and contradicts his statement on p.663 that this Artaxerxes is Darius Hystaspes who follows Cambyses. He does not identify Cambyses with any of the kings named in Ezra 4:5-7; 6:14.
56. Bullinger's statement on p.615 that the wall was completed in 419 contradicts his assertion everywhere else that it was completed in 454.
57. A reading of Nehemiah leads naturally to the conclusion that the 20th year of Artaxerxes the king mentioned in 2:1 and 5:14, and assumed in 13:6, refers to the same king and date of reign. But Bullinger says 2:1 refers to the 20th year of the reign of Astyages, whereas in 5:14 and 13:6 it is the 20th year of the life of Darius Hystaspes, a later king. When Ezra goes to Jerusalem in the 7th year of Artaxerxes (Ezra 7:7), this is said to refer to the reign of Darius Hystaspes(!).
58. If Nehemiah was governor during this time would we not read of him protesting the work being stopped?
59. This is to be assumed from Bullinger's construction of the events. In the one chapter (Ezra 6) dealing with the Temple's completion and dedication, Nehemiah is not mentioned.
60. Thus this breakdown in separation (Ezra 9) would have continued during the prophetic ministry of Haggai and Zechariah (Hag.1:1-7; 2:19), and during the renewed work on the Temple, for Ezra to have to deal with this matter so soon after the Temple's dedication. The question of how long is the *after these things* of Ezra 7:1 is the crucial issue of the entire debate. Bullinger gives one year, while the traditional span is 59 years (516-457 BC). Bullinger's one year, as we will show, is probably right!
61. Why, if the wall was rebuilt in 454 BC, is it only dedicated now? Bullinger is silent as to a reason for this 51-year gap.
62. Jones, p.215.
63. Anstey, p.49.
64. *Ibid.* p.154.
65. *Ibid.* p.139.
66. *Ibid.* Anstey counts his revised dates from Adam; these are here converted to the BC reckoning.
67. *Ibid.* pp.232, 233.
68. *Ibid.* p.19.
69. *Ibid.* pp.19,20.
70. *Ibid.* p.25.
71. *Ibid.* p.31.

CHAPTER 1: SEVEN CHRONOLOGIES COMPARED

72. Anstey, pp.244,251.
73. Chronologists who have developed Denny's principles during the 20th century have said that the years from Creation to the Exodus were lunar years of 354 days. Therefore it is possible, they say, to convert from lunar back to solar for the totals. Thus the 2008 years would be reduced to 1946 solar years, and the 505 to 490 years. This would give a creation date of 4075 BC rather than 4152 BC. But whether what the Bible calls *years* can be converted back and forth in this manner is doubtful. The Hebrew year was luni-solar, with the moon determining the length of the months and the sun the length of the year. And as twelve lunar months were eleven days short of one solar year, the Hebrew year was found in a most remarkable way to be self-adjusting. Each year the Jews would look for the appearance of the almond tree blossoms (in February) followed several weeks later by the appearance of the ripened ears of barley. The next new moon after this would commence the first month of the new year. This was called Abib or "first ear of ripe grain." Thus yearly they were to look to the Lord of the harvest and of the heavens (Gen.8:22; Job 38:33). The lunar cycles would determine their monthly feasts and the solar cycle their agricultural year. But as both are intertwined, to say that you can measure an extended period by "lunar" rather than solar years as Denny, Anderson and others have, must surely be a fallacy. For a full discussion see Floyd Jones pp.109-113.

"And about the time of <u>forty years</u> suffered he their manners in the wilderness. And <u>when he had destroyed seven nations</u> in the land of Chanaan, he divided their land to them by lot. And after that he gave unto them judges about the space of <u>four hundred and fifty years</u>, until Samuel the prophet. And afterward they desired a king: and God gave unto them Saul the son of Cis, a man of the tribe of Benjamin, by the space of <u>forty years</u>. And when he had removed him, he <u>raised up unto them David</u> to be their king…"

(Acts 13:18 – 22)

CHAPTER TWO

FIRST DIVIDE: THE EXODUS TO THE TEMPLE

The Bible's *Crux Chronologorum* may be readily seen by adding up the years recorded from Exodus 12 to I Kings 6. This count, over 600 years, will be found to be in harmony with Paul's statement in Acts 13:18-22a.

> And about the time of <u>forty years</u> suffered he their manners in the wilderness. And when he had destroyed seven nations in the land of Chanaan, he divided their land to them by lot. And after that he gave unto them judges about the space of <u>four hundred and fifty years</u>, until Samuel the prophet. And afterward they desired a king: and God gave unto them Saul the son of Cis, a man of the tribe of Benjamin, by the space of <u>forty years</u>. And when he had removed him, he raised up unto them David...

The Scriptural times will be found to be as follows:

40 years	In the wilderness
7 years	To conquer and divide the land (Josh.14:8-10)
450 years	"after that, until Samuel the prophet"
20 years	Unto Samuel's victory at Mizpeh
10 years	Unto Saul's reign
40 years	Saul's reign
40 years	David's reign
<u>4 years</u>	Unto the Temple's construction in Solomon's 4th year.
611 years	

The figures from Acts and Judges seem to be in conflict with I Kings 6:1.

> And it came to pass in <u>the four hundred and eightieth year</u> after the children of Israel were come out of the land of Egypt, in the fourth year of Solomon's reign ... that he began to build the house of the LORD.

The reader will want to look again at Edward Denny's explanation of this apparent contradiction in Chapter One. He shows that if the years recorded in Judges when Israel because of apostasy was under foreign domination are subtracted, the result will take us to the 480 years of I Kings 6:1. As the purpose of the Exodus was fellowship in the Temple - *He brought us out that He might bring us in* (Deut.6:23) - the years out of fellowship are not counted.

This appears to me to be the correct approach. But while some have followed it - Anstey, The Companion Bible, Dakes Bible etc. - most of the better-known chronologists have not. Instead they have proposed that the 450 years of Acts, rather than being lineal, are the sum of overlapping time increments. By doing this, Floyd Jones, for example, shortens the span to 299 years and is thereby able to make all of the events fit into the 480-year time frame.

Before examining how this 151-year reduction is made, we will first show that in a natural reading of the chronological portions there is -

1. NO OBVIOUS OVERLAPPING IN JUDGES

Except for Samson's 20-year judgeship occurring within the 40-year Philistine oppression - a fact clearly indicated - reading through Judges does not give the impression of overlapping reigns and servitudes. There is no hint, let's say, of a judge ruling in the north of Israel while another was active in the south. Nor is there indication that the judges' rule somehow ran concurrently with the period of oppression. All seems to follow in an orderly, consecutive progression.

First Cycle 3:8-11

and the children of Israel served Chushan-rishathaim <u>eight years</u>. And when the children of Israel cried unto the LORD, the LORD raised up ... Othniel ... And the land had rest <u>forty years</u>. And Othniel the son of Kenaz <u>died</u>.

Second Cycle 3:12-31

And the children of Israel did evil again ... and the LORD strengthened Eglon ... So the children of Israel served Eglon the king of Moab <u>eighteen years</u> (3:14). But when the children of Israel cried unto the LORD, the LORD raised them up a deliverer, Ehud ... And the land had rest <u>fourscore years</u> (3:30). And <u>after him</u> was Shamgar ... which slew of the Philistines six hundred men.

Third Cycle 4:1 - 5:31

And the children of Israel again did evil in the sight of the LORD, <u>when Ehud was dead</u>. And the LORD sold them into the hand of Jabin king of Canaan ... and <u>twenty years</u> he mightily oppressed the children of Israel (4:3). And Deborah ... sent and called Barak ... And the LORD discomfited Sisera, and all his chariots ... And the land had rest <u>forty years</u> (5:31).

CHAPTER 2: FIRST DIVIDE: THE EXODUS TO THE TEMPLE

Fourth Cycle 6:1 - 8:32

And the children of Israel did evil in the sight of the LORD: and the LORD delivered them into the hand of Midian <u>seven years</u> (6:1). But the Spirit of the LORD came upon Gideon (6:34) ... Thus was Midian subdued before the children of Israel ... And the country was in quietness <u>forty years</u> in the days of Gideon (8:28).

Fifth Cycle 8:33 - 9:57

And it came to pass <u>as soon as Gideon was dead</u> that the children of Israel turned again ... And Abimelech the son of Jerubbaal went to Shechem ... When Abimelech had reigned <u>three years over Israel</u> (9:22) ... a certain woman cast a piece of a millstone upon Abimelech's head ... and <u>he died</u>.

Sixth Cycle 10:1,2

And <u>after Abimelech</u> there arose to defend Israel Tola ... And he judged Israel <u>twenty and three years, and died</u>.

Seventh Cycle 10:3-5

And <u>after him</u> arose Jair a Gileadite, and judged Israel <u>twenty and two years</u> ... And <u>Jair died</u>.

Eighth Cycle 10:6 - 12:7

And the children of Israel did evil again in the sight of the LORD ... and he sold them into the hands of the children of Ammon. And <u>that year</u> they vexed and oppressed the children of Israel: <u>eighteen years</u>, all the children of Israel that were on the other side of Jordan (10:8) ... Moreover the children of Ammon passed over Jordan ... so that Israel was sore distressed. And the children of Israel cried unto the LORD ... Then the Spirit of the LORD came upon Jephthah ... And he smote them ... And Jephthah judged Israel <u>six years</u>. <u>Then died Jephthah</u> (12:7).

Ninth Cycle 12:8-10

And <u>after him</u> Ibzan of Bethlehem judged Israel ... <u>seven years</u>. <u>Then died Ibzan</u>.

Tenth Cycle 12:11-12

And <u>after him</u> Elon, a Zebulonite, judged Israel ... <u>ten years</u>. And <u>Elon died</u>.

Eleventh Cycle 12:13-15

And <u>after him</u> Abdon ... judged Israel <u>eight years</u>. And <u>Abdon ... died</u>.

Twelfth Cycle 13:1 - 16:31

And the children of Israel did evil again in the sight of the LORD; and the LORD delivered them into the hand of the Philistines <u>forty years</u> (13:1) ... Then three thousand men of Judah went to the top of the rock Etam, and said to Samson, Knowest thou not that the Philistines <u>are rulers over us</u> (15:11)? ... And he judged Israel <u>in the days of</u> the Philistines <u>twenty years</u> (15:20) ... But the Philistines took him, and put out his eyes (16:21) ... And Samson said, Let me <u>die</u> with the Philistines (16:30) ... And he judged Israel <u>twenty years</u> (16:31).

Thirteenth Cycle I Sam 1 - 7

Now Eli the priest sat upon a seat by a post of the temple of the LORD. (I Sam.1:9) ... And the Philistines fought and Israel was smitten ... And the ark of God was taken ... Now Eli was ninety and eight years old ... And it came to pass, when he made mention of the ark of God, that he fell from off the seat backward ... And he had judged Israel <u>forty years</u> (4:10,11,16,18). And the men of Kirjath-jearim came, and fetched up the ark ... And it came to pass while the ark abode in Kiriath-jearim, that the time was long; for it was <u>twenty years</u>; and all the house of Israel lamented after the LORD (7:1,2) And Samuel spake unto all the house of Israel ... And gathered together to Mizpeh ... And Samuel judged the children of Israel in Mizpeh (7:3,6).

Reading through these thirteen cycles several times gives the distinct impression that it is a consecutive presentation of the oppressions and the judges' rule. This impression becomes virtual certainty when we discover that by adding the underlined years the total is 450 years.

<u>Oppression</u>	<u>Rest</u>	
8 yrs.	40 yrs.	First Cycle - Othniel
18 yrs.	80 yrs.	Second Cycle - Ehud, Shamgar
20 yrs.	40 yrs.	Third Cycle - Deborah, Barak
7 yrs.	40 yrs.	Fourth Cycle - Gideon
3 yrs!		Fifth Cycle - Abimelech
23 yrs.		Sixth Cycle - Tolah
22 yrs.		Seventh Cycle - Jair
18 yrs.	6 yrs.	Eighth Cycle - Jephthah
7 yrs.		Ninth Cycle - Ibzan
10 yrs.		Tenth Cycle - Elon
8 yrs.		Eleventh Cycle - Abdon
40 yrs.		Twelfth Cycle - Samson
40 yrs.		Thirteenth Cycle - Eli
20 yrs. [1]		To Samuel's Victory
131 yrs.	+	319 yrs. = 450 yrs.

CHAPTER 2: FIRST DIVIDE: THE EXODUS TO THE TEMPLE

The fact that the stated periods in Judges and I Samuel equal 450 years (as in Acts 13:20) is a convincing argument that they are to be taken as consecutive rather than overlapping. And as Denny shows, when the 131 years of being out of fellowship are subtracted from the total years for the exodus to the Temple (611 years), they equal the 480 years of I Kings 6:1. This is one of the great wonders in Bible Chronology.

Nevertheless, Biblically sound chronologists as Floyd Jones believe that the 480 years is an absolute figure, and that the figures of Judges and Samuel and Paul's statement in Acts 13:20 are to be brought into line with it. They advance several arguments against the longer chronology, the chief being -

2. THE GENEALOGY OF DAVID

It is argued that the rule of the judges could not have extended to 450 years and must overlap, for in the line of David there are only four generations from the entry into Canaan unto Saul's reign.

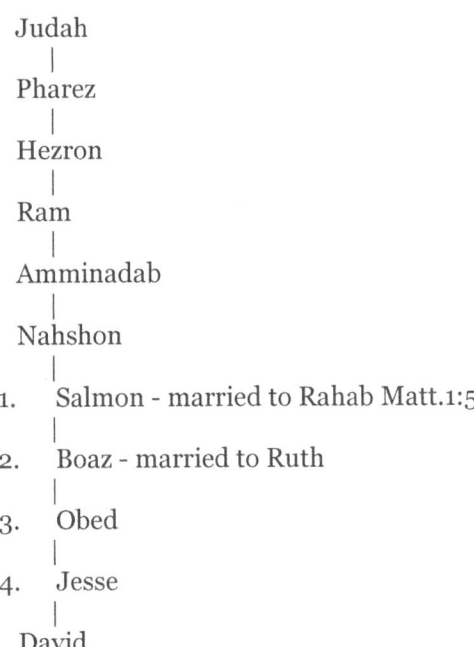

```
      Judah
       |
      Pharez
       |
      Hezron
       |
      Ram
       |
      Amminadab
       |
      Nahshon
       |
1.    Salmon - married to Rahab Matt.1:5
       |
2.    Boaz - married to Ruth
       |
3.    Obed
       |
4.    Jesse
       |
      David
```

BIBLE CHRONOLOGY: THE TWO GREAT DIVIDES

Therefore, if we use Denny's figures and count 611 years from the Exodus to Solomon's fourth year, and if we say that Salmon was about twenty when he entered Canaan and married Rahab, we are faced with a highly unlikely scenario -

Year

1	The Exodus
41	Entry into Canaan, Salmon at 20 years marries Rahab
c.165	Salmon at *124 years* begets Boaz
c.289	Boaz at *124 years* begets Obed
c.413	Obed at *124 years* begets Jesse
c.537	Jesse at *124 years* begets David
607	David dies after reigning 40 years
611	Solomon's fourth year

This would certainly represent four *miracle* births! The 480 year view, however, does not fare a great deal better for we still have these four men begetting at the age of one hundred. While it might be tempting to look for gaps in the line of David, the several places where the line is given is always as we have it here, and there is no indication in other passages of missing generations. In fact it should be noted that there are ten generations from Judah to Jesse, with David the eleventh. Pharez had been born illegitimately (Gen.38), thus disqualifying the line of Judah (Gen.49:10) from producing a king until the tenth generation (Deut. 23:2).

This is the chief argument against the longer chronology. Neither Denny and his particular school nor Anstey (surprisingly!) addresses the problem. Bullinger, however, believes that it is to be explained by gaps in David's line:

> The inference therefore seems clear that, as in a *Royal* line it is not necessary to include every link (as it is in the case of an ordinary man) certain names are omitted in this pedigree, in order that "the generations of Pharez" may be reckoned as ten generations, to accord with the principle which we observe from Adam to Zedekiah (viz. Adam to Noah, ten; Shem to Abraham, ten; Solomon to Zedekiah, twice ten). So here Pharez to David is given in ten generations. [2]

Bullinger then goes on to cite Matthew 1 as an example of abridgement in royal genealogy.

But of course the line of Christ does not divide into the royal and natural (i.e. to Mary) until the generation *after* David. Further, unless a gap exists between Obed and Jesse the inclusion of the mother's names in Matt. 1:5 rules out the possibility of missed generations between the other names.

CHAPTER 2: FIRST DIVIDE: THE EXODUS TO THE TEMPLE

> And Salmon begat Booz of Rachab; and Booz begat Obed of Ruth; and Obed begat Jesse.

With regard to Obed and Jesse, the wording of Ruth 4:17 needs to be carefully considered:

> And the women her neighbours gave it a name, saying, There is a son born to Naomi; and they called his name Obed: he is the <u>father</u> of Jesse, the <u>father</u> of David.

Is it likely that "father" would be used in the first instance as grand- or great-grandfather, if in the second it is the actual father?

The Bible records a number of much longer genealogies in the line of Levi. These span the same period. Ezra 7 records ten high priests from the crossing of Jordan to the generation before David.

	Aaron	
1.	Eleazar	Death mentioned in Josh.24:33
2.	Phineas	High priest at the beginning of the judges. Jdg.20:28
3.	Abishua	
4.	Bukki	
5.	Uzzi	
6.	Zerahiah	
7.	Meraioth	
8.	Azariah	
9.	Amariah	
10.	Ahitub	In Saul's reign, II Sam.8:17
	Zadok	One of two high priests in David's reign, II Sam.8:17

The genealogies for David's choir leaders Asaph (I Chr.6:39-43) and Ethan (I Chr.6:44-47) record about the same number of generations as that of the high priest. It is, however, in the genealogy of the third choir leader Heman that we find a more than adequate number of generations to span 450 years. Remarkably, Heman is the grandson of Samuel.

I Chr. 6:33-38 records -

	Levi	
	Kohath	
	Izhar	
	Korah	
1.	Elisaph	He did not die when the ground swallowed his father (Num. 16:27-33; 26:11) and would likely have lived into the time.
2.	Assir	

    3. Tahath
    4. Zephaniah
    5. Azariah
    6. Joel
    7. Elkanah
    8. Amasai
    9. Mahath
    10. Elkanah
    11. Zuph
    12. Toah
    13. Eliet
    14. Jeroham
    15. Elkanah
    16. Shemuel   - Samuel
         Joel
         Heman   - Appointed to the Levitical choir in David's time.

While believing that the Bible is clear as to there being only four generations in David's line spanning the period of the judges, we agree it is highly unusual. Perhaps they alert us to a series of miracle births before David, and indeed to prepare the world for the miraculous birth of the Son of David. Perhaps the phrase "root of Jesse" is a reference to this (cp. Isa.11:10 with 53:2). But whatever the reason, the line of David cannot be used as a conclusive argument against the longer chronology. The <u>parallel line of Samuel</u> with its sixteen generations averaging 28 years would easily span 450 years.

Before looking at some of the other means chronologists use to reduce these 450 years we must first test the longer chronology in the light of –

3. SIX DISPUTED TIME PERIODS

Note again what Scripture seems clearly to show concerning the main time divisions from the exodus to the Temple dedication.

    40 yrs.   In the wilderness
    7 yrs.   To conquer and divide the land
    450 yrs.   (*20 + 430) "after that, until Samuel the prophet"
    20 yrs.   Unto Samuel's victory at Mizpeh
    *10 yrs.   From Samuel's victory to Saul's reign
    40 yrs.   Saul's reign
    40 yrs.   David's reign
    4 yrs.   To Solomon's 4th year, and beginning of the Temple
    7 yrs.   To completion of Temple

CHAPTER 2: FIRST DIVIDE: THE EXODUS TO THE TEMPLE

<u>*3 yrs.</u>   To furnishing and dedication of the Temple
621 yrs.

There are three time periods (*) where Scripture does not directly state the number of years. The first of these unstated periods is -

(1) From the Division of Canaan to the First Oppression - Twenty Years

When chronologists reject the 450 years as a consecutive span, they have removed the one clear pointer for determining this unstated period and have been left instead to give what is frequently little more than an estimate. These vary widely; for example, Ussher has 31 years, while Jones makes it 44 years. But when the 450 years are accepted for what they say they are, a definite conclusion can be reached. The time is 20 years.

Note the wording of Acts 13:19,20:

> And when he had destroyed seven nations in the land of Chanaan, he divided their land to them by lot. And after that he gave unto them, judges about the space of four hundred and fifty years, until Samuel the prophet.

A reasonable and natural understanding of these words is to count 450 years from the dividing of Canaan to the end of Eli's judgeship, during which time Samuel was being increasingly recognized as Israel's prophet.

Before the account of Eli's death (I Sam.4:18), I Sam.3:20,21 says:

> And all Israel from Dan even to Beersheba knew that Samuel was established to be a prophet of the LORD. And the LORD appeared again in Shiloh: for the LORD revealed himself to Samuel in Shiloh by the word of the LORD.

As there are 430 years from the beginning of the servitude to Chushan-rishathaim to the death of Eli, there must therefore be 20 years for the unstated period.

This approach seems preferable to that of Anstey (and Bullinger with some differences) who counts the 450 years from the first servitude to Samuel's victory at Mizpeh, 20 years after Eli's death (I Sam.7:1-12). But by this time Samuel would have been a prophet for at least and probably well over 20 years. And this means they must rely on some other factor to determine the length of the unstated period.

Anstey describes the method used:

> The determination of the length of this period has been a great puzzle to the chronologers. To all of them except the author of the *Companion Bible* ...
>
> The number of years in the so-called Joshua-Judges chasm ... is 13. This is involved in the length of the long period from the conquest and occupation of Heshbon by Joshua in the year before the entry into Canaan (Deut.2) to its reconquest by Ammon 300 years later. Now we know the length of every constituent portion of this period from the division of the land to the oppression of Cushan, and they amount altogether to 287 years. Therefore we conclude by an inevitable historical induction that that period must have contained exactly the remaining 13 years. [3]

But as Anstey goes on to show, it is not nearly so simple as this. For, from the first years of Cushan (Jdg. 3:8) to the 22nd year of Jair (Jdg. 10:3) is 301 years. And then there is the further 18 years (Jdg. 10:8) that the Philistines and Ammonites "vexed" the children of Israel. Thus it is after 319 years of history in the Book of Judges added to the length of the chasm itself that Jephthah asks the king of Ammon:

> *And now art thou any thing better than Balak ... king of Moab? did he ever strive against Israel or did he ever fight against them, While Israel dwelt in Heshbon and her towns, and in Aroer and her towns, and in all the cities that be along by the coasts of Ammon, <u>three hundred years</u>? why therefore did ye not recover them within that time? (Jdg.11:25,26).*

We will shortly examine the relationship of these 300 years to our proposed longer chronology. But for now we must stress that Bullinger and Anstey have had to alter the natural reading of Judges 10:3-9 in order to arrive at their conclusion. Notice carefully this passage:

> *And after him arose Jair, a Gileadite, and judged Israel <u>twenty and two years</u> ... And <u>Jair died</u> ... And the children of Israel did evil again in the sight of the LORD ... and he sold them into the hands of the Philistines, and into the hands of the children of Ammon. And <u>that year</u> they vexed and oppressed the children of Israel: <u>eighteen years</u>, all the children of Israel that were on the other side Jordan ... in Gilead. Moreover the children of Ammon passed over Jordan to fight also against Judah, and against Benjamin, and against the house of Ephraim; so that Israel was sore distressed.*

Shortly after Jair died (cp. 8:33) Israel did evil, and immediately, *that year*, they began to be oppressed by the Philistines and Ammonites. This oppression lasted 18 years unto the judgeship of Jephthah. Now this seems quite plain. Anstey however says:

> *The words "that year" refer to the 1st year of the Judgeship of Jair, in which the children of Ammon "broke and crushed" the children of Israel, and thereby recovered possession of Heshbon, and some part of the land of Israel, which they held during the 22 years of Jair; whilst the words "eighteen years" refer to the time when, immediately after the death of*

CHAPTER 2: FIRST DIVIDE: THE EXODUS TO THE TEMPLE

> *Jair, they subdued and oppressed "all the children of Israel" on both sides of the river Jordan.* [4]

Thus by this reckoning, neither Jair's 22 years nor the following 18 years are included in the 300 years, and he makes the 300 years end in the 1st year of Jair. [5]

He then shows:

1 yr.	Conquest of Heshbon to crossing of Jordan
7 yrs.	Crossing to division of land
....	Unstated period
<u>279 yrs.</u>	First servitude to Tola's judgeship (before Jair)
287 yrs.	+ 13 yrs. = 300 yrs.

But, as we are following and upholding the Authorized Version in these chronological studies, this proposal must be rejected. No one reading these verses would ever imagine that "that year" in Judges 10:8 refers back to 10:3 and the 1st year of Jair's 22-year term. The passage simply does not say that. Further, other considerations show that 13 years is too short a time for this period.

Floyd Jones also uses the 300 years to determine the Joshua-Judges chasm, but as his system is based on a reduction of the 450 years we will wait until later to look at his method. Suffice it for now to say that the 44 years he proposes seems certain to be too long.

Having introduced these 300 years we must now examine how they fit in with the longer chronology.

(2) The Three Hundred Years

Let us note again that in his appeal to the aggression of the king of Ammon, Jephthah argued that -

> *... Israel dwelt in Heshbon and her towns, and in Aroer and her towns, and in all the cities that be along by the coasts of Arnon, <u>three hundred years</u>? why therefore did ye not recover them within that time? (11:26).*

Israel conquered this region several months before the beginning of the year when they crossed Jordan, and for 300 years it had been her *possession*.

BIBLE CHRONOLOGY: THE TWO GREAT DIVIDES

> *Wilt not thou <u>possess</u> that which Chemosh thy god giveth thee to <u>possess</u>? So whomsoever the LORD our God shall drive out from before us, them will we <u>possess</u> (11:24).*

The following table (allowing the 20 years to be correct) shows 346 years from the year before the Jordan crossing to the beginning of Jephthah's judgeship. These 46 additional years must refer to times when civil rule east of Jordan lapsed and Israel could not have been said to be in *possession*.

(x months)	Conquest of Heshbon to entry
7 yrs.	Entry to division
20 yrs.	Division to 1st oppression
8 yrs.	Servitude to Cushan king of Mesopotamia
40 yrs.	Rest under Othniel
*18 yrs.	Servitude to Eglon king of Moab
80 yrs.	Rest under Ehud
20 yrs.	Servitude to Jabin king of Canaan
40 yrs.	Rest under Deborah and Barak
*7 yrs.	Servitude to Midianites
40 yrs.	Rest under Gideon
3 yrs.	Usurpation by Abimelech
23 yrs.	Judgeship of Tola
22 yrs.	Judgeship of Jair
*<u>18 yrs.</u>	Servitude to Philistines and Ammonites
346 yrs.	

There were three periods (*) totalling 43 years that would have directly affected Israel's possession of the eastern regions. In his remonstrance with the king of Ammon, Jephthah could not have included them, and when subtracted we come very close to the figure of 300 years.

Chronologists have used these 300 years to reduce the length of the Book of Judges. And as they frequently propose around 40 years for the chasm, they are forced to remove some 66 years from the stated times between Cushan and Jephthah. How much better to take all of the chronological statements at face value and see that when these servitudes are removed, and the servitudes from the 450 years, the three great time spans of 300, 450 and 480 years are found to be in complete harmony.

We now come to a further consideration which supports our view that the Joshua-Judges chasm is nearer 20 years than the 13 years proposed by Bullinger and Anstey or the 31 years of Usshur and certainly than the 44 years of Jones.

CHAPTER 2: FIRST DIVIDE: THE EXODUS TO THE TEMPLE

(3) The Ages of Joshua, Caleb and Othniel

Joshua and Caleb alone from the doomed generation were allowed to enter the Promised Land (Num.26:65). At the time of the Exodus, though said to be "one of Moses' young men" (Num.11:28; Ex.33:11), Joshua was old and mature enough to be made the leader of Israel's army (Ex.17:9). But 47 years later when Canaan is divided, he is said to be "old and stricken in years", while Caleb is strong and healthy at age 85 (Josh.14:10). Joshua died at 110 years (Josh.24:31), and was followed in death by the remainder of his generation.

> *And Israel served the LORD all the days of Joshua, and all the days of the elders that overlived Joshua, and which had known all the words of the LORD, that he had done for Israel (Josh.24:31).*

Israel then forsook the LORD for Baal and Ashtaroth (Jdg.2:13). They are sold to Cushan for 8 years (3:8). They cry out, God raises up a deliverer -

> *...even Othniel the son of Kenaz, Caleb's younger brother ... And the land had rest forty years. And Othniel the son of Kenaz died. And the children of Israel did evil (Jgd.3:9,11,12).*

The account of Othniel places a time constraint upon the period from the division to the servitude, and demonstrates that our calculated 20 years is entirely reasonable. In Joshua 15:15-17 (land divided) Othniel is old enough to conquer a city and marry the daughter of 85-year-old Caleb! Generally we would not expect an octogenarian's unmarried daughter to be a "spring chicken." Thus if Othniel was only twenty-five at his marriage - and he could easily have been older - we have the following years for his life.

- 25 ... at the division
- 45 ... beginning of first servitude (20 yrs. after the division)
- 53 ... defeats Cushan, becomes first judge
- 93 ... dies after 40 years rest

If, as Jones and other chronologists who give forty or more years to the chasm, then we meet with the unlikely scenario that Othniel defeated Cushan and became judge when he was above seventy.

Coming again to Joshua, with these factors in mind, and assuming that Joshua was somewhat older than Caleb who was thirty-eight at the Exodus, his history would be more or less as follows:

    48 ... at the Exodus
    95 ... at the division
    110 ... at death
    5 years of decline, culminating in servitude to Cushan (20 yrs. after the division)

It is argued that forty-eight is too old for a "young man" (Ex. 33:11). But, he was one of *Moses'* young men (Num.11:28) who was eighty at the time. Certainly today a man of forty-eight in high office is considered young. Others think that five years is not enough time for the other leaders of Joshua's generation to die off, and for such a fatal apostasy to take hold. But the remaining leaders are of course also old men, they are nameless (Jdg.1:1), and they do not begin to approach Joshua's stature and influence. With such a vacuum it would not take long for the nation to slide into terminal decline (cp.Jdg.8:33). When we consider the rapid changes of our day, five years can be a long time.

However, a study of the above tables will also show that the 13 years for the chasm proposed by Bullinger and Anstey would not likely provide enough time.

From these considerations our calculated twenty years appears to be the correct solution. We now come to the second unstated period in the time span from the Exodus to the Temple.

(4) From Samuel's Victory at Mizpeh to the Beginning of Saul's Reign - Ten Years

We are not directly told how many years elapsed from Samuel's victory over the Philistines at Mizpeh (I Sam.7:7-13) unto the beginning of Saul's reign (I Sam.9:1 - 10:1). But, as the total of the other periods (excluding the 131 years [6] when Israel was under foreign domination) add up to 470 years, and as I Kings 6:1 says that it is 480 years, we must assume that the unstated time is 10 years.

From our previous tables the reckoning is as follows:

    40 yrs.   From the Exodus to the crossing of the Jordan
    7 yrs.   From the crossing to the division of the land
    20 yrs.   From the division to the first oppression
    319 yrs.   For the period of the judges unto Samuel's victory at Mizpeh
                  (450 yrs.-131 yrs. = 319 yrs.)
    ....   From Samuel's victory to Saul's reign
    40 yrs.   Saul's reign
    40 yrs.   David's reign

CHAPTER 2: FIRST DIVIDE: THE EXODUS TO THE TEMPLE

<u>4 yrs.</u> To Solomon's 4th year and beginning of Temple
470 yrs. + 10 yrs. = 480 yrs. I Kings 6:1

A direct solution to this unstated period is possible only if both redemption and actual chronology are accepted as existing in Scripture. The wide variance among chronologists using the other approach aptly demonstrates the deficiency of a system based on conjectural overlaps. Ussher, for example, gives 15 years to this period and Jones 6 years. Bullinger and Anstey, whose chronology for Judges is not based upon overlaps but who nevertheless contorts the stated years prior to Jephthah, have 20 and 0 years (!) respectively. And as for this latter, I Sam.7:12-8:5 shows Anstey is certainly wrong to propose that Saul was anointed king almost immediately after Samuel's victory at Mizpeh.

This brings us now to the third unstated period, and as chronologists note that the 7 years Solomon was building the Temple and the 13 years he was building his own house equals the stated 20 years of I Kings 9:10, this period has gone virtually unnoticed.

(5) From the Completion of the Temple to its Dedication - Three Years

Redemption has its glorious conclusion in the building and dedication of the Temple. Here the purpose of the Exodus is consummated. *He brought us out that he might bring us in* (Deut.6:23). That I Kings 6:1 should link this beginning and consummation, and that the span in question is near to the Jubilee- significant 490 years is a matter to be carefully considered.

I Kings 6:1-36 describes the construction of the Temple, and then states in verses 37 and 38 that the House was finished in seven years. This according to redemption reckoning would bring us to 487 years from the Exodus. We are not told how long it took to make and adorn the Temple with its elaborate furnishings and appointments. That this work is subsequent to the actual Temple construction seems evident from the fact that its description is given in 7:13-51 *after* the statement of the seven years in 6:38.

> *And Solomon made all the vessels that pertained unto the house of the LORD ... So was ended all the work that king Solomon made for the house of the LORD (7:48,51).*

And as the Temple construction was completed in the 8th month of the 7th year (6:38), but is dedicated in the 7th month, (8:2), at the very least one year transpires before its dedication.

Edward Denny believed that the time spent on these furnishings was three years, so that as with the previous spans when the time came to dedicate the Lord's House (8:1-9:9) it was found to be in the 490th redemptive year since the Exodus.

We look now at one final and at first very puzzling time period in the Exodus to Temple span.

(6) Absalom's Forty Years

> *And on this manner did Absalom to all Israel that came to the king for judgement: so Absalom stole the hearts of the men of Israel. And it came to pass <u>after forty years</u>, that Absalom said unto the king, I pray thee, let me go and pay my vow, which I have vowed unto the LORD, in Hebron*
> *(II Sam.15:6,7).*

To what do these forty years refer? A study of the context will show that it could not be to the years Absalom stood at the gate, or his age (he was born some years after David's 40-year reign began), or David's age (David was much older than this), or the 40th year of David's reign. The key is to be found in the words that Absalom *stole the hearts of the men of Israel*. Who did he steal them from? He stole them from David! When does the Bible say that David *won the hearts of the men of Israel*? It was when he slew Goliath, and his victories over the Philistines in the months that followed.

> *And when the Philistines saw their champion was dead, they fled. And the men of Israel and Judah arose and shouted ... (I Sam.17:51,52).*
>
> *And [David] was accepted in the sight of all the people, and also in the sight of Saul's servants (I Sam.18:5).*
>
> *But all Israel and Judah loved David because he went out and came in before them (I Sam.18:16).*
>
> *... so that his name was much set by (I Sam.18:30).*

Therefore in about the 58th year of his life, 40 years after he slew Goliath, David *lost* the hearts of the men of Israel.

After giving a full discussion of this passage, Floyd Jones writes: "The Biblicist must exercise faith rather than doubt when he doesn't understand." [7] Yet, as we will now show, sound chronologists as Jones are forced to make what must surely be uncomfortable concessions when the stated years from the Exodus to the Temple are forced into the 480 years of I Kings 6:1.

CHAPTER 2: FIRST DIVIDE: THE EXODUS TO THE TEMPLE

4. FITTING 611 YEARS INTO 480 YEARS!

Many who construct a chronology of the Old Testament show no qualms in altering the text and translation (not to mention the punctuation) of the Authorized Version. The work of Floyd Jones is different. It stands firm for the Massoretic Text and Authorized Version, and displays many years of spiritually diligent research. There are few works that we go to with greater confidence. Yet in taking the position that Acts 13:18-21 must *fit into*, rather than *coexist* with I Kings 6:1, he and other chronologists have had to resort to the following:

(1) Straining the Text

On the Acts 13:18-21 account of the 40 years in the wilderness, 450 years of judges, and the 40-year reign of Saul, Jones says:

> ... rather than adding 40+450+40=530 years, the 40s were found to overlap the period of 450 and thus should be subtracted from the total. [8]

Despite his attempts to explain this, few indeed reading the passage and noting especially the *after that*, *until*, and *after* would come to this conclusion.

Another example concerns the Judges account of the second servitude and deliverance:

> *So the children of Israel served Eglon the king of Moab eighteen years (3:14)....*
> *So Moab was subdued that day under the hand of Israel, And the land had rest fourscore years (3:30).*

Of this Jones writes:

> The problem is that English punctuation and syntax suggest that the land had rest for a period of 80 years after Moab's defeat, however Hebrew contains no punctuation. Thus Judges 3:30 should be understood as saying "and the land had rest" followed by a pause in thought whereby the following 80 years" is a summary statement referring to the entire period of time covered by the story." [9]

Thus he places the 18 years within the 80. It would take a long pause indeed to leave the reader with the impression that "fourscore years" is not directly referring to "rest"! Following this precedent, Jones places several of the other servitudes within the stated periods of rest.

And then, in order to make the years fit, some respected and supposedly Bible-believing chronologists have taken the further step of -

(2) Denying the Text

Ivan Panin shortens Saul's reign from forty to two years. Regarding the statement of Acts 13:21 that it was forty years, he says:

> As to Paul's apparently assigning to Saul a forty years reign, exclusive of Samuel's judgeship - it is impossible. [10]
>
> Still, Paul's 40 years would be decisive, if no other meaning could be gotten out of his words. But Paul does not necessarily say this. [11]
>
> In any case, Saul did not reign 40 years ... [12]

Panin tries to show that God *gave* Saul a forty year reign, but because of his disobedience he removed him after only two years. This is not what Acts 13:21 *says*, nor is it what the I and II Samuel account *indicates*. For there we find that Saul at the beginning of his reign was a *young man* (I Sam.9:3), and five years after his death, his son Ish-bosheth is said to be *forty years old* (II Sam.2:10). Thus, I Samuel shows that the reign of Saul was about forty years. But the chief means used to reduce the stated years is through -

(3) Conjectural Overlaps

I call these overlaps *conjectural* because reading through Judges and I Samuel would never lead us to suspect that they exist. Yet, apart from a wholesale denial of the stated years this is the only option available if one accepts the 480 years as an absolute figure. A number of rather complex arrangements have been proposed. The following from Floyd Jones' work shows how the 450 stated years from the first oppression to Samuel's victory at Mizpeh are reduced to 299 years.

	stated	Jones
(1) 8 yrs. to Cushan included in the 40 yrs. under Othniel	48 yrs.	40 yrs.
(2) 18 yrs. to Eglon included in the 80 yrs. under Ehud	98 yrs.	80 yrs.
(3) 20 yrs. to Jabin included in the 40 yrs. under Deborah and Barak	60 yrs.	40 yrs.
(4) 7 yrs. to Midian included in the 40 yrs. under Gideon	47 yrs.	40 yrs.
(5) 3 yrs. under Abimelech	3 yrs.	3 yrs.
(6) 23 yrs. under Tola	23 yrs.	23 yrs.
(7) 18 yrs. to Ammon included in the 22 yrs. under Jair	40 yrs.	22 yrs.
(8) 6 yrs. under Jephthah	6 yrs.	6 yrs.

CHAPTER 2: FIRST DIVIDE: THE EXODUS TO THE TEMPLE

(9) 7 yrs. under Ibzan	7 yrs.	7 yrs.
(10) 10 yrs. under Elon	10 yrs.	10 yrs.
(11) 8 yrs. under Abdon	8 yrs.	8 yrs.
(12) 40 yrs. to the Philistines (Samson is judge 20 yrs. during the second half, but with no deliverance). During the first half of these 40 yrs. Jones includes 2 yrs. of Ibzan, 10 yrs. of Elon, 8 yrs. of Abdon: 40-2,-10,-8=20	40 yrs.	20 yrs.
(13) 40 yrs. under Eli. Jones overlaps Eli with Jair (10 of his 22 yrs.), Jephthah, Ibzan, Elon, Abdon, and places his death just *before* the 20 yrs. of Samson begin	40 yrs.	0 yrs.
(14) 20 yrs. under Samuel's prophetic ministry to his victory at Mizpeh. Jones overlaps this with the 20-yr. judgeship of Samson	20 yrs.	0 yrs.
	450 yrs.	299 yrs.

Others have proposed different arrangements, but this is one example of how the stated times are reduced so that they fit into the 480 years. Again I must refer the reader back to the beginning of this second section where the chronological passages of Judges were written out, and ask if there is any hint -

> (1) that in the first four cycles the stated years of oppression are to be *included* in the stated years of rest? Certainly not!
> (2) that among the latter judges the tenures of Jephthah and four others coexist with Eli and Samuel? Or that during the same twenty years that Samuel is engaged in his prophetic ministry (I Sam.5-7), Samson is struggling against the Philistines (Jdg.13-16)? This is indeed very hard to imagine.

CONCLUSION

It is here that we close our examination of the first of two major divides of Bible Chronology - the famous *Crux Chronologorum*. Most, including the standard chronology by Ussher, have accepted that I Kings 6:1 presents an absolute figure, with Acts 13:20 and the stated times of Judges being made to fit in. I think the material presented above makes this position untenable. Such a reduction can only come about by straining, and indeed contorting and wresting the chronological statements of the Authorized Version. In fact, by taking such a tortuous course they have demonstrated that the *Crux Chronologorum* remains just that!

On the other hand there is a perfect harmony of *all* the stated times when it is accepted that I Kings 6:1 reveals a redemption chronology existing alongside the Bible's actual chronology. A convincing demonstration of this is that when the years of servitude are subtracted from the total stated times, they exactly equal the 480 years of I Kings 6:1. Thus, in redemption chronology the years out of fellowship are not counted.

Most today who know of this principle have seen it second-hand in the work of Bullinger and Anstey, but I think that Edward Denny, who first wrote on the subject, and his more immediate followers give a better presentation.

It is through this seeming contradiction that Scripture opens up the marvellous truth of seventy-times-seven forgiveness (Matt.18:22). And as Denny sought to show, this may well be the chronological key to redemption history from Adam right on through to the Second Coming of Christ.

As we come now to the investigation of the Second Divide, we will find it to be a daunting challenge. It brings us to a time of history that Anstey called "the most difficult period in the whole realm of Bible Chronology." It appears to be a time in which a battle raged to dislodge (at least in the minds of men) the cornerstone of chronology - the Seventy Weeks of Daniel.

CHAPTER 2: FIRST DIVIDE: THE EXODUS TO THE TEMPLE

NOTES: CHAPTER TWO

1. As these 20 years are a *stated* period (I Sam.7:2), for the sake of illustration I have added them here as part of the 450 years. In fact they are subsequent to the 450 years, which as Denny shows begin with the division of Canaan and end with Eli's term as judge. In this way Acts 13:20 is the means of determining the *unstated* time from the division to the start of the Canaanite oppression.
2. *Companion Bible*, p.365.
3. Anstey, pp.137,139.
4. Anstey, p.140.
5. *Ibid.* p.146.
6. This as we have shown is: 8 yrs. to Chushan, 18 yrs. to Eglon, 20 yrs. to Jabin, 7 yrs. to the Midianites, 18 yrs. to the Philistines and Ammonites, 40 yrs. to the Philistines during Samson's time and 20 yrs. to the Philistines at the beginning of Samuel's time = 131 yrs.
7. pp.104,105.
8. *Ibid.* p.74.
9. *Ibid.* pp.74,75.
10. Ivan Panin, *Bible Chronology*, (Burnaby B.C.: The Association of the Covenant People, 1950), p.97.
11. *Ibid.* p.99.
12. *Ibid.* p.101.

"I have raised him (Cyrus) up in righteousness, and I will direct all his ways: <u>he shall build my city</u>, and he shall let go my captives, not for price nor reward, saith the LORD of hosts."

(Isaiah 45:13)

CHAPTER THREE

SECOND DIVIDE: CYRUS TO ALEXANDER

As we appear to have an unbroken *genealogy* from Adam to Christ (Luke 3) we would expect also to have an unbroken *chronology* over the same span of time. And indeed we do from Adam to the end of the captivities. But then remarkably as this long chronicle of years comes to an end, Daniel is given the prophecy of the Seventy Weeks, and with this we are able to link and bridge the last of the stated years all the way to the Cross of Christ. Or so it would seem! Because for most this is not the case. Ptolemy, the chronicler of Alexandria, entered the scene in the 2nd century AD and presented figures which push Daniel and the weeks back some eighty-eight years (to 538 BC) with the result that if they begin with the decree of Cyrus they will run out 55 years *before* the birth of Christ.

Ptolemy's Canon has received near universal acceptance, and it, rather than the Seventy Weeks, has been the bridge from the captivities to Christ.

The following dates of Biblical events down to Alexander are based on the Canon and accepted by nearly all.

BC
- 539 (late) Babylon falls to Persia; Darius the Median takes the kingdom being 62 years of age (Dan. 5:31). He reigns two years with Cyrus.
- 538 Daniel is given the Seventy Weeks prophecy in the 1st year of Darius "the son of Ahasuerus"(Dan. 9:1).
- 536 Cyrus in his 1st year is charged by God to let the Jews return and build the Temple (IIChr. 36:22,23). 49,897 return to Israel. Cyrus reigns as sole-rex seven years.
- 529 Cambyses becomes king, halts work on the Temple, reigns eight years.
- 521 Darius Hystaspes becomes king, reigns thirty-six years.
- 520 Haggai and Zechariah stir the people to renew work on the Temple. Darius Hystaspes in the 2nd year of his reign (519 BC) re-enforces the decree of Cyrus (Ezra 4:24; 5:1-6:14).
- 516 The Temple is dedicated in the 6th year of Darius Hystaspes (Ezra 6:15).
- 486 Xerxes becomes king, reigns twenty-one years.
- 479 Xerxes (=Ahasuerus) makes Esther queen in the 7th year of his reign (Est. 2:16).
- 474 Haman plots to kill the Jews in the 12th year of Ahasuerus' reign (Est. 3:7). Mordecai is made Prime Minister in the following year.
- 465 Artaxerxes Longimanus becomes king, reigns forty years.

458	Artaxerxes in his 7th year grants the "request" of Ezra (Ezra 7:6-8), and allows him to return and "beautify" the Temple (7:27). This permission took the form of a "decree" (7:13,21), and seems to be linked to the original decree of Cyrus (6:14).
445	Artaxerxes in his 20th year grants the "request" of Nehemiah (Neh. 2:1-4), and allows him to return and build the walls of Jerusalem. The king writes "letters" enabling Nehemiah to obtain the necessary materials (2:7,8). Many see this as <u>the starting point of the 69 weeks</u> (=483 years). But as this would come to 39 AD, they have followed Sir Robert Anderson who considers these to be prophetic years of 360 days thus reducing the span to about 476 solar years and resulting in 32 AD for the crucifixion. It is, however, questionable whether such a long period of time should ever be figured in any other but solar years. And would the Jews who measured time according to their *observed* luni-solar year (see ch.1, note 72) have known to calculate the time of Messiah's death according to this other measure? On the other hand, it is argued that as according to Rev. 11:2,3; 12:14; 13:5 the 70th week is composed of 360 day years can we not then assume that the sixty-nine weeks would be the same? The debate will continue, but as we shall see there is a far more problematic issue involved here.
433	Artaxerxes in his 32nd year (Neh. 13:6, called here the "king of Babylon") grants further leave to Nehemiah. This is the last recorded date in the Old Testament.
424	Xerxes becomes king, reigns one year. This is the first of six remaining Persian kings listed by Ptolemy. There is, however, but little near-contemporary historical evidence.
423	Darius II Nothus becomes king, reigns nineteen years.
404	Artaxerxes II Mnemon becomes king, reigns forty-six years.
358	Artaxerxes III Ochus becomes king, reigns twenty years.
338	Arses becomes king, reigns three years.
335	Darius III Codomannus becomes king, reigns four years.
331	Persia falls to Alexander the Great.

This is the Traditional Chronology. It is virtually "fixed in stone" and apart from minor revision is seldom to be seriously questioned. Many, though, are not aware of how little evidence there is to corroborate the six kings and one hundred years or so of Persian history between Artaxerxes Longimanus and Alexander. As far as Persia is concerned it hangs on not a great deal more than the historian Diodorus (50 BC), and the thread of Ptolemy's Canon. Therefore how stable is the historical basis for these years? Do all or most of these years, in fact, exist? And if the Persian evidence is weak, can this period be bridged with firm data from Greek and Jewish sources? We will be looking at these questions.

Few also are aware that by assigning ninety-two years from Cyrus to Nehemiah, and a total of 205 years from Cyrus to Alexander, serious conflicts arise with the statements of Scripture, but also with well-known secular sources such as Josephus.

Thus, we want to be absolutely clear as to what the Bible, the Authorized Version, says about this matter, and examine to what extent it is in opposition to Ptolemy's Canon. Below are seven

CHAPTER 3: SECOND DIVIDE: CYRUS TO ALEXANDER

areas of Scriptural and historical evidence which on the face of it shows that Ptolemy cannot possibly be right for the Persian period.

1. THE SEVENTY WEEKS SEEM CERTAIN TO BEGIN WITH THE CYRUS DECREE

Given its emphasis in Scripture and the fact that it is the subject of a two hundred year old prophecy (Isa. 44,45), and occurring so soon after Daniel received the prophecy, it seems highly unlikely that any decree other than that of Cyrus could be considered as the starting point for the Seventy Weeks. It is *the* decree, and the basis and precedent for any further decrees. Nevertheless, according to the Canon it cannot be considered, for the weeks would fall some fifty years short of the birth of Christ. And further we are told by virtually all commentators of our premillennial school:

> Daniel was told that this 490-year period would begin "from the going forth of the commandment to restore and to build Jerusalem" (Dan. 9:24). In the Scriptures are contained several decrees that have to do with the restoration of the Jews from the Babylonian captivity. There was the decree of Cyrus in II Chr. 36:22,23; the decree of Darius in Ezra 6:3-8; and the decree of Artaxerxes in Ezra 7:7. However, in all these permission was granted for the rebuilding of the temple and nothing was said about the rebuilding of the city ... When we turn to the decree of Artaxerxes, made in his twentieth year, recorded in Neh. 2:1-8, for the first time is permission granted to rebuild the city of Jerusalem (emphasis mine).[1]

This standard answer is in fact conditioned by the Canon and not by the actual facts as revealed in Scripture. Yet, despite Ptolemy, there is compelling Scripture evidence which points to Cyrus.

(1) It was prophesied that Cyrus would indeed *build* Jerusalem

> *That saith of Cyrus, He is my shepherd and shall perform all my pleasure: even <u>saying to Jerusalem, Thou shalt be built</u>; and to the temple, Thy foundation shall be laid* (Isa. 44:28).

> *I have raised him up in righteousness, and I will direct all his ways: <u>he shall build my city</u>, and he shall let go my captives, not for price nor for reward, saith the Lord of Hosts (Isa. 45:13).*

What could be plainer! Notice that, *he shall build my city*, is mentioned with, and in fact before, *he shall let go my captives*. It is noteworthy that writers pass over these passages and concentrate instead on II Chr. 36:22,23 and Ezra 1:1-11 where it mentions the Temple rather than the city aspect of Cyrus' decree. For example, Floyd Jones does not mention Isa. 44:28 and

45:13. And while John Walvoord makes brief references, he does not discuss their significance.[2] And further, the fact that Cyrus in II Chr. 36 and Ezra 1 stresses the Temple, must certainly presuppose the redevelopment of the city around the Temple. The Temple would be at the heart of the city's restoration. Where indeed is it to be thought that some of the nearly 50,000 returnees will be living? The *going forth of the commandment to restore and to build Jerusalem* is precisely what happened with the Cyrus decree.

(2) It is likely that God "stirred" the heart of Cyrus by acquainting him with the prophecy of Isa. 44:28-45:13

> *Now in the first year of Cyrus king of Persia, that the word of the LORD by Jeremiah might be fulfilled, the LORD stirred up the spirit of Cyrus king of Persia, that he made a proclamation throughout all the kingdom, and put it also in writing saying, Thus saith Cyrus king of Persia, The LORD God of heaven hath given me all the kingdoms of the earth; and he hath charged me to build him an house in Jerusalem, which is in Judah (Ezra 1:1,2).*

Cyrus' recognition that *God had given him all the kingdoms of the earth* was precisely what Isaiah had prophesied.

> *Thus saith the LORD to his anointed, to Cyrus, whose right hand I have holden to subdue nations before him ... (Isa. 45:1).*

Indeed it would have been incredible for Cyrus to proceed as he did and not to know the Isaiah prophecy.

Perhaps Daniel showed it to him, or as Josephus says:

> *This was known to Cyrus by his reading the book which Isaiah left behind him of the Prophecies. (XI.5-7).* [3]

None of the later "decrees" was in any sense a subject of prophecy as this one was.

(3) Even allowing for exaggeration, the Jews' enemies are adamant that the early returnees had begun to rebuild the city

This point was the basis of their accusation to the king of Persia.

CHAPTER 3: SECOND DIVIDE: CYRUS TO ALEXANDER

> *Be it known unto the king, that the Jews which came up from thee to us are come unto Jerusalem, <u>building the rebellious and the bad city</u>, and have set up the walls thereof, and joined the foundations (Ezra 4:12).*

It is doubtful that much if any work had been done on the actual walls of the city. But the Jews' accusers saw work on the Temple walls as but a preliminary to rebuilding the city walls (cp. Ezra 4:13,16,21; 5:3,8). It is also pointed out that when Nehemiah came to build the walls, the city was severely underpopulated (Neh.2:3; 7:4; 11:1). Questions, however, concerning the *extent* of the city's rebuilding are beside the point. The decree of Cyrus clearly gave them the right to build both the city and Temple, and thus we read that the returnees with Zerubbabel *came again unto Jerusalem and Judah, every one unto his city* (Ezra 2:1; Neh.7:6). During the remaining six years of Cyrus' reign, they naturally would have begun some rebuilding work, at the very least their own accommodation. We can hardly imagine them living in tents all that time!

(4) The repetition of *the commandment going forth* in 9:23,25 indicates that they are one and the same, thus showing that the Weeks are in the process of beginning

Many see the command in verse 23 as given to the angel, but this is not what the passage actually says:

> *O Daniel. I am now come forth to give thee skill and understanding. At the beginning of thy supplications <u>the commandment came forth</u>, and I am come to show thee ... therefore understand the matter and consider the vision (9:22,23).*

> *Know therefore and understand, that from <u>the going forth of the commandment</u> to restore and to build Jerusalem unto the Messiah the Prince shall be seven weeks, and threescore and two weeks: the street shall be built again, and the wall, even in troublous times (9:25).*

Rather than a command to Gabriel, verse 23 speaks of a command that has *gone forth*, i.e. issued from the Lord. Gabriel has now come to *show* it to Daniel. After which, Cyrus himself will hear, either through Daniel or some other means of revelation, this same command. He will then issue it forth to the Jews. Scripture places great emphasis upon the fact that a Divine constraint was placed upon Cyrus.

> *the LORD stirred up the spirit of Cyrus king of Persia, that he made a proclamation ... All the kingdoms of the earth hath the LORD God of heaven given me; and <u>he hath charged me</u> to build him an house in Jerusalem*
> (II Chr.36:22,23).

This is repeated in Ezra 1, where again we hear Cyrus' testimony "He hath charged me." In none of the subsequent decrees do we read even remotely of such Divine obligation being placed upon the king. It could only be Cyrus who was the recipient of the commandment going forth.

(5) The decree of Cyrus was the basis and precedent for actions of subsequent Persian kings

Cyrus' decree was primary, while those of Darius in his 2nd year (Ezra 5:9-6:8) and Artaxerxes in his 7th and 20th years (cp. Ezra 6:14) were secondary, and but an adjunct to the original. Therefore Cyrus is the logical starting place of the Seventy Weeks.

Notice how Josephus confirms this principle and also that Cyrus had intended to restore Jerusalem:

> And all that Cyrus intended to do before him, relating to the restoration of Jerusalem, Darius also ordained should be done accordingly. (XI.63).

(6) The revelation of the Seventy *Weeks* was the Lord's answer to Daniel's prayer concerning the seventy *years* (Dan.9:2), and are therefore linked

Given that the decree of Cyrus provided the *conclusion* to the seventy years, there is every likelihood that it provided the *commencement* to the Seventy Weeks.

(7) The start of the Seventy Weeks was something Daniel could *know*

As Daniel actually saw the decree go forth from Cyrus and was perhaps party to it, he would likely assume that this was the fulfilment of that which Gabriel revealed to him a short time before and would also assume the Weeks were now beginning. Thus it was something he would know experientially. This explains the emphasis on the word "know".

> *Know* therefore and <u>understand</u> that from the going forth of the commandment to restore and to build Jerusalem ... (Dan.9:25).

The prophecy of the Weeks would not have been in any practical and personal sense an answer to Daniel's prayer unless he actually saw them begin.

CHAPTER 3: SECOND DIVIDE: CYRUS TO ALEXANDER

(8) Only the Cyrus decree would alert the Jews to begin a count to the Messiah

While most premillennialists believe the 20th year of Artaxerxes Longimanus is the starting point to the Seventy Weeks, few have considered how minor this so-called decree was in comparison with that issued by Cyrus. In fact it is not called a decree but is rather the granting of the request of Nehemiah (Neh.2:4,8). The king provided a guard and wrote letters of authorization to the Persian authorities enabling Nehemiah to reach Judah and to obtain timber for the work (2:7-9), but in all other respects his coming to Jerusalem was unannounced, and with but few accompanying him (2:11,12,16). The extent of the rebuilding was limited to a three-fold objective:

> *that he may give me timber to make beams for the gates of the palace which appertained to the house, and for the wall of the city and for the house that I shall enter into (2:8).*

The reader must ask whether the Jews would be sufficiently alerted by such a restrained and unannounced event to "know" (Dan.9:25) that the counting of Weeks to Messiah was then to begin. Contrast this with the worldwide proclamation given to Cyrus' decree:

> *the LORD stirred up the spirit of Cyrus king of Persia, that he made a proclamation throughout all his kingdom, and put it in writing, saying, Thus saith Cyrus king of Persia, The LORD God of heaven hath given me all the kingdoms of the earth; and he hath charged me to build him an house at Jerusalem ... (Ezra 1:1,2).*

No one could miss this, a fact which leads naturally to our next point.

(9) Only the Cyrus decree would be a basis for the calculations of the Wise Men

Scripture specifically points to a linkage between Daniel and the wise men of Babylon, and it may be reasonably assumed that the wise men that came to pay homage to the infant Christ based and timed their journey according to the Seventy Weeks prophecy.

> *Then the king made Daniel a great man, and gave him many great gifts, and made him ruler over the whole province of Babylon, and chief of the governors over <u>all the wise men</u> of Babylon (Dan. 2:48).*

With the other "decrees" so little known, it is difficult to conceive the wise men commencing the count from anything other than the decree of Cyrus. And the very fact that they were looking for

Christ's birth (Mt. 2:2), rather than his ministry and death 33 years later shows that the decree of Cyrus must have been about 451 BC; i.e. 451 + 33 -1 for BC/AD = 483 years.

(10) Jerusalem's desolation was to be *limited* to seventy years and its rebuilding would span forty-nine years

> *In the first year of his reign I Daniel understood by books the number of the years, whereof the word of the LORD came to Jeremiah the prophet, that he would accomplish <u>seventy years in the desolations of Jerusalem</u> (Dan. 9:2).*
>
> *that from the going forth of the commandment to restore and to build Jerusalem ... shall be <u>seven weeks</u> ... the street shall be built again, and the wall even in troublous times (Dan. 9:25).*

Realizing that this revelation was in answer to Daniel's prayer, it would be natural for him to assume that though he could not personally return to Jerusalem he *could* have the joy of knowing that work was shortly to begin and would be largely completed in forty-nine years. But there would be no personal satisfaction if major restoration were only to start in ninety-three years (538-445 BC), and completion not until 142 years. Certainly this would not be an answer to the *immediacy* of Daniel's prayer.

> *O Lord, according to all thy righteousness, I beseech thee, let thine anger and thy fury be turned away from thy city Jerusalem, thy holy mountain ... <u>Now therefore</u>, O Our God, hear the prayer of thy servant, and his supplications, and cause thy face to shine upon thy <u>sanctuary</u> that is desolate ... and behold our desolations, and the <u>city</u> which is called by thy name ... O Lord, hear; O Lord, forgive; O Lord <u>hearken and do; defer not</u>, for thine own sake, O my God; for thy city and thy people are called by thy name (Dan. 9:16-19).*

Daniel asked the Lord to *defer not* in the restoration of Jerusalem. Reading onward from verse 20 gives the clear impression that the Lord would not delay. Yet virtually all today follow a chronology in which He did defer and that by *nearly a century!*

Further, and this is the crucial point, Daniel had been reading the prophecy of Jeremiah which foretold that God "would accomplish *seventy years* in the desolations of Jerusalem" (Dan 9:2). How many chronologists have ignored the simple force of these words! Jerusalem will be a desolation for seventy years, not 160 years. Therefore, the decree to rebuild must occur at the close of the seventy years, and this must be the starting point of the Seventy Weeks.

Ezra in his prayer acknowledges that repairs to the desolations were well in place by the time of his own arrival in Jerusalem.

CHAPTER 3: SECOND DIVIDE: CYRUS TO ALEXANDER

> *For we were bondmen; yet our God hath not forsaken us in our bondage, but hath extended mercy to us in the sight of the kings of Persia, to give us a reviving, to set up the house of our God, and to <u>repair the desolations</u> thereof, and to give us a wall in Judah and in Jerusalem (Ezra 9:9).*

It is to be further noted that these seven weeks are not very well "nailed down" by commentators on Daniel Nine. They frequently pass over the clear distinction Dan. 9:25 makes between the seven and the sixty-two weeks. The reason is obvious. No natural conclusion is to be found for forty-nine years in the 536/445 BC chronology.

Unger gives the common view:

> An interesting but difficult question arises in connection with the division of the sixty-nine weeks from Artaxerxes' decree to the Messiah the Prince into a period of seven plus sixty-two weeks. There is no clear reason given for distinguishing the two periods ... The best explanation seems to be that, although Nehemiah finished the walls, it took a whole generation to rebuild the desolated city, and restore it as the beautiful, well-arranged capital it once was... [4]

"Whole generation" is hardly a precise equivalent for forty-nine years. And the proposal is further flawed on its premise that after nearly a century the seven weeks commence rather than conclude with Nehemiah's governorship, and then extend into a period where there is no known *terminus ad quem*.

If, on the other hand, the 12th year of Nehemiah's governorship coincides with the 32nd year of Darius Hystaspes rather than the 32nd of Artaxerxes Longimanus (cp. Neh 13:6), and this is added to the reigns of Cyrus and Cambyses (seven and eight years), the sum will be found to be about two years short of the forty-nine years.

The remaining years can be accounted for by noting that after his 12th year Nehemiah returned to Persia "and after certain days obtained leave" to return to Judah (Neh.13:6). These certain days were long enough for Eliashib to give Tobiah a lodging place in the Temple court and for the other declensions mentioned in Neh.13 to occur. The time Nehemiah then took to put these matters right and institute reforms would likely bring us up to the 49th year.

It has also been noted that Nehemiah's reforms coincide on a number of points with the subject matter of Malachi. This final book of the Old Testament may well have been written at the same time.

Consider the following examples from Nehemiah's reforms: [5]

1. He restored the Temple services (Neh. 13:11 with Mal. 1:7-14).
2. He restored the payment of the tithes (Neh. 13:12-14 with Mal. 3:8).
3. He put a stop to heathen marriages (Neh. 13:25-27 with Mal. 2:11-16).
4. He cleansed the priesthood (Neh. 13:29 with Mal. 2:1-8).

With this last event of the Old Testament we find a fitting conclusion to the seven weeks and the reason for the division of seven and sixty-two weeks - all of which is lacking in the Ptolemaic reckoning.

(11) How could Nehemiah be shocked over the report of Jerusalem's broken walls if ninety-one years had passed since the return from Babylon?

> *And they said unto me, The remnant that are left of the captivity there in the province are in great affliction and reproach; the wall of Jerusalem is also broken down, and the gates thereof are burned with fire. And it came to pass, when I heard these words, that I sat down and wept, and mourned certain days (Neh. 1:3,4).*

Merrill Unger's comment on this passage demonstrates the conflict and contradiction faced by those holding to the 536/445 BC chronology:

> Though many scholars refer this to the destruction in 586 BC, it is difficult to see why Nehemiah should be shocked at what happened almost a century and a half before. It is much more probable that the walls of Jerusalem had been partially restored and again demolished.[6]

Of this "second demolishing" Scripture makes no mention. Josephus, however, does have something to say; but first we need to be clear as to the Bible's description of the city's destruction by Nebuchadnezzar:

> *And he burnt the house of the LORD, and the king's house, and all the houses of Jerusalem, and every great man's house burnt he with fire. And all the army of the Chaldees, that were with the captain of the guard, broke down the walls of Jerusalem round about (IIKings 25:9,10; also IIChr. 36:19; Jer.52:).*

> *The LORD hath purposed to destroy the wall of the daughter of Zion: he hath stretched out a line, he hath not withdrawn his hand from destroying: therefore he made the rampart and the wall to lament; they languished together. Her gates are sunk into the ground; he hath destroyed and broken her bars (Lam. 2:8,9).*

> *The LORD hath accomplished his fury; he hath poured out his fierce anger, and hath kindled a fire in Zion, and it hath devoured the foundations thereof (Lam. 4:11).*

CHAPTER 3: SECOND DIVIDE: CYRUS TO ALEXANDER

Here is a picture of total desolation, and to say that Cyrus' decree gave no mandate to repair the city itself, and that significant repair did not begin until ninety-one years later, is completely untenable. Among all the lines of contrary evidence, what, for example, are the proponents of this view to do with Hag.1:4?

> *Is it time for you, O ye, to dwell in your cieled houses, and this house lie waste?*

The building of expensive houses certainly indicates that the rebuilding of Jerusalem had begun.

Coming now to the point of a possible second destruction of the walls, Josephus gives the following embellishment of Neh.1: 1-3:

> Now there was one of those Jews who had been carried captive, who was cupbearer to king Xerxes; his name was Nehemiah. As this man was walking before Susa, the metropolis of the Persians, he heard some strangers that were entering the city, after a long journey, speaking to one another in the Hebrew; so he went to them and asked them whence they came; and when their answer was that they came form Judaea, he began to enquire of them again in what state the multitude was, and in what condition Jerusalem was; and when they replied that they were in a bad state, for that their walls were thrown to the ground, and that the neighbouring nations did a great deal of mischief to the Jews... (XI.159-161).

He then goes on to relate Nehemiah's shock and sorrow, and his approach to the king. Now, whatever our view may be of Josephus here, one thing is certain: he did not believe that Nehemiah had heard a report describing a situation that had existed for 141 years! And further, if, as Unger, it is argued that there had been a destruction of partially restored walls, then their basic premise is contradicted that the decrees of Cyrus did not include the city, and that important rebuilding work did not begin until Nehemiah. Either way, proponents of the 586/536/445 BC chronology are upon the horns of a dilemma.

And consider further, that if the more common view be accepted that ninety-one years have elapsed since the return, how can it be explained that Nehemiah's response was not only of sorrow but also of surprise. With travellers going back and forth, surely he would have heard long before now.

And still further, does it seem likely or even possible that for seventy-one years after the Temple dedication Israelites made their way through fallen walls and burnt gates to worship at Jerusalem? Could there have been a fully functioning Temple in the mist of a desolate city? Yet this is what we are asked to believe if the Temple was finished in 516 BC, while the city remained waste until 445 BC.

From this and factors which we will soon discuss, Nehemiah's work on the walls must have taken place not nearly so long after the exiles' return and rebuilding of the Temple. It most likely occurred within the seven week (forty-nine year) framework from Cyrus' decree. As twenty or twenty-one years had expired by the time the Temple was dedicated, Nehemiah must have come during the remaining twenty-nine years. This, however, raises the question as to the identity of the Artaxerxes who granted him permission for the building work. We will examine this shortly.

(12) Josephus says that Cyrus' decree applied to the city

Whatever modern interpreters may think, Josephus, who lived before Ptolemy, leaves us in no doubt that Cyrus' decree mandated the city at large:

> In the <u>first year of Cyrus</u>, which was the <u>seventieth</u> from the day that our people were removed out of their own land ... God stirred up the mind of Cyrus, and made him write this throughout all Asia:- "Thus saith Cyrus the king; Since God Almighty hath appointed me to be king of the inhabited earth, I believe he is that God which the nation of the Israelites worship; for indeed he foretold my name by the prophets, and that I should build him a house at Jerusalem, in the country of Judaea." (XI.1-4).

> This was known to Cyrus by his reading the book which Isaiah left behind him of his prophecies ... Accordingly when Cyrus read this, and admired the divine power, an earnest desire and ambition seized upon him to fulfil what was so written; so he called for the most eminent Jews that were in Babylon, and said to them that he gave them leave to go back to their own country, and <u>to rebuild their city Jerusalem</u>, and the temple of God. (XI.5-6).

> When Cyrus had said this to the Israelites, the rulers of the two tribes of Judah and Benjamin, with the Levites and priests, went in haste to Jerusalem, yet did many of them stay in Babylon ... so they performed their vows to God, and offered the sacrifices that had been accustomed of old time; I mean this upon <u>the rebuilding of their city</u>, and the revival of the ancient practices relating to their worship ... Cyrus also sent an epistle to the governors that were in Syria, the contents whereof here follow:- ... I have given leave to as many of the Jews that dwell in my country as please to return to their own country, <u>and to rebuild their city</u>, and to build the temple of God at Jerusalem. (XI.8-9,12).

Three times in these paragraphs Josephus shows that Cyrus would not only decree the rebuilding of the Temple, but also and equally the city. With this we conclude twelve compelling reasons from Scripture that Cyrus did indeed build Jerusalem, and therefore the only conclusion to be drawn is that the Seventy Weeks begin with his decree.

To conclude this first section we note again that most fundamental of statements:

> *[The Lord] would accomplish seventy years in the desolations of Jerusalem (Dan.9:2).*

Seventy years and seventy years only! From then onward the decree goes forth to remove the desolations. This being the case, we can rely solely upon the Bible to give us the number of years from Adam to Christ.

We come now to a second witness from the Scriptures which further shows how far adrift the Traditional Chronology is.

2. THE SCRIPTURE LISTS SHOW THAT THE 586/536/445 CHRONOLOGY IS UNTENABLE

In the first example, Neh.10 records those who sealed the covenant with Nehemiah after the walls were built, and Neh.12 gives the leading priests and Levites who returned with Zerubbabel. We frequently find the *same names* in the *same order* in both lists, yet ninety-one years are supposed to separate them!

What would be the age of these men, if in 536 BC they were old enough to be *leaders* of the people and in 445 BC we find them sealing a covenant with Nehemiah?

More specifically, in Neh.10 we have a list of the priests, Levites and chief of the people who sign a covenant of consecration (cp. Neh.6:15;8:1,2,9;9:1). In ch.11 a plan is put forward to increase Jerusalem's population (cp. Neh 7:4). But before describing the dedication of the walls in 12:27, a list is given of the priests and Levites who returned *with Zerubbabel*. This contains the names of seventeen men who also signed the covenant in ch.10!

(1) Seventeen Priests and Levites

Covenant Signers with Nehemiah Neh. 10:1-10	Returning Exiles with Zerubbabel Neh.12:1-8
Seraiah	Seraiah
Jeremiah	Jeremiah
Amariah	Amariah
Malluch or Malchijah	Malluch

Hattush	Hattush
Shebaniah	Shechaniah
Meremoth	Meremoth
Ginnethon	Ginnetho
Abijah	Abijah
Mijamin	Miamin
Maaziah	Maadiah
Bilgai	Bilgah
Shemaiah	Shemaiah
Jeshua	Jeshua
Binnui	Binnui
Kadmiel	Kadmiel
Shebaniah	Sherebiah

The *order* in which the seventeen[7] names appear is virtually identical in both lists. This, despite a few spelling variations, clearly demonstrates that the individuals are the same. The enormity of this problem for the Traditional Chronology cannot be overstated. As Floyd Jones says:

> Not having noticed the problem inherent in comparing these two registers in relation to the dates they have assigned to them, nearly all scholars have failed to fathom the true extent and depth of the perplexity ... Unless a solution is found, the time disparity between the Nehemiah 10 and 12 lists invalidates not only Sir Robert Anderson's solution ... but all other accepted scenarios in use today as well. [8]

Notice how Merrill Unger in his comments on Neh.12:1-9 acknowledges that the names are the same but completely ignores the implications:

> These are the names of twenty-two priests and eight Levites who apparently returned with Zerubbabel. Fifteen of these priests sealed the covenant in Nehemiah's day. These and the numerous lists in Ezra-Nehemiah show how important pure Jewish descent was to the LORD's chosen covenant people. [9]

Frankly, from a Bible-believing standpoint, if one holds to the 536/445 BC chronology, there is little else one can do but pass over the matter. In Chapter One, however, we did look at one attempt. This we termed the "flash back" theory of Sir Isaac Newton. He proposed that after the description of Nehemiah's return to build the walls in Neh.1:1-7:4, Neh.7:5-12:26 (and thus the registers in chs.10 and 12) is a "flashback" to the time of the return under Zerubbabel in 536 BC. Thus the problem of the enormous ages of the covenant signers is immediately resolved.

But, as this view reckons Ezra and Nehemiah (Neh. 8:9) being present in Jerusalem in 536 BC for the start of the Temple and the covenant signing (Neh.9:38; 10:1), how old would they be in 445 BC (Artaxerxes' 20th year) and Nehemiah in 433 BC (Artaxerxes' 32nd year, Neh.13:6)?

CHAPTER 3: SECOND DIVIDE: CYRUS TO ALEXANDER

Could a man well in excess of 130 years show such physical energy as Nehemiah does in Neh.13:21-27? Any attempt to resolve this by suggesting that Nehemiah the wall-builder is different from Nehemiah the covenant-signer is of course countered by "both" being the son of Hachaliah (Neh.1:1; 10:1).

There are other and probably more serious problems in Newton's proposal. Apart from the two registers in Neh. 7:5-13 and 12:1-26, we are not given the impression that Nehemiah in chs.7-12 is narrating events that occurred ninety-one years earlier. These chapters seem naturally contemporary and sequential to the wall-building, and lead just as naturally to the wall-dedication (12:37) And if chs.7-12 go back to Zerubbabel's return in 536 BC, which was twenty-one years before the Temple was completed and dedicated, how is it that these same chapters speak of the Temple as an accomplished fact?

> *8:16 So the people went forth ... and made themselves booths ... in the court of the <u>house of God</u>.*
>
> *10:32 Also we made ordinances for us, to charge ourselves yearly with the third part of a shekel for the service of the <u>house of our God</u>.*
>
> *10:33 ... for all the work of the <u>house of our God</u>.*
>
> *10:34 ... for the wood offering, to bring it into the <u>house of our God</u>.*
>
> *10:35 And to bring the firstfruits ... unto the <u>house of the LORD</u>.*
>
> *10:38 ... shall bring up the tithe of the tithers unto the <u>house of our God</u>, to the chambers, into the treasure house.*
>
> *10:39… we will not forsake the <u>house of our God</u>.*
>
> *11:22 Of the sons of Asaph, the singers were over the business of the <u>house of God</u>.*

These verses show that the Temple had already been built, and therefore Newton's proposal is wrong that chs.7-12 go all the way back to the exiles' return. This is further demonstrated in ch.10:28 which speaks of a separation that had taken place.

> *And the rest of the people, the priests, the Levites, the porters, the singers, the Nethinims, and all they that had separated themselves from the people of the lands ...*

It is hardly likely that this mingling and subsequent separation would have taken place immediately upon their return from Babylon. This could only describe a situation which arose some considerable time later.

The verses and chapters do demonstrate, however, that while they occur after the Temple was built and dedicated (twenty-one years from the exiles' return), they seem not to have occurred so long after as is usually supposed. They express the kind of instruction and dedication that we would expect to see after the Temple began to function normally. Notice especially Neh.8:17:

> And all the congregation of them that were come again out of the captivity made booths, and sat under the booths: for since the days of Jeshua the son of Nun unto that day had not the children of Israel done so.

This along with Nehemiah's shock over Jerusalem's state (Neh.1:1-4) best harmonizes with a time not so far removed from the Temple dedication. Certainly the traditional seventy years (515 BC to 445 BC) is much too long.

Nowhere will the reader find a more thorough examination of the facets of this issue than in Floyd Jones' work. Accepting the Ptolemaic 536 BC as the correct date for the return from Babylon, we saw in Chapter One his reasons for revising the 20th year of Artaxerxes and Nehemiah's wall-building from 445 BC to 454 BC. But as this only marginally reduces the age problem, he utilizes Newton's proposal as an "acceptable answer" [10] to the Nehemiah 10 and 12 question. In doing this he is prepared to accept the excessive ages this gives to Ezra and Nehemiah, but does not explain how Nehemiah could be so physically active at 130 (Neh.13:6-31). Nor does he address the two further problems mentioned above.

What must certainly be the final and fatal blow to Newton's theory is to be seen in a comparison of the wall-builders in Neh.3 and the covenant-signers in Neh.10. According to Newton, Neh.10 took place in 536 BC and Neh.3. in 445 BC. But, in Neh.3:24 we read of a wall-builder, named Binnui the son of Henadad, and then among the covenant-signers we find Binnui of the sons of Henadad (10:9), A further search reveals that many of the names in these two chapters are the same.

(2) Sixteen Wall-Builders

Wall Builders Neh.3:1-32	Covenant-Signers Neh.10:1-27
Zaccur	Zaccur 10:12
Meremoth	Meremoth 10:5
Meshullam (2) 3:4,6	Meshullam (2) 10:7,20
Zadok (2) 3:4,29	Zadok 10:21
Hattush	Hattush 10:4
Malchijah	Malchijah 10:3

Hashub (2) 3:11,23	Hashub 10:23
Hanun ? (2) 3:13,30	Hanun ? (3) 10:10,22,26
Rehum	Rehum 10:25
Hashabiah	Hashabiah 10:11
Bavai ?	Bebai ? 10:15
Baruch	Baruch 10:6
Azariah	Azariah 10:2
Binnui	Binnui 10:9
Shemaiah	Shemaiah 10:8
Hananiah	Hananiah 10:23

Some sixteen of the wall-builders were also covenant-signers, which in addition to its implications for Newton's theory must show a not-too-far-removed proximity of the wall-builders to those listed in Neh.12.

Newton's proposal is therefore erroneous and can offer no help in relieving the Ptolemaic chronology of its dilemma.

The problems do not end here for the Traditional Chronology. In addition to the seventeen priests and Levites listed in Neh.10 and 12, there are fifteen "chiefs of the people" who signed the covenant with Nehemiah (Neh.10:14-18) and in Ezra 2 and Neh.7 11 are also listed among those who returned with Zerubbabel.

(3) Fifteen Chiefs of the People

Covenant-signers with Nehemiah Neh.10:14-18	Returning Exiles with Zerubbabel Ezra 2, Neh.7
Parosh	Parosh
Pahath-Moab	Pahath-Moab
Elam	Elam
Zatthu	Zattu
Bani	Bani, Binnui
Azgad	Azgad
Bebai	Bebai
Adonijah	Adonikam
Bigvai	Bigvai
Adin	Adin
Ater	Ater
Hizkijah[12]	Hezekiah
Hashum	Hashum

               Bezai   Bezai
               Hariph   Jorah, Hariph

"A threefold cord is not quickly broken" (Eccl.4:12). These two registers of the returnees from Babylon (Ezra 2, Neh.7) combine with the list of the covenant-signers to demonstrate that the return and wall-building took place in about the same generation. Notice again that the order of the names is virtually the same in each of the lists. Nor are Ezra 2 and Neh.7 a listing of ancestral names; they are precisely what Neh.10:14 calls them, "the chief of the people." If as some assume they were ancestral family names, dating long before the exile, then it is strange that they do not generally appear in the pre-exilic lists of I Chronicles and elsewhere. A search of each name in *Youngs Concordance* shows that with but few exceptions they occur only in Ezra and Nehemiah. Therefore it is during the exile that they become prominent as "chiefs" of large families and clans. In fact their sons were old enough to have taken strange wives after the return (Ezra 10:18-44), while other of their sons came with Ezra in the time after the Temple dedication (Ezra 8:1-14). Thus at the return these chiefs were not mere "thirty-year-olds." All of which makes it unthinkable that a further ninety-one years could be added to their ages as required by the 536/445 BC chronology.

Nehemiah Ten stands as a remarkable corrective in the study of Bible Chronology. This one chapter decisively exposes the fundamental error of Ptolemy's system.

But there is more to be seen in the Scripture lists.

(4) Thirteen "First Inhabitants" of Jerusalem

In I Chr.9 there is a list of the "first inhabitants" (9:2) who dwelt in Jerusalem after the return from Babylon (9:1-34). Many of these same men are listed in Neh.11, where they are introduced with the words:

> And the rulers of the people *dwelt* at Jerusalem: the rest of the people also cast lots; to bring one of ten to *dwell* in Jerusalem the holy city, and nine parts to dwell in other cities. And they blessed all the men that willingly offered themselves to *dwell* at Jerusalem. Now these are the chief of the province that *dwelt* in Jerusalem ... And at Jerusalem *dwelt* certain of the children of Judah, and of the children of Benjamin (Neh.11:1-4).

Reading this introduction does not give the impression that we are about to read a list of "rulers", "chiefs" and "others" who dwelt in Jerusalem nearly a century before the wall-building. But rather, in the general time frame of Nehemiah this is an account of those who chose of their own will to dwell in Jerusalem and those who were picked from among ten to live there, and as such, some are identified as "first inhabitants" (I Chr.9:2).

"First Inhabitants at Jerusalem" I Chr.9	"Now these dwelt at Jerusalem" Neh.11
Asaiah	Maaseiah
Sallu	Sallu
Jedaiah	Jedaiah
Jachin	Jachin
Azaraiah	Seraiah
Adaiah	Adaiah
Shemaiah	Shemaiah
1. Mattanaiah	Mattanaiah
2. Bakbakkar	Bakbukiah
3. Obadiah	Abda
4. Akkub	Akkub
5. Talmon	Talmon

The two lists present the names in the same order. And then a further indication that these men are *both* "first inhabitants" and yet also in Nehemiah's time, can be seen by comparing the last five names on the list with Neh.12:25,26:

Mattaniah and *Bakbukiah*, *Obadiah*, Meshullam, *Talmon*, *Akkub*, were porters keeping the ward of the thresholds of the gates. These were in the days of Joiakim the son of Jeshua, the son of Jozadak, and in the days of Nehemiah the governor, and of Ezra the priest, the scribe.

These five porters place a constraint on how much time could elapse from the return of the exiles to the "days of Joiakim" and the "days of Nehemiah." We now note two further men who do the same.

(5) Jeshua and Kadmiel

There is a remarkable linkage between the Levites - Jeshua (not the high priest) and Kadmiel. Together they span the time from the return to the building of the walls. Thus we see them:

Among the returning exiles.

The Levites: the children of Jeshua and Kadmiel, of the children of Hadaviah, seventy and four (Ezra 2:40).

> *The Levites: the children of <u>Jeshua,</u> of <u>Kadmiel</u>, and of the children of Hadevah, seventy and four (Neh.7:43).*

When the foundations of the Temple were laid.

> *and appointed the Levites ... then stood <u>Jeshua</u> with his sons and his brethren, <u>Kadmiel</u> ... to set forward the workmen in the house of God (Ezra 3:8,9).*

After the walls were built.

> *Then stood up upon the stairs, of the Levites, <u>Jeshua</u>, and Bami, <u>Kadmiel</u> ... and cried with a loud voice unto the LORD their God. Then the Levites, <u>Jeshua</u>, and <u>Kadmiel</u> ... said, Stand up and bless the LORD your God for ever and ever (Neh.9:4,5).*

At the sealing of the covenant.

> *And the Levites: both <u>Jeshua</u> the son of Azanaiah, Binnui of the sons of Henadad, <u>Kadmiel</u> (Neh.10:9).*

In the list of the returning priests and Levites.

> *Now these are the priests and the Levites that went up with Zerubbabel ... Moreover of the Levites: <u>Jeshua</u>, Binnui, <u>Kadmiel</u> ... (Neh.12:1,8).*

The linkage of their names makes it a virtual certainty that they are the same in each of the above passages. The lists do, indeed, present strong and consistent evidence that the time from the return of the exiles into Nehemiah's wall-building is not nearly so long as is usually presented.

We now come to a third major area of Scripture evidence against the Traditional Chronology.

3. MORDECAI AND EZRA WERE LIVING AT THE TIME OF JERUSALEM'S FALL

The Scripture shows that Mordecai and Ezra were born before Jerusalem fell to Babylon. This by Ptolemaic reckoning was 586 BC, yet the Ptolemaic dating also requires that these two men be alive and active some 130-140 years later.

CHAPTER 3: SECOND DIVIDE: CYRUS TO ALEXANDER

(1) Ezra's Genealogy

Ezra's father Seraiah was the high priest slain by Nebuchadnezzar. The high priestly line went from Seraiah to his son (and Ezra's brother) Jehozadak and then to Jeshua, the high priest who returned with Zerubbabel. Notice that except for some omissions in Ezra's genealogy, Ezra shares with Jehozadak the same line back to Aaron.

Ezra	Jehozadak
Ezra 7:1-5	I Chr.6:3-15
Aaron	1. Aaron
Eleazar	2. Eleazar
Phineas	3. Phineas
Abishua	4. Abishua
Bukki	5. Bukki
Uzzi	6. Uzzi
Zerahiah	7. Zerahiah
Meraioth	8. Meraioth
---	9. Amariah
---	10. Ahitub
---	11. Zadok
---	12. Ahimaaz
---	13. Azariah
---	14. Johanan
Azariah	15. Azariah
Amariah	16. Amariah
Ahitub	17. Ahitub
Zadok	18. Zadok
Shallum	19. Shallum
Hilkiah	20. Hilkiah
Azariah	21. Azariah
Seraiah	22. Seraiah
EZRA	JEHOZADAK

The slaying of Seraiah is described in II Kings 25:18-21 and also in Jer.52:24-27.

> *And the captain of the guard took Seraiah <u>the chief priest</u> and Zephaniah the second priest ... to the king of Babylon to Riblah; And the king of Babylon smote them and slew them.*

While in a few places "chief" is used in a general sense for leaders among the priests (I Chr.27:5; II Chr.36:14; Ezra 8:24,29; Neh.12:7,12), the designation "*the* chief priest" refers only to the high priest (II Kings 25:18; II Chr.19:11; 24:6; 26:20; Ezra 7:5; Jer.52:24). Thus, the passages above show clearly that the father of Ezra is the high priest slain by Nebuchadnezzar.

As this conflicts with the Traditional Chronology, the usual response is to make Ezra the great-grandson or more distant descendant of Seraiah. The McClintock and Strong Cyclopedia is typical:

> Ezra was a lineal descendant from Phineas, the son of Aaron (Ezra 7:1-5). He is stated to be the son of Seraiah, the son of Azariah; which Seraiah was slain at Riblah by order of Nebuchadnezzar ... But, as 130 years elapsed between the death of Seraiah and the departure of Ezra from Babylon ... we may suppose that by the term son here, as in some other places, the relationship of great-grandson or of a still more remote direct descendant, is intended. [13]

Nevertheless, in comparing Ezra's genealogy (Ezra 7:1-5) with I Chr.6:3-15 and the notice of the high priests in the Scripture history shows that in the eight generations to Seraiah there is no indication of a gap.

Azariah
Amariah
Ahitub
Zadok
Shallum
Hilkiah
Azariah
Seraiah
EZRA

Therefore it is reasonable for us to expect that as Seraiah was the son of Azariah, the son of Hilkiah, so in the same sense Ezra is the son of Seraiah. In view of Ezra's leadership in the nation, if he *were* a distant descendant, it would be appropriate to show the links to Seraiah. Certainly given the nature of Ezra's genealogy there is a great difference between being designated by Scripture "the son of Seraiah" and being merely one of Seraiah's many great-grandsons! There are no gaps between Seraiah and Jehozadak (I Chr.6:3-15) and we can be certain that the same is true for Ezra (Ezra 7:1-5).

There is, however, another Seraiah with a remarkably similar genealogy who might be thought to be Ezra's father.[14] He is listed among the priests who were "the first inhabitants" of Jerusalem after the return (cp. I Chr.9:2,3,10,11 with Neh.11:1,10,11).

> *Of the priests ... Seraiah the son of Hilkiah, the son of Meshullam, the son of Zadok, the son of Meraioth, the son of Ahitub, was the ruler of the house of God (Neh.11:10,11).*

CHAPTER 3: SECOND DIVIDE: CYRUS TO ALEXANDER

"Ruler of the house of God" here cannot mean high priest, for the high priest to the returning exiles was Jeshua followed by Joiakim, and then Elishib. This Seraiah was an "assistant to the high priest"[15] whereas the Seraiah of Ezra 7:1-5 was clearly the high priest. The similarity of the names and order in the genealogies can be attributed to the popularity of the high priestly names among the families of Levi. A comparison will show there are differences between the two lines, and in I Chr.9:11 this Seraiah is also named Azariah.

Thus, the Scripture evidence points strongly to the conclusion that Ezra was living at the time of Jerusalem's fall, that his father was Seraiah the high priest slain by Nebuchadnezzar, that his brother was the high priest Jozadak, and that his nephew was Jeshua, the high priest of the returning exiles.

This conclusion is impossible to reconcile with the 586/536/445 BC chronology. For Ezra to be contemporary with Nehemiah in 445 BC he would be at least 140 years old!

Regarding Nehemiah: apart from the fact that he was the son of Hachaliah and brother of Hanani (Neh.1:1,2; 7:2; 10:1), nothing further is revealed in Scripture of his or his father's and brother's genealogy.[16] The fact that he was made governor justifies the widely held view that he was of royal lineage.[17] It is also likely, and a matter we will look at shortly, that *he is* the Nehemiah whose name appears at the head of the list of returnees (Ezra 2:2; Neh. 7:7).

Coming now to Mordecai, we find that he has a genealogy in Scripture, but it is subject to two widely different interpretations.

(2) Mordecai's Genealogy

In Esther 2:5-7 we have the following:

> 5. Now in Shushan the palace there was <u>a certain Jew</u>, whose name was Mordecai, the son of Jair, the son of Shimei, the son of Kish, a Benjamite:
>
> 6. <u>Who had been carried away</u> from Jerusalem with the captivity which had been carried away with Jeconiah king of Judah, whom Nebuchadnezzar the king of Babylon had carried away.
>
> 7. <u>And he brought up Hadassah</u>, that is, Esther, his uncle's daughter: for she had neither father nor mother, and the maid was fair and beautiful; whom Mordecai, when her father and mother were dead, took for his own daughter.

"And he brought up Hadassah" (7), refers back as naturally to "who had been carried away" (6) as it does to "a certain Jew" (5). As the subject of verses five and seven are Mordecai, it seems far more likely that the entirety of verse six refers to him rather than his great-grandfather Kish. Therefore, it is Mordecai who was carried away with Jeconiah. But as this is reckoned by the Ptolemaic Chronology to be 597 BC, and as it is asserted that Xerxes is the Ahasuerus during whose 12th year (=474 BC) Mordecai is elevated (Est. 3:7; 10:3), commentators are forced to refer verse six to Kish.

A good example of the struggle that this entails can be seen in the following quotation from an earlier edition of *Encyclopaedia Britannica*.

> It must, however, be observed, that the serious chronological difficulty in Esther 2:5,6 (where Mordecai is apparently said to have been carried captive with Jeconiah) can hardly be removed by maintaining with Canon Rawlinson (contrary to Hebrew usage) that Kish, not Mordecai, is the person referred to. [18]

Floyd Jones has no doubt on this point:

> The solution to the dilemma, accepted by nearly all, has been to impose an unnatural rendering of the Esther 2:5-6 passage, compelling the verse to read as though it were Kish, Mordecai's Grandfather, who was carried away ... Notwithstanding, this interpretation is neither true nor an accurate rendering of the Hebrew construction which affirms that it was Mordecai who was carried away with Jeconiah. Only by a tortured, forced grammatical construction could this sentence ever be applied to his Great Grandfather Kish. [19]

As it would conflict with the Traditional Chronology, C. F. Keil doubts that it could be Mordecai who was carried away to Babylon. Yet, he acknowledges that Mordecai rather than Kish would grammatically be the subject of the "who" at the beginning of verse 6:

> Nevertheless it is more in accordance with the Hebrew narrative style to refer *asher* to the chief person of the sentence preceding it, viz. Mordecai, who also continues to be spoken of in ver. 7. [20]

Kiel gives a further reason why he does not believe it was Kish who was carried away:

> Jair, Shimei, and Kish can hardly mean the father, grandfather, and great grandfather of Mordecai ... Shimei was probably the son of Gera, well known to us from the history of David, II Sam. 16:5 sq. and I Kings 2:8,36 sq., and Kish the father of Saul, I Chron. 8:33, I Sam. 9:1. [21]

Which of course begs the question, "was anyone carried away?" According to Kiel the clause -

> ...need not be so strictly understood as to assert that Mordecai himself was carried away; but ... it involves only the notion that he belonged to those Jews who were carried to Babylon....[22]

Thus this learned author, because of the constraints of Ptolemy, has stripped from the passage its obvious meaning, in fact, any specific meaning at all!

Esther 2:5-7 shows that Mordecai was living at the time of Jerusalem's fall. This then raises the question as to which Persian king is the Ahasuerus of the Book of Esther. The question of the kings and priest will be discussed later, but for now it should be noted that Floyd Jones presents convincing arguments that it is Darius Hystaspes rather than Xerxes. And, Matthew Henry quotes the opinion of Lightfoot that it may be an even earlier king:

> Which of the kings of Persia this Ahasuerus was the learned are not agreed. Mordecai is said to have been one of those that were carried captive from Jerusalem (ch. 2:5,6) whence it should seem that this Ahasuerus was one of the first kings of that empire. Dr. Lightfoot thinks that he was that Artaxerxes who hindered the building of the temple, who is called also Ahasuerus (Ezra 4:6,7).[23]

This raises a question as to Esther's age (cp. Est. 2:7), of which several possibilities would seem to exist. But here we submit that the genealogies of Mordecai and Ezra show conclusively that both were living before the fall of Jerusalem, and could not have been actively engaged 130-140 years later as required by the Ptolemaic Chronology.

Our next point carries this argument further and is supported by what has been previously shown.

4. EZRA, NEHEMIAH AND MORDECAI ARE LISTED AMONG THE RETURNEES FROM BABYLON

While the Ptolemaic Chronology requires that the Ezra, Nehemiah and Mordecai of the returnees be different than those whose history we are familiar with, yet the Scriptures indicate otherwise.

> *Now these are the children of the province that went up out of the captivity, of those which had been carried away, whom Nebuchadnezzar the king of Babylon had carried away into Babylon, and came again unto Jerusalem and Judah every one into his own city; which came with Zerubbabel: Jeshua, Nehemiah, Seraiah, Reelaiah, Mordecai ... (Ezra 2:1,2).*

> *And my God put into mine heart to gather together the nobles, and the rulers, and the people, that they might be reckoned by genealogy. And I found a register of the genealogy of them which came up at the first, and found written therein, These are the children of the province ... who came with Zerubbabel, Jeshua, <u>Nehemiah</u>, Azariah, Raamiah, Nahamani, <u>Mordecai</u> ... (Neh.7:5-7)*
>
> *Now these are the priests and the Levites that went up with Zerubbabel the son of Shealtiel, and Jeshua: Seraiah, Jeremiah, <u>Ezra</u> (Neh.12:1).*

It is the *prominent* men that we have at the head of these lists. Given the rarity of their names in Scripture, is it likely that we would have two prominent Ezras (cp.Neh. 12:1,7 with Ezra 7:1-12), Nehemiahs and Mordecais, the one trio active in 536 BC and the second some eighty years later?

Apart from the above, there is only one other Ezra, a descendant of Judah (I Chr. 4:17); one other Nehemiah, a repairer of the wall (Neh. 3:16); and *no other* Mordecai. And then there is the distinguishing point made about Mordecai and Nehemiah in Ezra 2:1 and Neh.7:6, that they were among those "whom Nebuchadnezzar the king of Babylon had carried away unto Babylon." As Ezra and Mordecai have a genealogy which shows they were living at the time of Jerusalem's fall, and with the same confirmation for Nehemiah, it all points to a virtual certainty that these three returnees are the Ezra, Nehemiah and Mordecai we know from the rest of the Scriptures.

This of course requires that Ezra, Nehemiah and Mordecai returned to Persia after the exiles were settled and had begun work on the Temple. Mordecai would have returned permanently, while Ezra and Nehemiah came back to Jerusalem in the 7th and 20th years of Artaxerxes.

That this was a common view among earlier writers is seen in John Gill's comments on the list of returnees in Ezra 2:2:

> Dr. Lightfoot thinks that Nehemiah is the same, whose name the following book bears, and that Mordecai is he who was uncle to Esther, so Aben Ezra; but if so, they must return again ... and the same writer is of the opinion that Seriah, who is called Azariah, Neh. 7:7, is the same with Ezra, who therefore must and did return. [24]

And then going back to Josephus:

> Now there was one of those Jews who had been carried captive, who was cupbearer to King Xerxes; his name was Nehemiah. (XI.159).

Matthew Henry is of the same opinion:

CHAPTER 3: SECOND DIVIDE: CYRUS TO ALEXANDER

> Nehemiah and Mordecai are mentioned here; some think not the same with the famous men we afterwards meet with those names: probably they were the same, but afterwards returned to court for the service of their country. [25]

It is only because of Ptolemy's Canon that "some think not the same".

5. THERE DOES NOT APPEAR TO BE A LONG INTERVAL BETWEEN THE GOVERNORSHIPS OF ZERUBBABEL AND NEHEMIAH

Zerubbabel was the leader and the governor of the returning exiles. From I Chr. 3:16-19 (cp.Mt.3:12) he is the grandson of Jeconiah, the king, who at the age of eighteen (II Kings 24:8) had been carried into Babylon sixty-one years earlier. Thus Zerubbabel's maximum age at the return would not likely be above forty, and it was probably around thirty. This would make him about fifty at the time of the Temple's dedication (cp. Ezra 5:12; 6:15). After the dedication he is not seen further in the Scripture record.

It is in Neh. 12:47 where mention is made of the provision for the Temple singers and porters that we see the apparently close proximity between Zerubbabel and Nehemiah:

> *And all Israel in the days of Zerubbabel, and in the days of Nehemiah gave the portions of the singers and the porters every day his portion.*

Scripture does not mention any governor between these two men, though on first reading the following statement by Nehemiah might indicate otherwise:

> *But the former governors that had been before me were chargeable unto the people, and had taken of them bread and wine, beside forty shekels of silver (Neh. 5:15).*

Beginning with Gedeliah at the start of the exile, Jewish governors were appointed over Judah (II Kings 25:22,23), and thus Neh. 5:15 likely refers to the governors generally assigned by Babylon and Persia from that time.

It is further likely that if according to the Traditional Chronology the last mention of Zerubbabel is 515 BC and Nehemiah takes up his post in 445 BC Scripture would make some mention of an intervening governor. But none is made. Nor does Josephus (XI. 3-5), nor the apocryphal book, I Esdras (chs. 3-8). However, John Gill in his comments on Neh. 5:15 refers to the Seder Olam Zuta which lists the son and grandson of Zerubbabel as further governors.

> [A]ccording to the Jewish chronology, when Ezra came to Jerusalem, Zerubbabel returned to Babylon, and there died, and his son Methullam was in his stead, and after him succeeded Hananiah his son.[26]

This is not the son and grandson ascribed to Zerubbabel in our Lord's genealogies (Mt. 1:13; Lk. 3:27), but in I Chr. 3:19 Meshullam and Hananiah are both said to be the *sons* of Zerubbabel. In Ezra 8:16 (cp. 10:15) there is a Meshullam who is mentioned last among nine "chief men" called by Ezra to assist in dealing with the problem of the strange wives. And in Neh. 10:20 a Meshullam is listed 22nd among 45 "chief of the people" who signed the covenant with Nehemiah. Neither of these references would lead us though to think that the person named is the governor. As for Zerubbabel's son Hananiah, Neh. 7:1,2 may possibly be a reference to him.

> *Now it came to pass, when the wall was built, and I had set up the doors, and the porters and the singers and the Levites were appointed, that I gave my brother Hanani, and Hananiah the ruler of the palace charge over Jerusalem: for he was a faithful man, and feared God above many.*

But the point to emphasize is this: that if the Seder Olam is correct and Zerubbabel's governorship lasted until Ezra's coming to Jerusalem, then there would be only thirteen years between him and Nehemiah (Ezra 7:7; Neh. 2:1). And I think that the general tenor of the material presented above points to this kind of proximity between these two governors.

6. THE LINE OF THE HIGH PRIESTS SHOWS THAT THE PTOLEMAIC CHRONOLOGY FROM CYRUS TO ALEXANDER IS TOO LONG

Both Scripture and Josephus list six post-exilic high priests from Jeshua to Jaddua. Jeshua was the priest of the return, and according to Josephus, Jaddua was in office at the time of Persia's fall to Alexander the Great. Thus, if the Ptolemaic Chronology is followed, these six would span a period of 205 years (536 BC to 331 BC). As the high priest has to reach the age of at least thirty before his service began, this would give an average term of about thirty-three years. This compares with twenty-three years for the seventeen high priests who served during 390 years[27] from the schism to the destruction of Jerusalem. A much greater problem, however, for the Ptolemaic Chronology is that each of the post-exilic priests seems to have been living during the lifetime of Nehemiah, and *four* during his governorship!

Two passages in Neh. 12 list the six priests:
> *And Jeshua begat Joiakim, Joiakim also begat Eliashib, and Eliashib begat Joiada, And Joiada begat Jonathan, and Jonathan begat Jaddua (12:10,11).*

CHAPTER 3: SECOND DIVIDE: CYRUS TO ALEXANDER

> *The Levites in the days of Eliashib, Joiada, and Johanan, and Jaddua, were recorded chief of the fathers: also the priests to the reign of Darius the Persian (12:23).*

"This enumeration was of great importance, not only as establishing their individual purity of descent, but because the chronology of the Jews was henceforth to be reckoned, not as formerly by the reigns of their kings, but by the succession of their high priests."[28] Thus it is not likely that there would be gaps in this list.

As these six give a crucial insight to the chronology of the period, we will look at them in order.

(1) Jeshua

The son of Jozadak, and grandson of the Seriah slain by Nebuchadnezzar, Jeshua was high priest to the 50,000 who returned in the <u>1st year</u> of Cyrus (Ezra 1:1; 2:2). His great work was to direct the rebuilding of the altar and laying of the Temple foundations (3:2,8). After the death of Cyrus in what secular historians reckon to be the <u>7th year</u> from the Return, Cambyses the new king brought the work to a halt. His reign is said to have lasted <u>eight years</u>, and was followed by Darius Hystaspes who in his <u>2nd year</u> allowed the work on the Temple to begin again.

> *Then ceased the work of the House of God which is at Jerusalem. So it ceased unto the <u>second year</u> of the reign of Darius king of Persia. Then the prophets, Haggai the prophet, and Zechariah the son of Iddo, prophesied unto the Jews that were in Judah and Jerusalem in the name of the God of Israel, even unto them. Then rose up Zerubbabel the son of Shealtiel, and Jeshua the son of Jozadak, and began to build the house of God which is at Jerusalem (Ezra 4:24-5:2).*

It took from the 2nd year of Darius to his <u>6th year</u> (Ezra 6:15) to finish the Temple. Ezra shows that Jeshua was active in the 2nd year (4:24-5:2), but does not tell us how long he lived and ministered after that. In Zechariah, however, there is indication of further ministry:

> *And the angel of the LORD protested unto Joshua, saying, Thus saith the LORD of hosts; If thou wilt walk in my ways, and if thou wilt keep my charge, then thou shalt also judge my house, and shalt also keep my courts, and I will give these places to walk among those that stand by (Zech. 3:6,7).*

And in a passage which prefigures Christ Himself:

> *Then take silver and gold and make crowns, and set them upon the head of Joshua the son of Josedech, the high priest; And speak unto him, saying, Thus speaketh the LORD of hosts, saying, Behold the man whose name is The BRANCH; and he shall grow up out of his place, and he shall build the temple of the LORD (Zech. 6:11,12).*

But on the negative side, we find Jeshua in Zech. 3:3 clothed in filthy garments, which beside the wider implications, may well have signified some failure in his own life and ministry. Like Eli, the failure that Scripture mentions had to do with his sons. [29]

> *And among the sons of the priests there were found that had taken strange wives; namely, of the sons of Jeshua the son of Jozadak (Ezra 10:18).*

If, as is likely, Jeshua was approaching forty[30] at the return, then, as the visions of Zechariah take place in the 2nd year of Darius (Zech. 1:1), Jeshua would be in his mid-fifties, and his sons of marriageable age. Therefore in order for Ezra to deal with this problem (Ezra 9-10), his coming to Jerusalem could not be too long after the Temple was dedicated. The Traditional Chronology places Ezra's coming fifty-seven years after the Temple dedication (515-458 BC). This would put Jeshua's sons in their seventies and eighties, hardly the picture presented in Ezra 10 and Neh. 13.

How long Jeshua "judged" the Lord's house and "kept" His courts after the 2nd year of Darius is not known (Zech. 3:6,7). He is not mentioned at the Temple dedication in Darius' 6th year. And as we will show, it is possible that his son Joiakim was high priest at that event.

As demonstrated previously, it is likely that the Ezra (Neh. 12:1), and Nehemiah and Mordecai (Ezra 2:2) who came from exile with Jeshua are the same men we know from the other passages. Thus, though Jeshua is their contemporary, he would have passed from the scene before Ezra and Nehemiah returned to Jerusalem.

It is further to be noted that if the seven years of Cyrus and the eight years of Cambyses recorded by secular history are correct, then when added to Darius' 6th year (Ezra 6:15) the Temple would have been dedicated twenty-one years or *three weeks* after Cyrus' decree.

(2) Joiakim

Joiakim the son of Jeshua and father of Eliashib is mentioned three times (Neh. 12:10,12,26). And while Eliashib was high priest at the time Nehemiah built the walls (Neh. 3:1), Joiakim's priesthood seems to have extended reasonably near to the time of Nehemiah's arrival in Jerusalem, for in Neh. 12:26 we read:

> *These [Levites] were in the days of Joiakim the son of Jeshua, the son of Jozadak, and in the days of Nehemiah the governor, and of Ezra the priest, the scribe.*

CHAPTER 3: SECOND DIVIDE: CYRUS TO ALEXANDER

As Nehemiah 12 and 13 is our key source of information for the post-exilic priests, in our examination of Joiakim, it is necessary to note the basic structure of Neh. 12:1-26.

    12:1-7   The priests who returned with Jeshua
    12:8,9   The Levites who returned with Jeshua
    12:10,11   Explanation: Genealogy from Jeshua to Jaddua
    12:12-21   The priests in the days of Joiakim
    12:22,23   Explanation: Recording of the priests and Levites
    12:24-26   The Levites in the days of Joiakim

According to the Ptolemaic Chronology the last specific mention of Jeshua is 520 BC when work recommenced on the Temple, and the first mention of Eliashib is 445 BC at Nehemiah's wall-building. Jeshua, as we have shown, would have been in his mid-fifties in 520 BC. And as Neh. 12:36 and Josephus (XI.157-158) state that Joiakim was still in office when Ezra came to Jerusalem (458 BC), this means that Joiakim would have had to be in office for 50 years or more. This has provided quite a problem for commentators to wrestle with:

> [Joiakim] fills the gap between Jeshua and Eliashib ... A name may have fallen out, or there may have been some discontinuity in this period of about seventy years during which more than one political crisis occurred. [31]

The reader may be assured that nothing has fallen out of God's Word (II Kings 10:10), and the "discontinuity" has been caused by allowing Ptolemy's Canon to dictate these times.

A comparison of Neh. 12:1-7 with 12:12-21 gives further confirmation that Joiakim's is the only generation between Jeshua and Eliashib. In 12:12-21 we have listed the generation of <u>priests</u> associated with Joiakim along with their immediate forebears. In eleven to fifteen instances these are "chief of fathers" (12:12) who also returned with Jeshua (12:1-7).

Further, three <u>Levites</u> who returned with Jeshua, seem also to be serving with Joiakim:

<u>Returnees with Jeshua</u>	<u>Servers with Joiakim</u>
Neh. 12:8,9	Neh. 12:24,25
Sherebiah	Sherebiah
Mattaniah	Mattaniah
Bakbukiah	Bakbukiah

Their listing in the same order makes it a virtual certainty that they are the same. It is also likely that they were old enough to be "chief" (cp. 12:7) among the Levites at the return. And, as active service ended at fifty (Num. 8:23-26), these provide a constraint on the amount of time that would have elapsed between Jeshua and Eliashib.

Josephus states that Joiakim followed his father Jeshua, but also (probably wrongly) places this about the time that the throne of Persia passed from Darius Hystaspes to Xerxes. (XI.120-121). He says also that Joiakim was still in office when Ezra came to Jerusalem and seems to indicate that he died about the time of the Feast of Tabernacles in the following year. [32] (XI.120-130,145-158).

There is also "an early tradition, which survived for centuries, that Ezra replaced or deposed Joiakim."[33] One thing is clear from Scripture, thirteen years later when Nehemiah arrived in Jerusalem Eliashib was the high priest (Neh. 3:1).

Our study of the Persian kings will in fact show that Joiakim was high priest for only a short time.

(3) Eliashib

Our first sight of Eliashib the son of Joiakim (Neh. 12:10) is shortly after Ezra arrives in Jerusalem (the 7th year of Artaxerxes, Ezra 7:7). Ezra hearing of the people's unseparated state, and having sought the Lord in the Temple retires to the chamber of Johanan the son of Eliashib.

> *Then Ezra rose up from before the house of God, and went into the chamber of Johanan the son of Eliashib (Ezra 10:6).*

This is clearly the Eliashib recognized by his contemporaries as the man shortly to take Joiakim's place as high priest. Yet with the mention of Johanan an entire range of problems and implications arise for the Ptolemaic Chronology, and over these, commentators fundamentally disagree. Most notably, this verse coupled with other factors has led a number of writers to the erroneous conclusion that Ezra *followed* (by at least a generation) rather than preceded Nehemiah to Jerusalem.

Indeed, the evidence appears strong that this Johanan is Eliashib's grandson, who is to be identified with Jonathan, the 5th high priest (cp. Neh. 12:10,11 with 12:22,23). This view as we will show is supported by Josephus and the Elephantine Papyri. And while Scripturally it cannot result in placing Ezra after Nehemiah, it does place an impossible burden on the Traditional Chronology by showing that the time span of these priests is much shorter than can

CHAPTER 3: SECOND DIVIDE: CYRUS TO ALEXANDER

be allowed. And, of course, it also raises the question as to how Eliashib's grandson could at this time have a chamber in the Temple.

Some, obviously feeling the above leads into too much uncharted territory, suggest that Johanan is an otherwise unknown son of Eliashib.[34] And others make "Eliashib" to mean the head of the priestly course set up in David's day (I Chr. 24:12) and Johanan, again, an unknown descendant.[35] But these proposals, as we will see when we come to the fifth high priest, are not really credible.

Returning to Eliashib himself, we next see him working on the walls of Jerusalem with Nehemiah (in the 20th year of Artaxerxes, Neh. 2:1).

> *Then Eliashib the high priest rose up with his brethren the priests, and they builded the sheep gate (Neh. 3:1; also 3:20,21).*

However, this positive aspect of his work and office is not carried through, and our final look at the third high priest is not a good one. Nehemiah in the years following his 12th year as governor (the 32nd year of Artaxerxes) must take action against Eliashib's alliance with Tobiah.

> *And before this, Eliashib the priest, having the oversight of the chamber of the house of our God, was allied unto Tobiah; And he had prepared for him a great chamber, where aforetime they laid the meat offerings ... But in all this time was not I at Jerusalem: for in the two and thirtieth year of Artaxerxes king of Babylon came I unto the king, and after certain days obtained I leave of the king: And I came to Jerusalem, and understood of the evil that Eliashib did for Tobiah, in preparing him a chamber in the courts of the house of God. And it grieved me sore: Therefore I cast forth all the household stuff of Tobiah out of the chamber (Neh. 13:4-8).*

Tobiah, though an Ammonite and opponent to Jerusalem's reconstruction (Neh. 4:1-3), had married into a prominent Jewish family and was held in esteem by the nobles of Judah (Neh. 6:17-19). And now we discover that Eliashib had even given him the large chamber on the Temple court where the nation's tithes were gathered.

For Tobiah to have been given such an honour it is assumed by some that he had married into a *priestly* family, and was perhaps also related to Eliashib. As this has implications for the chronology of the time we need to look into Tobiah's background.

From Neh. 6:17,18 and Neh. 3:4 we find:

Arah   Meshezabeel

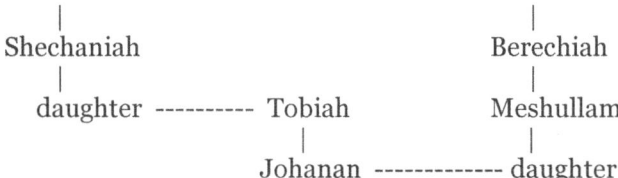

Thus, Tobiah married the daughter of Shechaniah, and Tobiah's son, Johanan, married the daughter of Meshullam. He is in this way linked to two important families of Israel, but as the following shows they were not priestly families.

The Arah who is shown to be the grandfather of Tobiah's wife is likely the prominent family leader who returned with Zerubbabel (Ezra 2:5). Indeed, the mention of this name would lead people in that day to think of no other. But as he was not of the tribe of Levi (cp. Ezra 2:36-42) then he would not be the father of the priest Shechaniah, who also returned with Zerubbabel (Neh. 12:3), nor the Shechaniah whose son built the wall and was keeper of the east gate (Neh. 3:29). [36]

As for the family that Tobiah's son married into, he likely married the daughter of the Meshullam, the son of Berechiah, the son of Meshezabeel who worked on the wall (Neh. 3:4). There is a Meshezabeel among the "chief of the people" who sealed the covenant with Nehemiah (Neh. 10:14,21), and also a Meshazabeel whose son was an aide to the king of Persia with regard to the returnees (Neh. 11:24); but in neither case is the person in question of Levi.

Therefore the frequent assertion that Tobiah was related by marriage to the tribe of Levi and possibly also to the high priest cannot be demonstrated. However, given the fact that he has a Jewish name (Jehovah is good) may well indicate that he was a Jew by race, but an Ammonite by choice because of the high office he had gained.[37] Certainly an ordinary Ammonite would not be given a place to live in the Temple!

> *An Ammonite or Moabite shall not enter into the congregation of the LORD; even to their tenth generation shall they not enter into the congregation of the LORD for ever (Deut. 23:3).*

There is a reasonable possibility that this is the "prominent" Tobiah (or his son) who returned with Zerubbabel, but could not prove his genealogy (Ezra 2:59,60). Such would explain how he could show such enmity[38] and yet maintain great influence among the Jews. Therefore while Tobiah's wife is of Eliashib's generation Tobiah himself is likely much older.

CHAPTER 3: SECOND DIVIDE: CYRUS TO ALEXANDER

The reforms connected with Nehemiah casting Tobiah's "household stuff" from the Temple some fourteen years after he became governor (Neh. 13:8; cp. 13:6) is the last recorded event of the Old Testament. In point ten of our discussion of the Seventy Weeks, reasons were given to show that this reformation provided the fitting conclusion to the first seven weeks of Daniel's prophecy. Therefore we have a forty-nine year time-frame (a Jubilee!) from the Return to the Reformation.

When the Scripture witness to the lineages of the different personalities of this time are viewed in the light of this forty-nine year time-frame, a reasonable harmony is the result. There is no need to talk of extreme ages, or missing generations, or dislocations of the text. But when the return is made to be 536 BC and Nehemiah's reformation about 430 BC, then all of this must be resorted to and confusion ensues.

Eliashib at the time of these reforms is old enough to have a married grandson (Neh. 13:28). Guidelines to this approximate age and to other personalities of this time will be given after our examination of the Persian kings. We now come to the fourth priest after the exile.

(4) Joiada

Eliashib's son and successor as high priest is Joiada (Neh. 12:10,11). He is mentioned twice further in Scripture.

> *The Levites in the days of Eliashib, Joiada, and Johanan, and Jaddua, were recorded chief of the fathers: also the priests, to the reign of Darius the Persian (Neh. 12:22).*
>
> *And one of the sons of Joiada, the son of Eliashib the high priest, was son in law to Sanballat the Horonite: therefore I chased him from me (Neh. 13:28).*

Josephus, who calls him Judas, gives this same order and number:

> When Eliashib the high priest was dead, his son Judas succeeded in the high priesthood: and when he was dead, his son John took that dignity (XI.297).

But it is with Neh. 13:28 that we are especially interested. Though many chronologists are more than a little hasty to pass over this verse, its importance for a right chronological understanding of the times cannot be overstated. The passage shows that Nehemiah at this time was contemporary *with the third, fourth and fifth* generations of the post-exilic high priestly line.

Eliashib
|

BIBLE CHRONOLOGY: THE TWO GREAT DIVIDES

While a number of age-variables are possible here, Neh. 13:28 gives further evidence of the time constraints that exist for this period. If the fifth high priest did not come to office before the death of Nehemiah, it would not have been long after.

With these factors in mind we come now to -

(5) Jonathan (Johanan)

Our next to last high priest mentioned in Scripture has two names. In the list of Neh. 12:10,11 he is Jonathan the son of Joiada. But elsewhere he is Johanan.

> *The Levites in the days of Eliashib, Joiada, and Johanan, and Jaddua, were recorded chief of the fathers: also the priests, to the reign of Darius the Persian (Neh. 12:22).*

These two passages make it clear that Jonathan or Johanan is the son of Joiada, and show that in the two further passages where he is called the son of Eliashib (one being the next verse) it must mean "grandson".

> *The sons of Levi, the chief of the fathers were written in the book of the Chronicles, even until the days of Johanan the son of Eliashib (12:23).*

> *Then Ezra rose up from before the house of God, and went into the chamber of Johanan the son of Eliashib (Ezra 10:6).*

This indicates that when Ezra came to Jerusalem (some twenty-seven years before Neh. 13) there was already a designated chamber for this future high priest. And from the names, "Johanan son of Eliashib", it may likely be assumed that Joiada was not in office for so long, and was generally passed over in the recognition and remembrance of the people.

That Eliashib could have a grandson at the time of Ezra's arrival receives strong confirmation from Neh. 13:28, when some twenty-seven years later, another of his grandsons is confronted by Nehemiah for marrying a foreign wife.

> *And one of the sons of Joiada, the son of Eliashib the high priest, was son in law to Sanballat, the Horonite; therefore I chased him from me (Neh. 13:28).*

CHAPTER 3: SECOND DIVIDE: CYRUS TO ALEXANDER

The one expelled would then be Johanan's brother. Thus, when examined together, we find that Ezra 10:6; Neh. 12:10,11; 12:22,23; 13:28 present a clear and harmonious picture of the generations following Eliashib.

Josephus, who gives the same order of succession as the Scripture, shows that Johanan's administration was a turbulent one:

> When Eliashib the high priest was dead, his son Judas succeeded in the high priesthood: and when he was dead, his son John took that dignity; on whose account it was also that Bagoses, the general of another Artaxerxes' army, polluted the temple, and imposed tributes on the Jews ... Now Jesus was the brother of John, and was a friend of Bagoses, who had promised to procure him the high priesthood. In confidence of whose support, Jesus quarrelled with John in the temple, and so provoked his brother, that in anger his brother slew him ... Accordingly, Bagoses made use of this pretence, and punished the Jews seven years for the murder of Jesus (XI.297-301).

A further remarkable insight into Johanan and his times comes from the Elephantine papyri. In the earlier part of the 20th century a collection of Aramaic letters was found at Aswan in Egypt. They had been written from a small island on the Nile named Elephantine (also Yeb), where for some considerable time a colony of Jews lived. The documents give a sad picture of how far they had departed from the True God.

Among these letters is one to Bagohi, the governor of Judah. Josephus refers above to the same official in the Greek form of the name, Bagoses. To Bagohi a complaint is made that a previous letter to Johanan the high priest has been ignored. They had asked Johanan's support to help rebuild their temple on Elephantine. In this letter they say that they had written about the same matter to Delaiah and Shelemaiah the sons of Sanballat governor of Samaria. [39]

Additional evidence comes from Dan Barag who has examined a small silver coin from Judaea on which "one can clearly read 'Johan(an)', and the word 'ha-kohen' (or priest)." [40]

On this and other coins from the time is the further inscription, "Hezekiah the governor". Nothing further is apparently known about this governor. But from these inscriptions Barag concludes:

> This demonstrates that Johanan was not merely an ordinary priest but was the high priest for he maintained a very important position - his status being equal to that of the governor nominated by the Persians.[41]

Thus Josephus, the Elephantine papyri and this silver coin combine to present a vivid picture of the power that the fifth high priest wielded. The material fits in well with the Biblical account, and all seems to be quite straightforward. But it does not combine well with the Ptolemaic dating. And if serious problems exist for the priestly succession down to Johanan - i.e. some even feeling it necessary to place Ezra after Nehemiah - with the mention of the next priest, the question of where and how to fit the various strands of evidence becomes chaotic.

Kidner reflects the prevailing confusion, when he says that Josephus "has enough names in common" with Nehemiah and the Elephantine papyri "to create a tangle which calls for some unravelling."[42] Frankly, his attempt to "unravel" the evidence, which of course means to bring it into line with Ptolemy, makes for some difficult and unconvincing reading.[43]

(6) Jaddua

Our sixth and final high priest is mentioned twice in Scripture, in the list of Neh. 12:10,11, and in Neh. 12:22:

> The Levites in the days of Eliashib, Joiada, Johanan, and Jaddua, were recorded chief of the fathers: also the priests, to the reign of Darius the Persian.

Josephus, in continuing the same order of succession, records two key events in the administration of Jaddua. The first has to do with the marriage of his brother to the daughter of Sanballat.

> Now when John had departed this life, his son Jaddua succeeded in the high priesthood. He had a brother whose name was Manasseh. Now there was one Sanballat, who was sent by Darius the last king [of Persia], into Samaria. He was a Cuthean by birth; of which stock were the Samaritans also. This man knew that the city of Jerusalem was a famous city, and that their king had given a great deal of trouble to the Assyrians, and the people of Celesyria; so that he willingly gave his daughter, whose name was Nicaso, in marriage to Manasseh, as thinking this alliance by marriage would be a pledge and security that the nation of the Jews should continue their good-will to him (XI.302-303).

> But the elders of Jerusalem being very uneasy that the brother of Jaddua the high priest, though married to a foreigner, should be partner with him in the high priesthood, quarrelled with him ... the high priest himself joining with the people in their indignation against his brother and driving him away from the altar. Whereupon Manasseh came to his father-in-law, Sanballat, and told him, That although he loved his daughter Nicaso, yet was he not willing to be deprived of his sacerdotal dignity on her account ... And then Sanballat promised ... if he would keep his daughter for his wife... he would build him a temple like that at Jerusalem, upon Mount Gerizzim ... and he promised that he would do this with the approbation of Darius the king. Manasseh was elevated with these promises and staid with Sanballat upon a supposal that he should gain a high priesthood as bestowed upon him by Darius, for it happened Sanballat was then in years. But there was now a great disturbance among the people of Jerusalem, because many of those

CHAPTER 3: SECOND DIVIDE: CYRUS TO ALEXANDER

priests and Levites were entangled in such matches; for they all revolted to Manasseh ... (XI.306-312).

As Josephus had previously recorded the death of Nehemiah (XI:183), this above account is after the one recorded in Neh. 13:28 in which we find Nehemiah expelling the brother of Johanan (and son of Joiada).

> *And one of the sons of Joiada the son of Eliashib the high priest, was son in law to Sanballat the Horonite; therefore I chased him from me.*

The question arises as to whether the Sanballat of Nehemiah's administration (Neh. 2:10; 13:28) could be the same mentioned by the Elephantine papyri in Johanan's time, and by Josephus in Jaddua's time, and indeed also at the time of Darius' defeat by Alexander (XI:321-325). The various strands of evidence present a consistent and progressive picture of but one Sanballat. We do not see him in connection with Ezra. But thirteen years later at Nehemiah's arrival, he is Israel's mocking foe (Neh. 2:10,19:4:1). During Nehemiah's term no mention is made of Sanballat's office.[44] It is only in the Elephantine papyri and Josephus that we see him in an official position as governor of Samaria. But by the time of the letter from the Jews of Elephantine, it is his sons, rather than Sanballat himself who is addressed, indicating that they were taking much of the responsibility of the governor's office.[45] And, by Jaddua's time, Josephus says that Sanballat "was then in years" and then shortly after gives the record of his death (XI.311,325).

Therefore from Nehemiah, to the Elephantine papyri, to Josephus we have a consistent record of Sanballat's ageing. Our reckoning shows that eighty-three years have passed since he first opposed Nehemiah unto Jaddua's administration at the time of Alexander (331 BC).

These years are figured as follows:

+14 yrs.	From Nehemiah's arrival to the completion of his reforms and the first seven weeks.
+434 yrs.	Sixty-two weeks to the death of Christ.
-33 yrs.	The years of Christ's life.
-331 yrs.	The BC date of Alexander's empire.
-1 yr.	BC to AD adjustment

83 yrs.

This will give us a date of 414 BC for Nehemiah's arrival, and 400 BC for the conclusion of his reforms, the completion of the seven weeks, and the commencement of the sixty-two weeks (434 years) to the Cross.

Eighty-three years is a long, yet certainly possible, time for Sanballat to influence events. However, the Ptolemaic date (445 BC) for Nehemiah's arrival means that Sanballat remained influential for 114 years unto Alexander. With this they are forced to postulate that there were two or even three Sanballats.

But as the Elephantine papyri point to a time during Johanan's term, and is therefore somewhere between the events presented by Nehemiah (Eliashib) and those of Josephus (Jaddua), it would seem likely that as the Elephantine Jews address Sanballat's two sons (Delaiah and Shelemiah)[46] they would also indicate that this was a different Sanballat or that there was "another" Sanballat in charge.

Nevertheless, evidence is claimed for a second Sanballat from papyri fragments discovered at Wadi ed-Daliyeh north of Jericho in 1962. Known as the Samaria Papyri, they are commonly purported to show the following:

> Sanballat II is known as governor of Samaria in the early fourth century BCE from an Aramaic papyrus and a clay sealing in Paleo-Hebrew ... Both inscriptions are of Sanballat II's elder son, whose name is to be restored as either [Jesh]ua or [Jadd]ua. The latter, also a governor, was apparently succeeded by his brother Hananiah who, in turn, was succeeded by Sanballat III. The practice of papponymy (naming a child for its grandfather) was common in the Persian and Hellenistic periods.[47]

This popularly held view is based on the research of Frank Cross Jr.[48] Yet in going through his material it is difficult to see anything in the Samaria Papyri that points to more than one Sanballat.

Cross dates the papyri fragments and clay seals over a period of forty years from about 375 to 335 BC.[49] Sanballat's name occurs twice, one being an inscription on a clay seal and written in Hebrew. Cross translates this as follows:

> ... iah, son of (San)ballat, governor of Samaria.[50]

On the basis of later study, Cross thinks the first name should read "Hananiah", and, indeed, Papyrus 8, which he dates 354 BC, has the words "before Hananiah governor of Samaria."[51]

The second fragment with Sanballat's name is translated:

CHAPTER 3: SECOND DIVIDE: CYRUS TO ALEXANDER

> (before) Jesus son of Sanballat (and) Hanun the prefect.[52]

This then is what has been so eagerly latched upon! When viewed in clear light it seems incredible that it somehow points to there being two or three Sanballats. These inscriptions simply show that Sanballat had sons or grandsons (none of whom is called Sanballat) who became prominent in the government of Samaria. Cross himself admits that his three-Sanballat reconstruction is "hypothetical".[53] One thing is certain: none of the sources - Nehemiah, Elephantine, Samaritan, Josephus[54] - mentions more than one Sanballat. This singular personage casts a long shadow from Nehemiah to Alexander, and over the Ptolemaic Chronology as well!

Coming back now to Jaddua the high priest, we note Josephus' further account of his times and his remarkable meeting with Alexander the Great.

> About this time it was that Darius heard how Alexander had passed over the Hellespont, and had beaten his lieutenants in the battle of Granicum, and was proceeding farther; whereupon he gathered together an army of horse and foot, and determined that he would meet the Macedonians before they should assault and conquer all Asia.
>
> So he passed over the river Euphrates and came over Taurus, the Cilician mountain; and at Issus of Cilicia he waited for the enemy, as ready there to give him battle. Upon which Sanballat was glad that Darius was come down; and told Manasseh that he would suddenly perform his promises to him and this as soon as ever Darius should come back, after he had beaten his enemies ... but the event proved otherwise than they expected, for the king joined battle with the Macedonians, and was beaten, and lost a great part of his army. His mother also, and his wife and children, were taken captives, and he fled into Persia. So Alexander came into Syria, and took Damascus, and when he had obtained Sidon, he besieged Tyre, when he sent an epistle to the Jewish high priest ... that what presents he formally sent to Darius he would now send to him, and choose the friendship of the Macedonians ... but the high priest answered his messengers, that he had given his oath to Darius not to bear arms against him and he said that he would not transgress this while Darius was in the land of the living. Upon hearing this answer, Alexander was very angry;
>
> But Sanballat thought he had now gotten a proper opportunity to make his attempt, so he renounced Darius, and taking with him seven thousand of his own subjects, he came to Alexander; and finding him beginning the siege of Tyre, he said to him, that he delivered up to him these men who came out of places under his dominion, and did gladly accept of him for their lord instead of Darius. So when Alexander had received him kindly, Sanballat thereupon took courage, and spake to him about his present affair. He told him, that he had a son-in-law, Manasseh, who was brother to the high priest Jaddua; and that there were many others of his own nation now with him, that were desirous to have a temple in the places subject to him; that it would be for the king's advantage to have the strength of the Jews divided into two parts ... Whereupon Alexander gave Sanballat leave so to do; who used the utmost diligence, and built the temple, and made Manasseh the priest, and deemed it a great reward that his daughter's children should

have that dignity; but when the seven months of the siege of Tyre were over, and the two months of the siege of Gaza, Sanballat died. Now Alexander, when he had taken Gaza, made haste to go up to Jerusalem; and Jaddua the high priest, when he heard that, was in an agony, and under terror, as not knowing how he should meet the Macedonians, since the king was displeased at his foregoing disobedience. He therefore ordained that the people should make supplications, and should join with him in offering sacrifices to God ... whereupon God warned him in a dream, which came upon him after he had offered sacrifice, that he should take courage, and adorn the city, and open the gates; that the rest appear in white garments but that he and the priests should meet the king in the habits proper to their order. ... Upon which, when he rose from his sleep, he greatly rejoiced; and declared to all the warning he had received from God.

And when he understood that he was not far from the city, he went out in procession, with the priests and the multitude of the citizens. ... [And] Alexander, when he saw the multitude at a distance, in white garments, while the priests stood clothed with fine linen, and the high priest in purple and scarlet clothing with his mitre on his head having the golden plate on which the name of God was engraved, he approached by himself, and adored that name, and first saluted the high priest. The Jews also did all together, with one voice, salute Alexander, and encompass him about: whereupon the kings of Syria and the rest were surprised at what Alexander had done, and supposed him disordered in his mind. However, Parmenio alone went up to him, and asked him how it came to pass, that when all others adored him, he should adore the high priest of the Jews? To whom he replied, "I did not adore him, but that God who hath honored him with that high priesthood; for I saw this very person in a dream, in this very habit, when I was at Dios, in Macedonia, who, when I was considering with myself how I might obtain the dominion of Asia, exhorted me to make no delay, but boldly to pass over the sea thither, for that he would conduct my army, and would give me the dominion over the Persians ... And when he had said this to Parmenio, and had given the high priest his right hand, the priests ran along by him, and he came into the city; and when he went up into the temple, he offered sacrifice to God, according to the high priest's direction, and magnificently treated both the high priest and the priests. And when the book of Daniel was showed him, wherein Daniel declared that one of the Greeks should destroy the empire of the Persians, he supposed that himself was the person intended; and as he was then glad, he dismissed the multitude for the present, but the next day he called them to him, and bade them ask what favors they pleased of him: whereupon the high priest desired that they might enjoy the law of their forefathers and might pay no tribute on the seventh year. He granted all they desired:

So when Alexander had thus settled matters at Jerusalem, he led his army into the neighboring cities; and when all the inhabitants, to whom he came, received him with great kindness, the Samaritans ... desired that he would come to their city, and do honor to their temple also.

Now when Alexander was dead, the government was parted among his successors ... About this time it was that Jaddua the high priest died, and Onias his son took the high priesthood. This was the state of the affairs of the people of Jerusalem at this time. (XI.313-347).

CHAPTER 3: SECOND DIVIDE: CYRUS TO ALEXANDER

This stirring account of Jaddua going out to meet Alexander and showing the great king Daniel's prophecy, strikes a chord with Bible believers. We have seen this before! Just as the king of Babylon and the king of Persia had been a subject of Daniel's prophecy, *and had been made to know that they were*, so we are not surprised that this same will be the case for the king of the third empire (Dan. 2:39; 7:6; 8:5-8:10:20-11:4). It needs to be kept in mind that the vivid account Josephus gives of these six high priests follows precisely the same order as that given in Nehemiah (12:10,11,22,23). The sources he drew upon were thus based upon the Scripture's structure. The Jews above all people would have sought to keep an accurate record of their high priests. And Josephus, from a priestly family, and educated as a Pharisee, would certainly have had access to this.

Therefore it is on Ptolemaic rather than Scriptural or historical grounds that writers such as Cross speak of Josephus' confusion, in not listing enough Sanballats, Jadduas and Dariuses.

> Of course Josephus confused Sanballat I and III, just as he confused Jaddua, high priest under Darius II (Neh. 12:22) and Jaddua, high priest in the time of Darius III.[55]

It is, however, to be noted, that Cross[56], Williamson[57] and other recent writers on the period generally do not seek support for their position from a passage in the Talmud which appears to contradict Josephus.

From Yoma 69a of the Babylonian Talmud, we have the following rabbinical discussion (Gemara) on statements in the Mishnah concerning the wearing of priestly vestments outside of the Temple precincts:

> Come and hear: As to priestly garments, it is forbidden to go out in them in the province ... Surely it was taught: The twenty-fifth of Tebeth is the day of Mount Gerizim, on which the Cutheans demanded the House of out God from Alexander the Macedonian so as to destroy it ... whereupon some people came and informed Simeon the Just. What did the latter do? He put on his priestly garments ... some of the noblemen of Israel went with him carrying fiery torches in their hands, they walked all the night ... As he [Alexander] reached Antipatris, the sun having shone forth, they met. When he saw Simeon the Just, he descended from his carriage and bowed down before him. They said to him: A great king like yourself should bow down before this Jew? He answered: His image it is which wins for me in all my battles. He said to them: What have you come for? They said: Is it possible that star-worshippers should mislead you to destroy the House wherein prayers are said for you and your kingdom that it be never destroyed! He said to them: Who are these? They said to him: These are the Cutheans who stand before you. He said: They are delivered into your hand. At once they perforated their heels, tied them to the tails of their horses and dragged them over thorns and thistles, until they came to Mount Gerizim, which they ploughed and planted with vetch, even as they had planned to do with the House of God. And that day they made a festive day.[58]

Simon the Just is said by Josephus to be Onias' son and Jaddua's grandson (XII.43). Chronologists such as Jones[59], Beecher[60] and Newton[61] have accepted the Talmud version in making Simon rather than Jaddua the high priest who met Alexander, thereby relieving pressure on the Ptolemaic Chronology.

However, the Babylonian Talmud's version of events does not seem to be so well attested as Josephus. It was written considerably later, perhaps some three or even four centuries after the *Antiquities*[62]. It is contradicted by passages in the earlier Jerusalem Talmud that place Simon the Just a century after Alexander.[63] It is concluded that the one or two possible candidates for the priest whom Jews revere as "Simon the Just" will not fit chronologically with Alexander's time. Of the Yoma 69a account *Encyclopaedia Judaica* says:

> [C]hronologically it can apply to neither of the Simeons ... However the suggestion that the origin of the story is to be found in a meeting that took place between Simeon (II) the Just and Antiochus III, who was his contemporary and ally, may be correct.[64]

Therefore, notwithstanding the problems it poses for the Traditional Chronology, Josephus' account is the one generally referred to. And with this we conclude our examination of the post-exilic high priests and the sixth major area of Biblical evidence. Jeshua, Joiakim, Eliashib, Joiada, Jonathan and Jaddua present a strong case for the shorter chronology from Cyrus to Alexander.

These six areas of Scriptural evidence demonstrate conclusively that despite its universal acceptance, the Ptolemaic reckoning for the Persian period is fundamentally and massively flawed. The fact that writers have chosen to gloss over the force of these arguments does not lessen their validity. But we do, nevertheless, wonder at how they can be so completely ignored. Like the theory of evolution, the Canon does indeed wield a powerful sway.

With the foregoing in mind we come now to the complex question of the Persian kings. At the outset we are met with Ptolemy's "orderly" list of ten or eleven kings spanning his 205 years from Cyrus to Alexander. But before examining the secular evidence for these kings, as always, we must be certain as to what the Scriptures say.

Our benchmark for this investigation is a passage in the Book of Daniel:

7. DANIEL 10:20-11:4 LIMITS THE TIMES AND NUMBERS OF THE PERSIAN KINGS

In the third year of Cyrus (Dan. 10:1) the following revelation is given to Daniel:

CHAPTER 3: SECOND DIVIDE: CYRUS TO ALEXANDER

20 Then said he, Knowest thou wherefore I come unto thee? and now will I return to fight with the prince of Persia: and when I am gone forth, lo, the prince of Grecia shall come.
21 But I will shew thee that which is noted in the scripture of truth: and there is none that holdeth with me in these things, but Michael your prince.

Chapter 11

Also I in the first year of Darius the Mede, even I, stood to confirm and to strengthen him.
2 And now will I shew thee the truth. Behold, there shall stand up <u>yet three kings</u> in Persia; and the fourth shall be far richer than they all: and by his strength through his riches he shall stir up all against the realm of Grecia.
3 And a mighty king shall stand up, that shall rule with great dominion, and do according to his will.

The words, "when I am gone forth the prince of Grecia shall come" (10:20), along with what follows, does not give the impression that Persian kings will reign for another 200 years before the "mighty king", Alexander, "stands up" (11:3).

This remarkable passage gives an insight into the role of angels in the rise and fall of empires. The same angelic speaker here who had helped to confirm the reign of Darius the Median some three years earlier (11:1 is parenthetical), would also place a restraint on the number of Persian kings before the rise of Alexander.

As the date of this final prophecy in Daniel is the third year of Cyrus the *Persian* (his sole reign 10:1; 6:28), it is clear that the three kings "yet to stand up" (11:2), are kings who will follow him and be of his same line. Thus Darius the Median does not figure in the reckoning.

It may be fair to conclude that this fourth king refers back to the third. That is, he is the third *after* Cyrus, but the fourth in the Persian line *from* Cyrus. But most take the fourth as following the third, and by counting Pseudo-Smerdis make Xerxes as the wealthy king who incites his empire against Greece.

The kings after Cyrus with their Ptolemaic dates are:

1. Cyrus	536-529 (sole reign)
2. Cambyses	529-522
(Pseudo-Smerdis)	522-521
3. Darius Hystaspes	521-486
4. Xerxes	486-465
(Artaxerxes Longimanus)	465-424

It seems unlikely that the seven month reign of the magi, i.e. Palizithes and his brother Gomates (Pseudo-Smerdis), could be counted as one of the kings "yet to stand up" (see Herodotus III.65).[65] Nor could Artaxerxes Longimanus be made the fourth king, for unlike Darius and Xerxes who invaded Greece, he for the most part is said to have followed a policy of co-existence. Thus by one or other reckoning, Xerxes must be the fourth king.

As the passage gives the impression that this fourth king takes us down to, or at least considerably closer to Alexander, how is it that there are 134 Ptolemaic years from the end of Xerxes' reign to Alexander (465-331)?

Merrill Unger gives the usual answer:

> After [Xerxes'] defeat at Salamis, Persia was envisioned as politically moribund. Therefore, prophetically, no notice was given of Xerxes' successors, and the telescope of prophecy focused at once on Alexander the Great.[66]

But does this really satisfy the emphatic nature of the passage?

> *And now will I shew thee the truth. Behold, there shall stand up yet three kings in Persia; and the fourth shall be far richer than they all; and by his strength through his riches he shall stir up all against the realm of Grecia. And a mighty king shall reign... (11:3,4).*

Is it an acceptable correspondence, to have four kings at the beginning of the statement and a 134 year gap at the end? Indeed, if as the Ptolemaic reckoning asserts, that there will be nine Persian kings after Cyrus, why this Scripture emphasis upon numbers three and four?

We now look at several further areas of evidence that seem to restrict the number of Persian kings.

(1) Xerxes rather than Artaxerxes Longimanus appears to be the last Persian king mentioned in Scripture

While the Artaxerxes of Ezra and Nehemiah is generally assumed to be Artaxerxes Longimanus (the long-handed) the son of Xerxes, a careful reading of Ezra 4 and following, with a consideration of the evidence presented above, will, I think, point to a different conclusion. Ezra 4 presents important guidelines and an interpretive key to the identity of the Persian kings.

Crucial to this question is Ezra 4:4-7.

CHAPTER 3: SECOND DIVIDE: CYRUS TO ALEXANDER

> *4 Then the people of the land weakened the hands of the people of Judah, and troubled them in building,*
> *5 And hired counsellors against them, to frustrate their purpose, all the days of **Cyrus** king of Persia, even until the reign of **Darius** king of Persia.*
> *6 And in the reign of **Ahasuerus**, in the beginning of his reign, wrote they unto him an accusation against the inhabitants of Judah and Jerusalem.*
> *7 And in the days of **Artaxerxes** wrote Bishlam, Mithredath, Tabeel, and the rest of their companions, unto Artaxerxes king of Persia; and the writing of the letter was written in the Syrian tongue, and interpreted in the Syrian tongue.*

I think a repeated reading of these verses, along with the rest of the chapter (especially 4:24), and then into chapter five where Darius allows work on the temple to resume, will show clearly that Ahasuerus and Artaxerxes are two titles for the same king, and that this is the king that reigned between Cyrus and Darius Hystaspes, i.e. Cambyses.

To identify Ahasuerus with Cambyses, and then give someone like Pseudo-Smerdis the august title of Artaxerxes looks to be untenable. Far worse is the currently popular proposal which sees in chapter four a "literary setting" [67] that allows this Artaxerxes to *follow* rather than precede Darius. This is but another example of manipulation and distortion of the Biblical text.

Chapter four of Ezra which introduces us to the kings following Cyrus most likely puts us on notice that a Persian king could have two titles, or advance from one title to another. Thus Cambyses is *Ahasuerus* (Aha = Mighty, Suerus = king) "in the beginning of his reign" (4:6). But as an acknowledgement of his "greatness" he then becomes *Artaxerxes* (Arta = Great, Xerxes = King or Shah) in Ezra 4:7.

Diodorus Siculus [68] (born c.90 BC) in speaking of a later king describes this Persian practice:

> [F]or since the first Artaxerxes had ruled well and had shown himself altogether peace-loving and fortunate, the Persians changed the names of those who ruled after him and prescribed that they should bear that name (XV.93).

Arta may also mean "justice" [69]; therefore it is incongruous to suggest that the Persians would bestow the title "Artaxerxes" upon Pseudo-Smerdis, a usurper and impostor who held the throne for only seven months before being slain by Darius Hystaspes.

From this we begin to see that the context rather than the title is the more important consideration in determining the identity of a Persian king. Esther 1:1 shows that other kings could be called Ahasuerus (Mighty King). Therefore this particular Ahasuerus is distinguished as the king who "reigned from India unto Ethiopia, over 127 provinces." And, as many of their kings, either out of appreciation or expediency, would be given the title Artaxerxes, it is necessary to search for other evidence before deciding on an identification.

Ezra 6:14 gives the second list of Persian kings.

> 14 And the elders of the Jews builded, and they prospered through the prophesying of Haggai the prophet and Zechariah the son of Iddo. And they builded, and finished it, according to the commandment of the God of Israel, and according to the commandment of **Cyrus**, and **Darius**, and **Artaxerxes** king of Persia.

It is generally assumed that this Artaxerxes, who unlike the previous one (4:7) reigned *after* Darius, is Artaxerxes Longimanus. And, that he is the same Artaxerxes of whom Ezra 7,8 and Nehemiah speak. But Biblical evidence is against this assumption.

Here in 6:17, Artaxerxes is probably Daniel's fourth king (Dan. 11:2), i.e. Xerxes, who as Josephus shows (XI.120) followed his father's benevolent policy towards the Jews, [70] and who during his massive preparations for the invasion of Greece would certainly be acknowledged as a Great (Arta) Xerxes. And, as already shown, if the king contemporaneous with Ezra and Nehemiah is Longimanus, then some really serious chronological problems arise, among which is the extreme ages this gives to Ezra and Nehemiah.

(2) The prominent king of Ezra-Nehemiah and Esther is the same, and is Darius rather than Xerxes

Ezra returned to Jerusalem in the seventh year of Artaxerxes' reign (Ezra 7:7), and Nehemiah returned in his twentieth year (Neh. 2:1). During this later period Ezra and Nehemiah were colleagues in the reformation (Neh. 8:9). Nehemiah's governorship extended at least unto the thirty-second year of Artaxerxes (Neh. 13:6). This is the last date in the Old Testament, and there is good reason to believe that when these thirty-two years are added to the reigns of Cyrus and Cambyses they will take us to just before the completion of the first seven weeks (forty-nine years) of the Seventy Weeks (Dan. 9:25). Finally, the Ahasuerus of Esther, whose third, seventh and twelfth years are mentioned (Est. 1:3; 2:16; 3:7), is likely to be the same as the Artaxerxes whose dates are given in Ezra and Nehemiah. Therefore we are proposing that this is but one king, and that his third, seventh, twelfth, twentieth and thirty-second years are recorded. And as we hope to demonstrate, also his second, fourth and sixth!

Evidence seems to point to the following conclusions:

CHAPTER 3: SECOND DIVIDE: CYRUS TO ALEXANDER

(a) Xerxes is not the Artaxerxes Ezra and Nehemiah dealt with

Having noted the huge chronological strains of placing the events of Ezra and Nehemiah in the reign of Longimanus, it is natural that we look first to see if Xerxes could be the king mentioned.

Ptolemaic reckoning gives a 486 to 465 BC reign to Xerxes. Surprisingly Herodotus (died 425 BC) closes his *Histories* in only the seventh year of Xerxes' reign, the year of his disastrous withdrawal from Greece. Neither Herodotus nor the other two classical historians, Thucydides and Xenophon, mentions the length of his reign. As with so many other "details" of this period we go to Diodorus (c. 50 BC) for the statement that he was slain after a reign of "more than twenty years" (XI.69). Thus as the Artaxerxes of Ezra and Nehemiah had a reign of at least thirty-two years (Neh. 13:6), we are faced with an immediate problem of making him Xerxes.

There does not seem to be a great deal of hard evidence confirming that Xerxes' reign was twenty-one years. [71] Indeed over a century after Diodorus, Josephus says that the king Ezra and Nehemiah dealt with was Xerxes the son of Darius. He further describes how Nehemiah completed the walls in the twenty-eighth year of Xerxes (XI.168,179).

But Josephus (or a later editor) is confused at this point, for while, as the Scriptures, he shows Ezra returning in the seventh year (XI.135), he contradicts Scripture by saying Nehemiah returned in the twenty-fifth rather than the twentieth year (XI.168).

Accepting that Xerxes reigned twenty-one years, Floyd Jones initially suggested that he reigned as co-regent with his father Darius for about nineteen years, thus giving him a total reign of some forty years (505 to 486 to 465 BC). This coupled with the further proposal that the sixty-nine weeks (483 years) extend to the birth rather than the death of Christ (486 to 4 BC), Jones was able to relieve the chronological pressures of the standard view. [72]

But as the Seventy Weeks are God's clock for Israel (Dan.9:24), why should the sixty-nine weeks end at Christ's birth? They must certainly end shortly before His crucifixion when the nation made its final and formal rejection of His Messiahship (9:26). This we believe is the fatal flaw to arrangements which see the birth of Christ as the fulfilment of the Seventy Weeks.

Further, while Herodotus does show that law forbade a Persian king to go into battle until he had named his successor (VII.2) [73], this does not appear to be the same as making him co-regent. And in the case at hand Herodotus indicates that Darius did not designate Xerxes until a year before his death (VII.3,4).

Therefore while Xerxes is almost certainly Daniel's fourth king (11:2), without any clear evidence that his reign extended beyond twenty-one years we conclude that he is not the Artaxerxes that Ezra and Nehemiah dealt with. [74]

Before considering the probable identity of Darius Hystaspes with Artaxerxes, we conclude that

(b) Darius and not Xerxes is the Ahasuerus of Esther

Most accept that Xerxes is the Ahasuerus of the Book of Esther, but as we will see there are considerable problems with this identification.

Merrill Unger gives three reasons for the popular view:

> That he is Xerxes I (485-464 BC) is shown by the following considerations: (1) Ahasuerus represents the Hebrew transliteration of the Persian name Khshayarsha, more popularly known by the Greek form, Xerxes. (2) The extent of his empire was "from India even unto Ethiopia" (1:1). India (the area drained by the Indus River) was not included in the empire of the previous Persian kings. (3) The character of Ahasuerus is strikingly similar to that of Xerxes, as reported by ancient historians (see Herodotus *History* VII.35 and Juvenal X.174-187). [75]

In the early nineteenth century, Georg Grotefend found a cuneiform inscription in Persepolis in which the name of the son of Darius Hystaspes was deciphered as Khshayarsha. The Greek equivalent is said to be Xerxes and when Khshayarsha is transliterated into Hebrew it reads Ahasuerus.. [76]

But rather than this confirming the king's identity, it demonstrates once again the interchange that takes place between the Persian titles. There are two earlier Ahasueruses: the king (Cambyses) who reigned between Cyrus and Darius Hystaspes (Ezra 4:5-7), and the father of Darius the Mede. Now, if as by the above reasoning, "Xerxes" and "Ahasuerus" are equivalent titles, why do we not find evidence of these kings also being called "Xerxes"?

But as Jones points out, there is something amiss with the above etymological reasoning inasmuch as "Ahasuerus" means "The Mighty" (Aha), and "king" (Suerus). How then in translating does this suddenly reduce to "Xerxes" which means only "Shah" or "King"? [77]

CHAPTER 3: SECOND DIVIDE: CYRUS TO ALEXANDER

Further examples of the interchange between royal titles is shown by the Septuagint using Artaxerxes in place of Ahasuerus throughout Esther. And, as Anstey notes, "Xerxes in his inscription at Persepolis, actually calls himself in one sentence 'Xerxes the great king' and in the next 'Darius the King'". [78] Darius, as the others, is a throne name meaning "restrainer" [79] or "worker" (Herodotus VI.98).

Therefore it is the Scriptural and historical content rather than the titles themselves which takes precedence in determining the identity of the Persian kings.

The common argument that the temperament of Xerxes is much like that of Ahasuerus in Esther is of course subjective and open to interpretation. Jones says that "from our knowledge of the classic literature there is nothing in the character of Ahasuerus which could not equally apply as well to Darius I Hystaspes". [80]

Many positive things could be said of Darius, as well as of Ahasuerus in Esther, yet another side of Darius' character is seen in the assessment of Herodotus.

> On account of this and other doings, the Persians say that Darius was a huckster ... for Darius looked to making a gain in everything (III.89).

While something of the character of Xerxes can be seen in his ordering the Hellespont to be scourged with "three hundred lashes" (VII.35), [81] or his love for his brother's wife (IX.108), yet to use examples like this as a link to the Ahasuerus in Esther is very tenuous.

Unger's other argument that no king prior to Xerxes could be said to reign "from India even unto Ethiopia" (Est.1:1) is contradicted by the evidence. In fact the opposite is true, for under Xerxes the Persian Empire began to contract. [82]

From the time of Darius the Mede when Persia defeated Babylon, unto Ahasuerus, the Persian Empire increased from "120 princes over the whole kingdom" (Dan.6:1) to "127 provinces (satrapies) from India to Ethiopia" (Est.1:1).

Cambyses during his reign conquered Egypt (Herodotus III.11ff). Moving further south, he invaded and "reduced" the Ethiopians but then withdrew (III.25,97). Some control, however, was maintained for an inscription speaks of Persian quarrying activity. [83] Also, tribute was sent back to Persia (III.97), ivory to Darius' palace, and troops for Xerxes' invasion of Greece (VII.69).

Darius Hystaspes, having inherited Cambyses' conquests in Egypt and Ethiopia, went on to invade and receive annual tribute from India (III.94). Thus, he reigned from "India even unto Ethiopia" (Est.1:1).

The identification of Darius with Ahasuerus becomes more compelling when we find that -

> *King Ahasuerus laid a tribute upon the land, and upon the isles of the sea (Est.10:1).*

It is for this that Darius was especially noted. Herodotus lists some seventy peoples, nations and districts which sent tribute to Darius (III.89-95), and then goes on to say:

> Such was the revenue which Darius derived from Asia and a small part of Libya. Later in his reign the sum was increased by the tribute of the islands, and the nations of Europe as far as Thessaly (III.96).

Thucydides says that Darius conquered the islands of the Aegean Sea (I.16).[84] And it should be especially noted that Ahasuerus "laid a tribute upon the land *and upon the isles of the sea*" in the twelfth year of his reign (Est. 10:1 with 3:7,12,13; 9:1,21). But with Xerxes' forces defeated at Salamis and Plataea in his seventh and eighth years (Diodorus XI.14-18,27-37), control of these islands weakened. Shortly after Samos and Mycale fell (XI.34,36), and "the Ionians [inhabitants of Asia Minor] and *islanders*" joined the Athenians in conquest of Sestos on the Hellespont (XI.37).

Therefore in Xerxes' eighth year Persian control of the Aegean was well on the way to collapse. Certainly by his twelfth year he would have been in no position to levy a tribute upon the isles of the sea.

The problem this poses for the Ahasuerus/Xerxes identification can be seen in the following attempt at an explanation.

> In the crippled state of Persia, after the unfortunate expedition into Greece, Xerxes could not lay tribute upon the nations of Europe, and the phrase, therefore, must be considered as bearing a more restricted meaning, viz., *the islands in the Persian Gulf* &c. [85]

Still further evidence that Ahasuerus is Darius rather than Xerxes is to be found in the apocryphal book of I Esdras. The first two verses of chapter three summarize Esther 1:1-3, except that "Ahasuerus" is called "Darius".

Unlike the other apocryphal books which tell their own unique and often fanciful story, I Esdras (Ezra) is different in that except for one section it presents a divergent account of several parts of the Old Testament. It reproduces the substance of II Chronicles 35:1 - 36:23, the whole of Ezra, Nehemiah 7:73 - 8:12 and Esther 1:1-3. Thus for our enquiry, it gives an insight into second century BC Jewish thought concerning the identity of these kings. [86]

Finally, by identifying Ahasuerus with Darius Hystaspes the problem concerning Mordecai's age (and Esther's!) is relieved somewhat. As demonstrated above, Mordecai was taken from Jerusalem with Jehoiachin (Est.2:5-7). If he was newly born at the time of the deportation he would be 113 years old in the third year of Xerxes (597-484 BC, Est. 1:3), while in the third year of Darius he would be about eighty.

It is not difficult to imagine Mordecai being this age or older, but it is difficult to resolve the implications this has for Esther's age - for she was Mordecai's *cousin* (Est. 2:7). That there was a large age gap between them is clear from the fact that "he took her for his daughter" (2:7).

Nevertheless, as explained above, most have imposed an unnatural reading upon the English and Hebrew and have made Kish, Mordecai's grandfather, the one who was carried away. And a few like Bullinger who followed Lumen have placed the events of Esther *before* Babylon fell to Persia.

Neither proposal is, we think, tenable, and it is best to look for a solution in circumstances that could have resulted in an unusually long age-span between Mordecai and Esther.

With this, then, we conclude that the evidence strongly indicates that Darius Hystaspes, rather than Xerxes, is the king in Esther.

(c) Darius Hystaspes is probably the Artaxerxes of Ezra and Nehemiah

Having shown that Xerxes rather than Artaxerxes Longimanus is likely to be the last Persian king mentioned in Scripture, and that Darius rather than Xerxes is the Ahasuerus of Esther, we come now to the question of the Artaxerxes who was associated with Ezra and Nehemiah.

While the popular view makes him to be Longimanus, few have encountered or addressed the substantial problems inherent in this. As presented above the evidence against Longimanus is probably conclusive.

A point that needs again to be made is that Daniel 11:2 speaks of four kings rising in Persia. This likely means that as far as the Biblical record is concerned we will not read about a king beyond the fourth king. This king as we have seen can only refer to Xerxes, whereas if Longimanus were the prominent monarch of Ezra and Nehemiah, then he would be the *fifth*. And the statements of emphasis so apparent in Daniel 11:2, i.e. *And now will I shew thee the truth, Behold...*, are to no obvious purpose.

Yet Xerxes cannot be the Artaxerxes of Ezra and Nehemiah, for there is no indication that his reign extended beyond twenty-one years (Diodorus XI.69). In fact after his eighth year very little is known about him. Apart from his death Diodorus mentions only the sanctuary he gave to the fleeing Themistocles. Xerxes is said to have urged Themistocles to lead the Persians in another invasion of Greece but the plan was abandoned with the latter's sudden death (XI.56-58). [87]

Thus after his huge defeats Xerxes appears for the remaining two-thirds of his reign to have had a moribund existence. This is not the kind of impression we have of the monarch Ezra and Nehemiah dealt with.

Herodotus says that Darius Hystapes reigned thirty-six years (VII.4), and thus meets the requirement of Neh. 13:6. This same historian presents an extensive account of a reign that was active throughout (III.86 - VII.4). In contrast, the near-contemporary material available for Artaxerxes Longimanus is very meagre.

Notwithstanding the problems with making Xerxes or Longimanus the Artaxerxes with Ezra and Nehemiah dealt, there is also a problem for the Darius Hystaspes identification. And this brings us back again to one of the great questions of Bible Chronology. How long is the time between the sixth and seventh chapters of Ezra? Between the sixth year of Darius when the Temple was completed (6:15) and the seventh year of Artaxerxes when Ezra went up "to beautify the house of the Lord" (7:1,7,27)?

Most without considering the inherent conflicts take it for granted that these are two different kings. Our proposal, that there is only one king, Darius Hystaspes, raises, of course, the question about the name or title change.

Certainly, as the following quotation from Matthew Henry shows, the one-king proposal is not new. Commenting on Ezra 7:1, he says:

> Some think that this Artaxerxes was the same with that Darius whose decree we had (ch.6), and that Ezra came the very year after the temple was finished; that was the sixth

CHAPTER 3: SECOND DIVIDE: CYRUS TO ALEXANDER

year, this the seventh (v.8), so Dr. Lightfoot, my worthy and learned friend, lately deceased. [88]

John Gill, with early rabbinical writers, held this view. Commenting on 7:1, he says that Artaxerxes -

[I]s the same with Darius in the preceding chapter; so Jarchi and Aben Ezra. [89]

A comparison of Esther and Ezra with the apocryphal *I Esdras* and *The Rest of Esther* demonstrates that this is also the view of Jewish writers during the second century BC.

This may be demonstrated as follows:

1. I Esdras (2:30-8:6 with 3:1,2) shows that the Darius who allowed work to recommence on the Temple during his second to sixth years is the Ahasuerus of Esther.

Chapter 2

30. Then king Artaxerxes [Cambyses] his letters being read ... the building of the temple in Jerusalem ceased until the second year of the reign of **Darius** king of the Persians.

Chapter 3

1. Now when **Darius** reigned, he made a great feast unto all his subjects, and princes of Media and Persia,
2. And to all the governors and captains and lieutenants that were under him, from India unto Ethiopia, of <u>an hundred twenty and seven provinces</u>.

Chapter 7

5. And thus was the holy house finished in the three and twentieth day of the month Adar, in the sixth year of **Darius** king of the Persians.

Chapter 8

1. And after these things, when **Artaxerxes** the king of the Persians reigned, came Esdras [Ezra] the son of Saraias ...
6. In the seventh year of the reign of Artaxerxes, in the fifth month, this was the king's seventh year; for they went from Babylon in the first day of the first month.

Compare now Esther 1:1-3 with I Esdras 3:1,2.

Chapter 1

BIBLE CHRONOLOGY: THE TWO GREAT DIVIDES

> 1. Now it came to pass in the days of **Ahasuerus** (this is Ahasuerus which reigned, from India even unto Ethiopia, over an hundred and seven and twenty provinces;)
> 2. That in those days, when the king Ahasuerus sat on the throne of his kingdom, which was in Shushan the palace,
> 3. In the third year of his reign, he made a feast unto all his princes and his servants; the power of Persia and Media, the nobles and princes of the provinces, being before him:

Thus as we have shown previously the writer of *I Esdras* identified Darius with Ahasuerus.

2. By further comparison with *The Rest of Esther* (i.e. apocryphal additions to Esther), Ahasuerus/Darius is also identified with Artaxerxes.

Chapter 11

> 2. In the second year of the reign of **Artaxerxes** the great, in the first day of the month Nisan, Mardocheus [Mordecai] the son of Jairus, the son of Semei, the son of Cisai, of the tribe of Benjamin, had a dream.
> 3. Who was a Jew, and dwelt in the city of Susa, a great man, being a servitor in the king's court.
> 4. He was also one of the captives, which Nabuchodonosor the king of Babylon carried from Jerusalem with Jechonias king of Judea (cp. Est.2:5,6).

Chapter 12

> 1. And Mordocheus took his rest in the court with Gabatha and Tharra, the two eunuchs of the king, and keepers of the palace.
> 2. And he heard their divices, and searched out their purposes, and learned that they were about to lay hands upon **Artaxerxes** the king; and so he certified the king of them (cp. Est.2:21-23).

Chapter 13

> 1. The copy of the letters was this: The great king **Artaxerxes** writeth these things to the princes and governors that are under him from India unto Ethiopia, in an hundred and seven and twenty provinces (cp. Est. 3:13-15).

Notice how the above witnesses link Darius (I Esdras 3:1), Ahasuerus (Est. 1:1), and Artaxerxes (Rest of Esther 13:1) with a reign over 127 provinces. As Est. 1:1 shows, this is a distinguishing feature, and therefore not likely to characterize the other kings. And certainly it is a description far more indicative of the reign of Darius than of Longimanus when the empire was in decline.

CHAPTER 3: SECOND DIVIDE: CYRUS TO ALEXANDER

Notice that the king who makes a great feast is both Darius (I Esdras 3:1) and Ahasuerus (Est.1:1).

Notice that the king Mordecai dealt with is both Ahasuerus (Est. ch. 2 etc.) and Artaxerxes (Rest of Esther 11:2 etc.). Therefore these apocryphal portions are a witness that Jews of the second century BC believed that the Darius who allowed the Temple to be completed, the Artaxerxes who gave Ezra and Nehemiah permission to return, and the Ahasuerus of Esther, are one and the same.

In addition to the Apocrypha, the Septuagint calls the king of the Book of Esther, "Artaxerxes". [90]

The view here presented is that in the providence of God, the Darius who in his sixth year oversaw the completion of the Temple (Ezra 6:15), becomes Artaxerxes (the great and just king[91]) in his seventh year (Ezra 7:1,7), and in this seventh year sends Ezra to further establish "the service of the house of thy God" (Ezra 7:19).

Rather than a fifty-eight year gap between chapters six and seven of Ezra, the one follows naturally and immediately upon the other, the completion of the Temple in the sixth year being the reason for Ezra's return in the seventh year.

(d) The regnal years in Ezra, Nehemiah and Esther are those of one king - Darius Hystaspes

Proceeding along the line we have proposed, a harmony and convergence of the different factors begins to emerge. This is especially true of the regnal years. Although the royal titles are different, the years of reign show the kind of development and harmonization we would expect if but one king is the subject.

Beginning with the second year of Darius, the years are as follows: [92]

2nd year, Darius
  6th month 1st day   Appeal to Zerubbabel and Joshua to build (Hag. 1:1).
  6th month 24th day   Zerubbabel and Joshua stirred to work (Hag. 1:15).
  7th month 21st day   The glory of the latter house (Hag. 2:1).
  8th month - day   Zechariah to appeal for repentance (Zech. 1:1).
  9th month 24th day   "From this day will I bless you" (Hag. 2:10).
  11th month 24th day   Zechariah's 1st vision, 70 yrs. Indignation (Zech. 1:7).

BIBLE CHRONOLOGY: THE TWO GREAT DIVIDES

3rd year, Ahasuerus
   - month - day   Ahasuerus' feast, Vashti deposed (Est. 1:1,3).

4th year, Darius
   9th month 4th day   Question of fasts during 70 yrs (Zech. 7:1).

6th year, Ahasuerus
   - month - day   Esther brought to Shushan (Est. 2:8,12,16).

6th year, Darius
   12th month 3rd day   Temple finished (Ezra 6:15).
   1st month 14th day   Passover observed (6:19).

7th year, Ahasuerus
   10th month - day   Esther's marriage and feast (Est. 2:16-18).

7th year, Artaxerxes
   1st month 1st day   Ezra leaves Babylon (Ezra 7:7,9).
   5th month 1st day   Ezra arrives in Jerusalem (7:9).
   9th month 20th day   Convocation begun, foreign wives (10:9).
   1st month 1st day   Convocation ended (10:17).

12th year, Ahasuerus
   1st month, to 16th day   Haman's plot foiled (Est. 3:7,12; 5:1,8).
   3rd month 23rd day   Mordecai's posts sent to 127 provinces (8:9).
   12th month, days 13-15 Jews defend themselves (9:1,15,18).

20th year, Artaxerxes
   9th month - day   Report of Jerusalem's broken state (Neh. 1:1).
   1st month - day   Nehemiah sent to Jerusalem (2:1).
   6th month 25th day   Wall finished in 52 days (6:15).
   7th month, days 1-2   Ezra reads the Law (8:2,13).
   7th month, days 15-24   Feast of Tabernacles, separation (8:14-9:1).

32nd year, Artaxerxes
   - month - day   Nehemiah's temporary leave (Neh. 5:14; 13:6).

This, we propose, is the chronicle of but one king, Darius Hystaspes. But if this is the record of two or three kings we are faced with the puzzling question as to why Darius disappears from the Biblical record after only six years of his thirty-six year reign. After his great kindness to the Jews in actively supporting the building and completion of the Temple it is very strange that we should not read any more about him.

Yet if indeed there is one king here, that which follows, i.e. his kindness towards Esther and Nehemiah, is but a natural continuance of what he had already displayed toward Israel.

It should also be noted that there is nothing contradictory in these regnal years which precludes them from referring to one monarch. Yet such would very likely be the case, if an attempt were made to take data from these kings and apply them to one.

CHAPTER 3: SECOND DIVIDE: CYRUS TO ALEXANDER

Nor do serious conflicts arise when we compare this Scriptural record with what early historians reveal of Darius. Such is certainly not the case, if for example Xerxes is Ahasuerus. For Ahasuerus in his seventh year marries Esther and celebrates with a great feast and "made a release to the provinces, and gave gifts, according to the state of the king" (Est. 2:16,18). But according to the archon dating of Diodorus, which makes Xerxes' reign to commence in 486 BC, the year 479 BC, which arguably is just after his seventh year, finds Xerxes far too busy to be involved in marriage celebrations. He is in the second year of the invasion of Greece. The campaign had taken a disastrous turn, and at Sardis after learning of further defeats, he leads his army back to Ecbatana (Diodorus XI.36). The march to Ecbatana would be roughly two thousand miles, and a further four hundred miles to Shushan (Est. 2:3). But of course Ahasuerus could not be marching back to Persia in his seventh year, for in his *sixth year* he was at Shushan awaiting the conclusion of Esther's twelve month purification rites
(Est. 2:12-16)!

These factors which make the Xerxes/Ahasuerus identification an impossibility are glossed over by commentators.

As to whether or not there would be historical conflicts if Longimanus were the Artaxerxes of Ezra and Nehemiah, so little is known of him, it is not easy to say. Diodorus, apart from the years of his accession and death, mentions him by name only in the revolt and defeat of his forces by Egypt in his third and fourth years, and the seventeenth year when he makes peace with Greece after a defeat at Salamis.

One aspect, however, does become apparent. Could Artaxerxes with honesty and candor refer to himself as *king of kings* if his father Xerxes had been massively defeated by the Greeks, and he had been defeated by Egypt in a revolt that was to last ten years? [93] Yet in his seventh year in a very upbeat and confident decree this is how Artaxerxes describes himself.

Artaxerxes, king of kings, unto Ezra the priest ... I made a decree ... (Ezra 7:12,13).

How can he be "king of kings" if his realm has been defeated by the kings of Greece and Egypt? Certainly there are serious "seventh year" conflicts for both Xerxes and Artaxerxes.

There is another point which indicates strongly that Darius Hystaspes is the king that is seen throughout these regnal years. In the last date of the Old Testament, notice again Nehemiah's return to the king for consultation (Neh. 13:6):

...for in the two and thirtieth year of Artaxerxes king of Babylon came I unto the king.

The inscriptions show that Darius Hystaspes is frequently given the title "King of Babylon", whereas only two instances are cited of it being given to Artaxerxes Longimanus. [94]

(e) The reign of Darius completes the first seven of the Seventy Weeks.

As we have seen, the Seven Weeks / Forty-nine Years (Dan. 9:26) provide the key bench mark in determining the post-exilic chronology. Daniel had earnestly requested *O Lord hearken and do; defer not ... for thy city* (9:19). In reply the Lord said the city would be restored and built within this seven week period. We have seen further that the entire thrust of these promises is meaningless if the seven weeks do not begin shortly after Daniel receives the prophecy.

Only Darius Hystaspes can fit comfortably into this forty-nine year framework. If the seven weeks begin with Longimanus' twentieth year, there is nothing recorded in history or Scripture that even remotely identifies itself as the concluding event of these forty-nine years. Thus, that which is presented as a specific timescale becomes open-ended.

But, if the last regnal year of the Old Testament (Neh. 13:6), and the last event (completion of Nehemiah's reforms), are shown to be under the reign of Darius, and if these years of Darius are added to those of his predecessors, Cyrus and Cambyses, the result will be close to forty-nine years.

Beginning with the first year of Cyrus when the decree went forth (Ezra 1:1), we have the following:

Cyrus reigns	7 years
Cambyses reigns	8 years
Pseudo Smerdis reigns	7 months
Darius' reign, to Nehemiah's departure	32 years
Nehemiah's return, and reforms	1-2 years est.
	49 years

This speaks for itself, and provides its own verification. Let someone set out an equally harmonious arrangement centred upon Longimanus. It cannot be done!

CHAPTER 3: SECOND DIVIDE: CYRUS TO ALEXANDER

(f) A 120-year harmony can be demonstrated between the kings and priests of Ezra and Nehemiah

Kings		Priests	Comments
	Certain		
Cyrus **450 BC** 7 yrs		Jeshua	Daniel's 1st King. Decree goes forth in 1st yr. Ezr. 1:1; Isa. 44:18.
Cambyses 8 yrs			Daniel's 2nd King. Called Ahasuerus and. Artaxerxes. Ezr. 4:6,7 Stops work on Temple.
Pseudo Smerdis 7 months			
Darius/Ahasuerus 36 yrs - 1st			Daniel's 3rd King
	2nd		Work on Temple recommences.
	3rd		Vashti deposed.
	6th	Joiakim	Temple finished. c. 3 of 7 weeks completed.
Assumes Artaxerxes title 7th			Ezra arrives. Goes into chamber of Johanan
		Eliashib	(grand)son of Eliashib Ezr. 10:6.
	12th		Haman's plot foiled.
	20th		Nehemiah arrives, <u>Sanballat</u> thwarts work.
	32nd		Nehemiah's absence.
SEVEN WEEKS=c.34th			Neh. Returns, chases a son of Joiada, the son of Eliashib the high priest, who had married the daughter of <u>Sanballat</u> Neh.13:28. Reforms conclude the 49th YEAR.
	49 yrs.		
	(Less certain)		
Xerxes (21 yrs)		Joiada	Daniel's 4th King. Little is known of Xerxes after 7th yr. Joiada's son married to <u>Sanballat</u>'s daughter Neh. 13:28.
		Jonathan	If Jonathan became high priest 45 yrs. after Ezra entered his chamber (Ezr.10:6), his accession would be 16 yrs after the death of Darius, 18 yrs after Nehemiah's encounter with his brother (13:28), and a further 53 yrs to Persia's defeat by Alexander.

BIBLE CHRONOLOGY: THE TWO GREAT DIVIDES

Arta. Longimanus (41 yrs)			Also during Jonathan's priesthood, "Bagoses the general of <u>another Artaxerxes</u>' army polluted the temple" (Josephus XI.297), and a letter is sent to the sons of <u>Sanballat</u> governor of Samaria (Elephantini papyri).
Darius II	<u>(19 yrs)</u>		
	(83 yrs)	Jaddua	"The Levites in the days of Eliashib, Joiada, and Johanan and Jaddua were recorded chief of the fathers ... to the reign of <u>Darius the Persian</u>" (Neh.12:22).
	((much less certain))		
(Artaxerxes II)	((45 yrs))		
(Artaxerxes III)	((21 yrs))		
(Arses)	((2 yrs))		
(Darius III)	((5 yrs))		Josephus mentions "<u>Darius the last king</u>" and <u>Sanballat</u> in connection with Jaddua (XI.302), and that after Persia fell Jaddua showed Alexander the prophecies of Daniel (XI.337).
	((73 yrs))		

Alexander defeats Persia **331 BC**

If, as Scripture seems certain to show, the decree to rebuild Jerusalem went out in the first year of Cyrus, and if, as all accounts indicate, 331 BC is a stable date for Alexander, then the period covered will be 120 years rather than the Ptolemaic 205 years.

Therefore the 483 years from Cyrus' decree to the Cross will be:

120 yrs	Cyrus to Alexander
331 yrs	Alexander to the Birth of Christ
- 1 yr	Crossing BC to AD
<u>33 yrs</u>	Birth of Christ to the Cross
483 years	= **Sixty-Nine Weeks**

These years thus expressed represent the building block and foundation stone of chronology and history.

In the above chart the center column shows the approximate length of service for the six priests during the 120 years. The comments on the right give some of the time constraints that point to the shorter rather than the longer chronology. Notice, for example, that Sanballat spans the

CHAPTER 3: SECOND DIVIDE: CYRUS TO ALEXANDER

years from Nehemiah to Alexander, and that Nehemiah is contemporary with several generations of the priests.

As for the kings, the regnal years of the first forty-nine years are well attested and in this instance agree with Ptolemy, but thereafter the chronology is much shorter - 71 years rather than 156 years.

It will also be noted that Ptolemy's 156 years are divided into two groupings of eighty-three and seventy-three years. Contemporary evidence for the eighty-three years is at best patchy, while for the Persian kings reigning during the seventy-three years the evidence becomes considerably less certain.

After adding the 70-year captivity to the 450 BC date for the decree of Cyrus, Nebuchadnezzar's first deportation from Jerusalem will have taken place in 520 BC rather than the Ptolemaic 605 BC. Therefore when the secular "bridges" are removed from the Bible's chronology, 520 BC is shown to be the likely date for the beginning of *the Times of the Gentiles* (Luke 21:24).

Having now examined this complex question from the standpoint of the Word of God, we must now leave this clear and certain revelation for the vagaries of secular evidence. Here we look at the writings of early historians and chronologists, at inscriptions on the walls of Persepolis, at clay tablets in Babylon, and at virtually anything that may give some further lead to this controversial period. But in this necessary review of the Persian and Greek evidence, it must always be kept in mind that we have left the certain for the uncertain.

NOTES: CHAPTER THREE

1. Dwight Pentecost, *Things To Come*, (Grand Rapids, USA: Dunham Publ. Co., 1958), p.244. Emphasis mine.
2. John Walvoord, *Daniel The Key to Prophetic Revelation*, (Chicago: Moody Press, 1971), pp.225,226.
3. Flavius Josephus, *The Works of Josephus*, Translated by William Whiston, (Peabody, Massachusetts: Hendrickson Publ., 1987), *Antiquities of the Jews* XI:5-7.
4. Merrill Unger, *Unger's Commentary on the Old Testament*, (Chicago: Moody Press, 1981), Vol.II, p.1666.
5. See Anstey, p.252.
6. Unger, Vol.I, p.639.
7. Anstey (p.254) believed the total was more, with Azariah = Ezra, Harim = Rehum, and Hodijah = Judah.
8. Jones, p.233.
9. Unger, Vol.I, pp.649,650.
10. Jones, p.245.
11. The register in Neh. 12 is limited to priests and Levites, while the lists of Ezra 2 and Neh. 7 include other leaders.
12. Probably the father of Ater, Ezra 2:16; Neh. 2:21.
13. "Ezra", *Cyclopedia of Biblical, Theological, and Ecclesiastical Literature*.
14. See Gordon Lindsay, *God's Plan of the Ages*, 4th edition, (Dallas: Christ For All Nations Inc., 1971), p.138.
15. Robert Jamison, *JFB Commentary* (London: Collins Sons Ltd., n.d.), Vol.II, p.626.
16. Lumen attempts to link him with the Zidkijah in Neh. 10:1, whom he thinks is the son of King Jehoiakim (I Chr. 3:16). But Zidkijah is not said to be linked genealogically to Nehemiah, but is simply the second in the list of covenant-signers (Neh. 10:1,2). Lumen, *The Prince of Judah*, (London:Elliot Stock, 1905), p.56.
17. *JFB* Vol.II p.606.
18. Quoted in Lumen, pp.36,37.
19. Jones, p.212.
20. C.F.Keil, "Ezra Nehemiah Esther", *Biblical Commentary on the Old Testament*, (Grand Rapids: Eerdmans Publishing Co. n.d.), pp.335,336.
21. *Ibid.*, pp.334,335.
22. *Ibid.*, p.336.
23. *Matthew Henry's Commentary*, (New York: Fleming H. Revell Co., n.d.), Vol.II, p.1122.
24. *Gills Commentary*, (Grand Rapids: Baker Book House, 1980).
25. Henry, Vol.II, p.1033.
26. *Gills Commentary, in loc.*
27. By Jones' count, p.206.
28. *JFB Commentary, in loc.*
29. *Gills Commentary, in loc.*

30. How old his father Jozadak was at the time Nebuchadnezzar slew Seriah cannot be determined. I Chr. 6:15 says "he *went* into captivity." Perhaps this is more likely a description of an adult than a child. He was also of such an age that he died during the remaining fifty years before the return (586-536 BC). Josephus throws no further light on this question, cp. *Antiquities,* X:151-153.
31. Charles Fensham, *The Books of Ezra and Nehemiah*, (Grand Rapids, USA: Eerdmans Publ. Co., 1982), p.338.
32. *Ibid.,* XI:120-130, 145-158. Ezra arrived in the fifth month (Ezra 7:8), his reforms took place from the 9th to the 1st months (10:9,16,17). Josephus gives the impression that this feast would then follow in the 7th month. However, his description is much like that given to the 7th month after Nehemiah's arrival (Neh. 8), 12/13 years later.
33. Fensham, p.338.
34. Gill, *in loc.*
35. Keil, pp.127,128.
36. Most likely a Levite porter of the east Temple gate, as the other gates were burned; so Gill.
37. Derek Kidner, *Ezra and Nehemiah*, (Leicester, U.K.: Inter-Varsity Press, 1979), pp.81,82.
38. *Ibid.,* cp. p.82, note 2.
39. Cowley, *Aramaic Papyri of the Fifth Century B.C.,* (Oxford Univ. Press, 1923). Cited by Kidner, p.143.
40. Dan P. Barag, "Some Notes on a Silver Coin of Johanan the High Priest," *Biblical Archaeologist,* (Sept.1985), pp.166-168. The coin is listed as (Mildenberg 1979:number 17).
41. *Ibid.* p.167.
42. Kidner, p.144.
43. *Ibid.* pp.144ff.
44. *Ibid.* p.82, note 1.
45. *Ibid.* pp.143,144.
46. *Ibid.* p.143.
47. "Sanballat", *Encyclopedia Judaica.*
48. Frank Moore Cross Jr., "The Discovery of the Samaria Papyri", *Biblical Archaeologist,* (1963,4), pp. 110-121.
49. *Ibid.,* p.115.
50. *Ibid.,* p.111.
51. *Ibid.,* p.115.
52. *Ibid.,* p.115.
53. *Ibid.,* p.121.
54. While Josephus does not specifically mention Sanballat in his account of Nehemiah, it is believed that his comments at XI:302 clearly project Sanballat back to Nehemiah's time. Thus Josephus is shown to describe but one Sanballat from Nehemiah to Jaddua and Alexander. See H.G.M.Williamson, "The Historical Value of Josephus *Jewish Anitquities* XI, 297-301", *The Journal of Theological Studies* (28, 1977), p.64.
55. Cross, "The Discovery of the Samaria Papyri", p.121.

56. See also, "Aspects of Samaritan and Jewish History in Late Persian Times", *Harvard Theological Review*, (59, July 1966).
57. "The Historical Value of Josephus".
58. Epstein ed., *The Babylonian Talmud*, (London: Soncino Press, 1938), Seder Mo'ed, Yoma 69a, pp.324-326.
59. Jones, p.207.
60. Willis J. Beecher, *The Dated Events of the Old Testament*, (Philadelphia: Sunday School Times, 1907), p.172, cited by Jones, p.207.
61. Newton, *The Chronology of Ancient Empires Amended*, pp.363-366.
62. According to its "Preface", the *Antiquities* were written in 93 AD, whereas the final editing of the Babylonian Talmud (Gemara) took place about 500 AD, and incorporated rabbinic opinion of the previous 250 years. The quotation given above appears to be a summary conclusion by the editor immediately before which are the opinions of Rabbi Asshi (dies 477 AD) and Rabbi Huna son of Joshua (dies 370 AD). See "Amoraim" and "Talmud, Babylonian", *Encyclopedia Judaica*.
63. "Simeon the Just", *Encyclopedia Judaica*, citing the Jerusalem Talmud, Yoma 6:3, 43c-d; Men. 109b, and *Avot*. These references show that Simon the Just's son built a temple in Egypt around the year 200 BC.
64. *Ibid.*
65. Herodotus, *The Histories*, Translated by George Rawlinson, (London: Everyman Library, 1996), pp. 249-50.
66. Unger, Vol.II, p.1677.
67. H.G.M.Williamson, *Ezra and Nehemiah in the Word Biblical Commentary*, (Waco, Texas: Word Books Publ., 1985), pp.56-60.
68. Diodorus Siculus, *The Library of History*, 12 Vols., The Loeb Classical Library, trans. by C.H.Oldfather, (London: William Heinemann Ltd.,1952).
69. Edwin H.Yamauchi, *Persia and the Bible*, (Grand Rapids: Baker Book House,1990), p.241.
70. Xerxes was apparently the last Persian king to practise a tolerant religious policy. C.J.Hayes and J.H.Hanson, *Ancient Civilizations*, (New York: Macmillan, 1968),p.182, cited from Jones, p.241.
71. For earlier evidence pointing to a 20/21 year reign, see *Cambridge Ancient History*, Second Edition, (Cambridge: Cambridge Univ. Press, 1992), Vol.V, p.13, n.47.
72. Jones, pp.240-244.
73. *Ibid.* p.243.
74. Jones later decided for Longimanus, but with some notable revision. While admirable as probably the best possible presentation of the Ptolemaic system, yet as we have shown it has serious and apparently fatal flaws.
75. *Unger's Commentary on the Old Testament*, Vol.I, p.657.
76. Yamauchi, p.187.
77. Jones, p.214.
78. The Romance of Bible Chronology, p.244.
79. *Companion Bible*, Appendix 57, p.80.

CHAPTER 3: SECOND DIVIDE: CYRUS TO ALEXANDER

80. Jones, p.213. See also the account of Darius' seven wives, Yamauchi, p.183-185.
81. In 1967 an inscription was found near Persepolis where Xerxes says "I am not hot-tempered ... I hold firmly under control by my will. I am ruling over myself", Yamauchi, p.188.
82. The discussion which follows is based on Jones' excellent presentation, pp.209-212.
83. Yamauchi, p.115.
84. Thucydides, *History of the Peloponnesian War*, translated by Rex Warner, (London: Penguin Books,1972), p.45.
85. *JFB Commentary*, Vol.II, p.650, emphasis mine.
86. Therefore the witness of I Esdras holds precedence over Josephus who wrote some two hundred years later. Josephus (or a later editor) says the king in Esther is "Cyrus whom the Greeks called Artaxerxes", the son of Xerxes (Antiquities XI.184).
87. This according to Diodorus' archon dating was 471 BC, and the fifteenth year of Xerxes reign. Later we will note Thucydides' quite different account as to which king protected Themistocles.
88. *Matthew Henry's Commentary*, Vol.II, p.1051.
89. *Gills Commentary*, in loc.
90. Anstey, p.243.
91. Yamauchi, p.241.
92. Based on Anstey's Chart, p.250, but without his textual alterations, p.240.
93. The Egyptian revolt was finally broken by Megabyzus, the Persian satrap of Syria. He in turn revolted against Artaxerxes, and defeated two expeditions that Artaxerxes sent against him. See Yamauchi pp.249,250.
94. Amelie Kuhrt, "Babylonia from Cyrus to Xerxes", *The Cambridge Ancient History*, Second Edition, (Cambridge: Cambridge Univ. Press, 1988), Vol. IV, pp.134,135.

"Know therefore and understand, that <u>from the going forth of the commandment to restore and to build Jerusalem</u> unto the Messiah the Prince shall be seven weeks, and threescore and two weeks: the street shall be built again, and the wall, even in troublous times."

(Daniel 9:25)

CHAPTER FOUR

FAULTLINES IN THE PERSIAN EVIDENCE

In his important book, *Persia and the Bible*, Edwin Yamauchi devotes his first seven chapters to the following subjects:

1. The Medes 31
2. Cyrus 65
3. Cambyses 93
4. Darius 129
5. Xerxes 187
6. Artaxerxes I 241
7. Susa 279 [!!!]

After describing so fully the reigns and times of these five kings, and allowing for the limitations of his subject (Persia *and* the Bible), we would, I think, expect him to take us further than Artaxerxes I. Instead there is only a brief footnote:

> For the confused situation that followed Artaxerxes I, in which there were several rivals for the throne, see D.M.Lewis, *Sparta and Persia*, (Leiden: Brill, 1977), pp.70-78. [1]

The indices show that Yamauchi makes numerous references to the kings following, and also of Alexander the Great, but I found it remarkable that formal discussion ends so abruptly with Artaxerxes I.

Actually, there is not much to say! And the above is not too far off the mark in illustrating this. From the end of the first third of Xerxes' reign unto the Darius defeated by Alexander, one is hard-pressed to find material for the mighty (!) Persian Empire.

Going over to Judea, and also Egypt, we find things quiet there also. Only in Greece do we seem to have a full history for this period. In fact, the history of these other places is usually written through "Grecian eyes". But as we will show, even in Greece the evidence is not as sound as may first appear.

The evidence that is known has been made to conform to Ptolemy's Canon. But as the Canon in the Persian period appears so sharply at variance with the Scriptures, it is necessary that we take a closer look. The characteristic word in the final two chapters is "faultlines". We will show first how apt this word is for the Persian evidence. Our first area of enquiry will be to see what the early historians say about the kings from Xerxes to Alexander. Here we find at the outset that there is very little of a near-contemporary nature.

1. THE EARLY HISTORIES

Daniel 11:2 alerts us to *four* Persian kings, and in the providence of God, near-contemporary historians, mainly Herodotus, write concerning *four* kings from Cyrus. Herodotus tells us a great deal about Cyrus, Darius, and Xerxes to his seventh year and defeat by Greece. But thereafter, and down to Alexander, there is only a smattering of information and that usually in the much later *Library of History* by Diodorus of Sicily.

The question may reasonably be asked whether all of the kings traditionally listed did in fact exist. And if they did, do they reign as long as Ptolemy says?

The following is the list as given by Diodorus (50 BC), and Ptolemy (150 AD).

Diodorus	Ptolemy [2]
Artaxerxes 465-425	Artaxerxes I 464-423
Xerxes and Sogdianus 425-424	
Darius 424-405	Darius II 423-404
Artaxerxes 405-362	Artaxerxes II 404-359
Artaxerxes (Ochus) 362-339	Artaxerxes III 359-338
Arses 339-337	Arses 338-336
Dareius 337-330	Darius III 336-331

As can be seen Diodorus and Ptolemy are virtually the same. And while Ptolemy gives only a list of the kings, it is from Diodorus that we have our earliest extant commentary on that list. But as for *near-contemporary* evidence very little exists. In fact, as a survey of the volumes on ancient Persia will show, it is Darius who features prominently in the reliefs, inscriptions and monuments. But from Artaxerxes onward the material is scant. This becomes apparent when we look at our "fullest" source.

(1) Diodorus of Sicily 50 BC

A search of his *Library of History* will show that Diodorus' year by year account gives only a relative little to the activities of the Persian kings. The following lists the years when Persian

CHAPTER 4: FAULTLINES IN THE PERSIAN EVIDENCE

activity is mentioned, and the number of pages the Loeb edition gives for each. The page size of the Loeb volumes is small. And while a great deal of space is alloted to Xerxes' defeat by Greece and Darius' defeat by Alexander, with but few exceptions, only a little is given in between.

Xerxes 21 years 486-465 BC

(Noting only the years from Xerxes' invasion of Greece to his death.)

480 (24 pages) Xerxes crosses into Greece and wins a costly victory at Thermopylae. But after a huge naval defeat off Salamis, he withdraws to Asia and Salamis.

479 (12 pages) Xerxes, hearing of the defeat and death of his general, Mardonius, sails back to Laconia.

471 (3.5 pages) Xerxes gives santuary to the disgraced Athenian general, Themistocles. Plans for a further invasion of Greece are abandoned after Themistocles' death.

470 (2.2 pages) Xerxes' son Tithraustes is defeated off Cyprus; many cities are returned to Greek rule.

465 (1.4 pages) Xerxes is slain by Artabanus after reigning for more than twenty years; his son Artaxerxes becomes king and reigns forty years.

Artaxerxes I Longimanus 40 years 465-425 BC

463 (1.2 pages) Artaxerxes establishes the kingdom in a favorable manner. Egypt, however, with the support of Athens revolts against his rule, to which Artaxerxes makes preparations for war.

462 (1.3 pages) Artaxerxes' forces under the command of Achaemenes are defeated in Egypt. He despatches further troops under Artabazus and Megabyzus.

461 (0.7 page) The Persian invasion force makes further preparations en route to Egypt.

460 (1.2 pages) The Persian force is victorious in Egypt.

450 (1.1 pages) Athens resolves to make war upon the Persians on behalf of the Greeks in Asia Minor. Artabazus and Megabyzus lead the Persian forces.

449 (1.5 pages) Cimon lays siege to a Persian garrison at Salamis, prompting Artaxerxes to conclude a treaty with the Greeks.

425 (0.1 page) Artaxerxes died after a reign of forty years; Xerxes succeeded to the throne and ruled one year or less.

Darius II Ochus - Nothus 19 years 423-404 BC

424 (0.2 page) Xerxes dies, his brother Sogdianus reigns nine months, but is slain by Darius who reigns nineteen years.

412 (1.6 pages) Darius, an ally of the Lacedaemonians, is urged to remain neutral in the latter's wars with Athens.

405 (0.4 page) Darius sends his son Cyrus to the aid of the Lacedaemonians in their was with Athens.

405 (0.4 page) Lysander, the admiral of the Lacedaemonians, receives substantial aid from Cyrus son of Darius in Asia Minor. After this, Darius died, having reigned nineteen years. His eldest son, Artaxerxes, succeeded to the throne, and reigned forty-three years.

Artaxerxes II Mnemon 43 years 405-362 BC

404 (1 page) Cyrus, Artaxerxes' brother, makes plans with the Lacedaemonians for a joint war against Artaxerxes.

403 (0.3 page) Cyrus continues with plans for war aginst Artaxerxes.

401 (20 pages) Cyrus marches to attack Artaxerxes and is slain, while Artaxerxes is wounded. The Lacedaemonians who aided Cyrus make their way back to Greece.

400 (2.9 pages) Artaxerxes despatches Tissaphernes to take over all the satrapies which bordered the sea.

399 (1.2 pages) Artaxerxes is persuaded to rebuild his fleet.

396 (2.1 pages) Artaxerxes is angry with the defeats Tissapherus suffered. He arranges his death and replaces him with Tithraustes. Conon and Pharnabazus receive funds from Artaxerxes to strengthen the Persian fleet.

CHAPTER 4: FAULTLINES IN THE PERSIAN EVIDENCE

395 (1.2 pages) The Persian fleet is victorious over the Lacedaemonians.

394 (0.7 page) Tiribazus the Persian land commander arrests Conon.

391 (1 page) Artaxerxes sends Hecatomnus to attack Evagorus on Cyprus.

390 (0.5 page) Artaxerxes sends Struthas to wage war against the Lacedaemonians.

387 (0.9 page) The Lacedaemonians send their admiral Antalcides to make peace with Artaxerxes. This freed Artaxerxes to attack Evagoras on Cyprus.

386 (3 pages) Artaxerxes sends his forces to Cyprus.

385 (4.8 pages) Artaxerxes concludes the war on Cyprus amidst conflict among his generals.

377 (0.8 page) Pharnabazus, general of the Persian forces, convinces Athens to recall Chabrias, who had offered to lead Egypt's war effort against Persia.

375 (0.5 page) Artaxerxes hoped to effect a resolution of the Greek wars so that they might aid him in the impending conflict with Egypt.

374 (4.5 pages) Artaxerxes sends an expedition against Egypt under the command of Pharnabazus, but after discord broke out, withdrew.

372 (0.2 page) Artaxerxes renews his appeal for peace among the Greek cities.

369 (0.1 page) Artaxerxes again appeals for peace among the Greek cities.

366 (0.1 page) Artaxerxes again appeals for peace among the Greek cities.

362 (4.3 pages) Artaxerxes seeks to quell revolts among the satraps and dies after a reign of forty-three years. He is succeeded by Ochus who ruled twenty-three years and assumed the name Artaxerxes.

Artaxerxes III Ochus 23 years 362-339 BC

351 (8 pages) Artaxerxes sends aid to the Thebans in their war aginst the Phacians. He also makes war upon the Egyptians.

350 (9 pages) Artaxerxes defeats the Egyptians.

349 (1.5 pages) Artaxerxes advances Mentor as a reward for his great successes in the war with Egypt.

341 (0.3 page) The Persian king viewing with alarm the conquests of Philip of Macedon, instructs his satraps on the coast to give all possible assistance to the Perinthians.

Arses 2 years 339-337 BC

Darius III Codomanus 7 years 337-330 BC

335 (2 pages) Under this year Diodorus describes how Bagoas poisoned Artaxerxes (Ochus) and placed his youngest son, Arses, on the throne. After reigning two years, he too was slain by Bagoas. Dareius (Darius III) was then placed on the throne.

334 (14 pages) Alexander crosses into Asia Minor to engage the Persian satraps.

333 (14 pages) Darius is defeated by Alexander at Issus in Syria.

331 (10 pages) Darius suffers a second defeat at Arbella.

330 (0.4 page) Bessus the satrap of Bactria murders Darius.

This then demonstrates the extent to which Diodorus, who is for the most part our sole and earliest available literary witness, describes the Persian Empire from Xerxes to Alexander. It is to be noted that Diodorus wrote nearly three hundred years after the fall of Persia. The great majority of the years are not commented upon. Most that are dealt with are given only a smattering of information.

Thus from 478 to 336 BC (i.e. after Xerxes' defeat and before Darius' defeat to Alexander) we find -

- Only thirty-eight years are touched upon.
- Only eleven of these years are given two or more of the small pages in the Loeb edition.
- Fifteen of the thirty-eight years are given less than one page.

CHAPTER 4: FAULTLINES IN THE PERSIAN EVIDENCE

In the following, evidence is brought forward for both sides of this question. Before looking at a number of witnesses who point to a shorter king list, we consider two historians whose fragmentary remains are thought to support the Diodorus/Ptolemy chronology.

(2) Berossus 281 BC

A priest of Bel in Babylon, Berossus wrote in Greek a history of Babylon down to the death of Alexander. The little which remains of his work is found in the pages of later authors. These include Apollodorus (144 BC), Josephus (93 AD), Africanus (220 AD), and Eusebius (260-340 AD).

His only available statements on the Persian kings after Xerxes are found in Eusebius' *Chronica*. S.M.Burstein translates this as follows:

> And Cyrus ruled over Babylon nine years... After him Cambyses ruled eight years, and then Darius thirty-six years. After him Xerxes and further the remaining Persian kings.
>
> (The Persians...) did not believe in wooden or stone images ... Artaxerxes, the son of Darius, the son of Ochus, introduced this practice. [3]

This is to some extent a rewriting of Berossus by Eusebius. Commenting on the last sentence of the first paragraph, Burstein says:

> Eusebius has drastically abridged Berossus' account of the Persian Period. [4]

But perhaps Berossus' account *was short!* The second paragraph presents Artaxerxes II as the son of Darius II, two kings who are supposed to have reigned nineteen and forty-five years. Assuming that this statement is original with Berossus, it is to be noted that unlike the kings before Xerxes, he does not give the length of their reigns.

In his widely influential *Chronica*, Eusebius followed the Diodorus/Ptolemy reckoning of the Persian kings, and the possibility of an editing of the statements of earlier writers towards this chronology cannot be ruled out.

Much of what remains of our next witness is also to be found in Eusebius. And like Berossus who dedicated his work to Antiochus I Soter (281-261 BC), this one is also a kind of "official" history.

(3) Manetho 258 BC

Commissioned by Ptolemy II Philadelphus (282-246 BC), Manetho, an Egyptian high priest, wrote in Greek a history of Egypt down to Alexander. The work is lost but portions remain in Josephus, Africanus and Eusebius.

Manetho touches upon the Persian period in his list of the kings who ruled Egypt during the dynasties XXVII-XXXI. In the accounts handed down to us by Africanus and Eusebius we have the following. [5]

XXVII	From Cambyses' 5th yr. to Darius II's 19th	124 years
XXVIII	Egyptian kings ruled	6 years
XXIX	Egyptian kings ruled, (Eusebius) [6]	21 years
XXX	Egyptian kings ruled, (Eusebius) [7]	20 years
XXXI	From 20th yr. of Arta. III Ochus to Darius III's last [8]	16 years
		187 years

Africanus' and Eusebius' accounts of Manetho disagree sharply for the final two dynasties. The overall figure arrived at by following Eusebius throughout is about nine years short of Ptolemy, but clearly fits into that mould.

With the passage of six hundred years, we must again ask whether with these figures Eusebius has recorded Manetho accurately.

We come now to a number of witnesses who show a lesser number of kings between Xerxes and Alexander.

(4) Josephus 93 AD

In chapter XI of his *Antiquities*, Josephus describes a transfer of reign in Persia.

> Upon the death of Darius, Xerxes his son took the kingdom (XI.120) ... Now about this time a son of Jeshua, whose name was Joacim, was the high priest (XI.121) ... After the death of Xerxes, the kingdom came to be transferred to his son Cyrus, whom the Greeks called Artaxerxes (XI.184) ... And this was the state of the Jews under the reign of Artaxerxes (XI.296). When Eliasib the high priest was dead, his son Judas succeeded in the high priesthood: and when he was dead, his son John took that dignity; on whose account it was also that Bagoses, the general of another Artaxerxes' army, polluted the temple (XI.297) ... Now when John had departed this life, his son Jaddua succeeded in

CHAPTER 4: FAULTLINES IN THE PERSIAN EVIDENCE

> the high priesthood. He had a brother, whose name was Manasseh. Now there was one Sanballat who was sent by <u>Darius</u>, the last king, [of Persia] into Samaria (XI.302).

Josephus goes on to describe Darius' defeat at the hands of Alexander, and Jaddua going out to meet Alexander (XI.313-339).

Therefore Between Xerxes and Alexander, Josephus mentions only three kings as compared with the six of Diodorus and Ptolemy.

- Artaxerxes
- another Artaxerxes
- Darius

The manner in which the ministry of the six high priests is connected with the account of these kings lessens the likelihood of much in the way of gaps occurring.

It is true that Josephus or a later editor of his work showed some confusion as to the relation of Xerxes and Artaxerxes to Ezra, Nehemiah and Esther.[9] But the important thing is that he clearly presented the shorter chronology for the Persian period.

Coming now to the traditional source for Jewish chronology, we see the presentation of an even shorter list of Persian kings. In fact it contains only <u>one</u> king!

(5) The Sedar Olam Rabbah 150 AD

This chronology, formulated in the Talmudic era, makes the Darius who allowed the post-exilic Jews to finish their Temple to be the same Darius who was defeated by Alexander. He is:

- Darius Hystaspes!

Now of course this is wrong, but this is the system the Jews have traditionally followed, and it has wielded great influence through the centuries. It is the basis for their current date (February 1999) being 5759.

In Chapter One we demonstrated how the rabbis of the second century AD deliberately shortened the Persian period and altered their own national chronology in order to make the Seventy Weeks point to Bar Kokhba (died 135 AD) rather than to Christ.

Therefore the Sedar Olam and Josephus demonstrate conclusively that the Jews of that time believed the Persian period to be much shorter than that given by the Greek chronologists. In fact it would have been impossible for the Talmudic rabbis to have succeeded in this radical abridgement were it not for the general belief that Greek chronology for the period was unstable.

Our next witness, though written much later, does reflect the traditional Persian understanding of their early history.

(6) Firdusi 1000 AD

As the Jews with the Sedar Olam, so also when the Persians are asked about their early history they will point to the epic poem of Firdusi. Though written in verse and in an uncritical manner, it is believed to gather and preserve some of the aspects of Persian national history. For the period in question, Firdusi records the following rulers after Darius Hystaspes. [10] Surprisingly he does not list Xerxes.

- Artaxerxes Longimanus
- Queen Homai, the mother of Darius Nothus
- Darius Nothus
- Darius, who was conquered by Alexander

As nearly all the Persian historical accounts were "swept away by the Greek and Mohammedan invasions" [11], Firdusi by preserving the national tradition is an impartial link to that time. He adds his voice to the two previous witnesses that Greek chronology makes the Persian king list too long.

Returning to a number of early witnesses we look next at a remarkable marble slab which had been set up on the Greek island of Paros and brought to London in 1627. It is now at the Ashmolean Museum in Oxford.

(7) The Marmor Parium 263 BC

The compiler of the inscriptions claims to list events from the first king of Athens down to Diognetus who was in office during the archonship of Astyanax (264/3 BC).

The marble mentions only two kings after Xerxes: [12]

CHAPTER 4: FAULTLINES IN THE PERSIAN EVIDENCE

- Artaxerxes (II) Mnemon
- Artaxerxes (III) Ochus

Therefore in addition to the Jewish and Persian witnesses we have a Greek voice which gives less than full support to the Diodorus/Ptolemy king list.

The above witnesses view the entire Persian period. The next three write (after Xerxes) while Persia is still in power.

(8) Thucydides, Xenophon and Ctesias

Thucydides[13] is acknowledged by all to be the finest historian of the Persian period, but his scope and years covered are limited - Greece and the Peloponnesian War (432-411 BC). He does however give a brief summary of important events from Xerxes' defeat down to this war (I.118). After Xerxes, he mentions Artaxerxes I and Darius II.

- Artaxerxes, the son of Xerxes (I.104,137; IV.50).
- Darius, the son of Artaxerxes (VIII.5,37,58-his 13th yr.).

Xenophon is not rated as highly as Thucydides, but his *A History of My Times* remains the primary source for the Ptolemaic years 411-362 BC. He is thought to have died in the late 350s.[14] He mentions only briefly Darius II and Artaxerxes II.

- Darius (I.2.19; II.1.8).
- Artaxerxes (V.1.31).

Ctesias was a Greek physician who for seventeen years resided at the Court of Persia in Susa. He accompanied Artaxerxes in putting down the rebellion of his brother Cyrus the Younger (401 BC). His literary work, the *Persica*, is an exaggerated account of Persian history designed to counter Herodotus whom Ctesias called a "lying chronicler".[15] The work ends with the year 398 BC,[16] which by Ptolemaic reckoning would be the seventh year of Artaxerxes II. The *Persica* mentions two kings who reigned very briefly between Artaxerxes I and Darius II (Xerxes II and Sogdianus, p.167), and with Artaxerxes II Ctesias mentions three kings after Xerxes.

- Artaxerxes I p.160
- Darius II Ochus p.167, reigned 35 yrs.(!) p.173.
- Artaxerxes II p.173

Ctesias is known to have exaggerated Persian history before Xerxes [17] and the thirty-five years he gives to the reign of Darius II may be an example of the same afterwards.[18]

Here then is the witness of the three contemporary historians available to us. Ctesias mentions three Persian kings. Thucydides (died probably 400 BC) mentions the first and second of these, and Xenophon the second and third. Except for the comments of Thucydides and Ctesias on the reign of Darius II, they say nothing further about the length of their reigns. In summary, for the six kings Diodorus/Ptolemy list from Artaxerxes I to Darius III, extant near-contemporary historians give us brief information on only the first three.

The situation is much the same in the considerable number of inscriptional items that have been discovered in various sites of the Persian Empire. Some of this evidence (a very small amount) does point to the kings after Xerxes. Yet there will always be reason to enquire as to whether the evidence has been made to "fit" into the Ptolemaic framework. And it must be kept in mind that when a particular object is said to "date to the reign of", for example, Artaxerxes II, it does not mean that this king's name is on this object, but only that in the received chronology this is where it "fits in".

2. INSCRIPTIONS FROM THE PALACES OF PERSIA

Most excavations and finds have centered on two sites, Susa and Persepolis. Susa (Shushan) was the capital and major city of ancient Elam until it was destroyed by the Assyrian, Ashurbanipal. Darius Hystaspes restored the city, and made it the administrative capital of the empire.

Persepolis was built by Darius and Xerxes to become the grand "city-palace" for the Achaemenid kings. Among the treasury and fortification tablets is one that shows construction ending after the seventh year of Artaxerxes I. [19] Though sacked and burned by Alexander, Persepolis has yielded a great deal of information about Darius and Xerxes, but far less of Artaxerxes. And, as with our other sources, there is very little direct mention in Susa, Persepolis and other sites for the kings after Artaxerxes. Given the great length of reign that chronology ascribes to these kings, the absence of inscriptional evidence is not easy to explain.

Of the great number of royal inscriptions for Darius and Xerxes, many are trilingual (Old Persian, Elamite and Akkadian). Thereafter they are usually written in a single tongue (Old Persian), follow a set formula, and show a deterioration in style. [20]

CHAPTER 4: FAULTLINES IN THE PERSIAN EVIDENCE

Some sixty Old Persian inscriptions (one hundred if duplicates are counted) are known to exist for Darius, and twenty-one for Xerxes. [21] Thereafter, they become rare. Ilya Gershevitch comments:

> [T]he brief inscriptions of Xerxes' successors - which are only thirteen, dictated over a period of about one hundred years - are merely correctly written impersonal stereotypes modelled on brief inscriptions of Darius. [22]

The following shows how most of those thirteen inscriptions to which Gershevitch refers are distributed among the kings following Xerxes.

(1) Artaxerxes I (464-423 BC)

A foundation marble states that Artaxerxes finished building the great throne hall of Persepolis begun by Xerxes.

> Artaxerxes the Great King says ... this house Xerxes my father began, and I finished... [23]

Four silver dishes bear the identical inscription:

> Artaxerxes the Great King ... son of Xerxes ... son of Darius ... in whose royal throne this silver saucer was made. [24]

An alabaster vase found in Russia contains a quadrilingual inscription of Artaxerxes. The Egyptian version of the text declares him to be "the Great Pharaoh". Four further quadrilingual vases bearing the Artaxerxes title are known to exist. [25]

(2) Darius II (423-404 BC)

Nothing for Darius II has been found at Persepolis, [26] but at Susa two inscriptions are known. [27]

> This palace of stone in its column(s), Darius the Great King built; Darius the king may Ahuramazda together with the gods protect.

> Saith Darius the king: This palace Artaxerxes previously built, who was my father; this palace, by the favor of Ahuramazda, I afterwards built (to completion).

149

(3) Artaxerxes II (404-359 BC)

For this Artaxerxes, there is a noteworthy inscription at Susa which reads:

> I am Artaxerxes, the Great King, the King of Kings, the son of King Darius ... Darius was the son of King Artaxerxes, Artaxerxes was the son of King Xerxes, Xerxes was the son of King Darius, Darius was the son of Hystaspes, the Achaemenian. This temple my ancestor Darius built. Afterwards my grandfather Artaxerxes (restored it). I placed in it (the images of) Anahita, Tanaitis and Mithras. [28]

Kent[29] lists three other inscriptions for Artaxerxes II at Susa. He gives only a partial translation, but as to lineage, these do not appear to go beyond stating that Artaxerxes is the son of Darius.

He lists three inscriptions from Hamadan (Ecbatana). Two of these are upon column bases, and the third is inscribed on a gold tablet. The first of these appears to give his lineage back to Darius Hystaspes. In the second he is Artaxerxes the son of Darius. And on the gold tablet his lineage goes back to Darius Hystaspes. [30]

Though Artaxerxes II is given forty-five years by Ptolemy, the only monument to him at Persepolis is said to be his tomb. [31] This, however, does not bear an inscription of his name.

(4) Artaxerxes III (359-338 BC)

Four sets of inscriptions with identical texts were found on palace ruins in southeast Persepolis.

> Saith Artaxerxes the Great King, the King of Kings ... I am the son of King Artaxerxes. Artaxerxes was the son of King Darius, Darius was the son of King Artaxerxes, Artaxerxes was the son of King Xerxes, Xerxes was the son of King Darius, Darius was the son of Hystaspes. [32]

Artaxerxes III is thought to have made some minor additions or alterations in this southeast corner of the city. [33]

(5) Arses (338-336 BC), Darius III (336-330 BC)

Little if anything has been found for these two kings. Anstey makes mention of a seal that bears the words: "Arsaces a son of the race of Ahyabusanus". [34] Yamauchi says that "there are no

CHAPTER 4: FAULTLINES IN THE PERSIAN EVIDENCE

monuments from the brief reign of Arses" [35] As for Darius III the same author only makes mention of a tomb that has been "ascribed" to him. [36] Again the tomb does not bear his name.

Here then are the thirteen or so inscriptions that Gershevitch says have been found for the kings after Xerxes. Given that these kings are supposed to have reigned for more than 130 years, we would expect considerably more than this. Thus while this evidence may be brought forward as a witness to their existence, it may also be a tacit indication that they did not reign as long as is supposed.

The current literature does not seem to question the validity of these inscriptions. Kent in his work, for example, describes five Old Persian inscriptions which are clearly spurious [37]. Anstey, however, expresses doubt and quotes a writer in his day who said that the "ring of metal seems less true in these later inscriptions". [38]

While the identification of the kings in these inscriptions may seem to be reasonably certain, we are of course dealing with titles rather than personal names. The titles could on occasion be interchanged. For example in one instance we find Xerxes referring to himself as Darius!

> A great god is Ormazd, who has made Xerxes king, sole king of many kings ... I am Xerxes the Great King ... the son of Darius the Achaemenian. Says Xerxes the Great King: By the grace of Ormazd, I have made this portal ... Says Darius the King. May Ormazd protect me ... and my father's work. [39]

The possibility of interchange needs to be taken into account in the identification of these latter kings.

(6) Tombs of the Kings

The tomb of Cyrus at Pasargadae is said by Arrian (VI.27; 2nd cent.AD) to have borne the inscription: "Mortal! I am Cyrus, son of Cambyses who founded the Persian Empire..." [40] That of Cambyses is thought to be the non-inscribed and unfinished tomb at Talcht-i-Rustam near Persepolis.

At Naqsh-i-Rustam near Persepolis is a rock face in which are carved four tombs. "Only the third tomb from the left is explicitly identified by an inscription as that of Darius. It is supposed that the other tombs are, from left to right, those of Darius II, Artaxerxes I, and on the extreme right, Xerxes." [41] Specific evidence for this, however, is lacking. Each of the tombs is placed within a large recessed cross that has been carved from the cliff face. As their appearance is very similar it is reasonable to enquire as to whether they were made at the same time, i.e. in the reign of Darius Hystaspes.

Two tombs on the slopes of Kuh-i-Rahmat beside Persepolis are thought to be those of Artaxerxes II and Artaxerxes III. But again, without inscriptional identification this must remain uncertain. The case is the same with the unfinished tomb proposed for Darius III. And, for Arses, no likely sites have been found. [42]

Our next area of evidence is considerably more vast and complex than that which we have seen to now.

3. THE TABLETS

Clay tablets numbering into the thousands have been discovered at Persepolis and sites in Babylonia. Frequently the size of a man's hand, they describe a wide range of subjects: business, agricultural, religious, astronomical etc. For our purpose, we are especially interested in those which are dated to the years of Persian kings.

(1) The Persepolis Tablets

Many hundreds of clay tablets written in the Elamite language have been found in the fortification walls and treasury of Persepolis. The Persepolis Treasury Tablets (PTT) number 114 pieces and date to the reigns of Darius Hysaspes, Xerxes and the first five years of Artaxerxes I. More than 2000 of the Persepolis Fortification Tablets (PFT) have been published, with thousands more awaiting publication. These also date to the reign of Darius. [43]

Both sets of tablets deal with the day-to-day running of the kingdom. Again we must ask why they do not extend into the reigns of the latter kings. The proposed explanation, that tablet records were replaced by Aramaic writing on perishable materials, can apparently account for only a small part of this gap. [44] Others, as A. T. Olmstead, in refering to the Persian evidence generally, speak of "linguistic decay" after Darius I. [45] But could it not be that it is the chronology rather than the linguistic remains that is at fault?

Coming now to the provinces of Babylon, the situation is much the same.

(2) The Babylonian Tablets

CHAPTER 4: FAULTLINES IN THE PERSIAN EVIDENCE

Babylonia's continued importance and activity after its fall to Persia is demonstrated by the large numbers of cuneiform tablets discovered there. Written in the Akkadian dialect, these have been divided into three categories.

(a) Chronicles

The governmental *chronicles* describe the affairs of state with reference to the years of a king's reign. A. K. Grayson, who has compiled the known chronicles from Assyrian down to Seleucid times, points out that there is a -

> ...complete absence of texts in some cases, particularly during most of the Achaemenid period. In fact ... only two texts are preserved. [46]

The one tablet apparently mentions Xerxes, and the second is assigned to Artaxerxes III (359-338 BC) - but not, I think, convincingly:

> The fourteenth [year] of Umasu, who is called Artaxerxes: In the month Tishri the prisoners which the king took [from] Sidon [were brought] to Babylon and Susa...[47]

"Umasu" is used of a Darius as well as an Artaxerxes in the Babylonian tablets.[48] And while Grayson assigns the tablet to the late Babylonian period, he says that it has features exhibited by chronicles of earlier Neo-Babylonia.[49] Thus the chronicle could refer to Artaxerxes I, or perhaps another king.

(b) Astronomical Tablets

A second group, the *astronomical tablets*, record a wide range of matters with reference to planetary and lunar positions. While the earliest is dated 652 BC, most of the 1648 tablets listed in LBAT [50] are from 330 BC to the 1st century AD, with a peak being reached in the 2nd century BC. Far fewer are available for the Persian period. The tablets were discovered in two sites: Babylon during the 1870s and 80s, and Uruk (some 150 miles to the southwest) in the early 1910s. Most are in the British Museum.

Consecutive Eclipse Cycles

A. J. Sachs has listed the astronomical tablets which give the names of Persian kings with reference to their regnal years.[51] Notable among these is the Saros Tablet, which is said to list the regnal years of Persian and later rulers at eighteen year intervals from 548-98 BC. Eighteen years was the standard Babylonian period for eclipse cycles (saros).

This tablet, and others which give a series of eclipses, are not based on contemporary observation, but on mathematical calculations made in many cases long after.[52] On the Saros Tablet we find the following:

From Xerxes' (Hisiarsu) 9th year (476/5 BC) [53] which is line five on the tablet, we next go to line six and the 6th year of Artaxerxes (458/7), eighteen years later.

Artaxerxes I

Line 6   "6 of Artaksatsu"
Line 7   [24 of Artaksat]su

Darius II

Line 8   (not given)
Line 9   "19 of Daramus"

Artaxerxes II

Line 10 (not given)
Line 11 "36 of Artaksatsu"

Artaxerxes III

Line 12 "8 of Umasu"

Darius III

Line 13 "3 of Darimus"

While these lines of text appear to fit in quite well with the reigns assigned by Sachs, this is after all a first century BC work in which the eighteen year eclipse cycle has been adapted to the chronological system then popular inthe Greek-speaking world - i.e. that found in Diodorus. This is not an account of actual observations, but only retroactive calculations based on the assumption that the chronology is correct.

Among the eight other *consecutive-eclipse tablets* assigned by Sachs to the Persian period,[54] only two give the names of kings. One, known as the Saros Canon, gives "consecutive lunar-eclipse possibilities, in eighteen year groups for the years 384/3 to 271/0 BC." [55] These, based

CHAPTER 4: FAULTLINES IN THE PERSIAN EVIDENCE

again on Greek chronology, are linked to the king's regnal year. The three royal names (!) on the tablet are abbreviated to the first syllable.
Sachs places them in the reigns of Artaxerxes III, Arses and Darius III respectively:

"1 of U."
"1 of Ar."
"1 of Da."

This is pretty slim! And we will have to leave it to those with the necessary expertise to explain why the eclipse data are linked only to the first year of their reigns.

One other eclipse tablet, based on the same eighteen year division (441/0 to 439/8; 423/2 to 421/0), places the accession of Darius II in the year 424/3 BC.

"Accession year of Umasu [called] Daramusu" [56]

Planetary and Lunar Observations

A second group of tablets is described by Sachs as *planetary and lunar observations*. Of the sixty-five tablet sets listed in LBAT, he dates and assigns the following eleven to the Persian kings:

Darius II

1. Observations of close approaches of Saturn and Mars to the moon, from 422/1 to 399/8 BC: "[Year 1 of Dariya]mus, son of Artakahisi." (422/1 BC).[57]

Artaxerxes II

2. Observations of close approaches of Saturn and Mars to the moon from 422/1 to 399/8 BC: "Year 1 of Ar." (403/2 BC).[58]

3. Venus observations from 462/1 BC onwards: "Year 2 of Arsu." (402/1 BC).[59]

4. Jupiter observations for the years 386/5 to 345/4 BC: "Observations of Jupiter from year 18 of Arsu called Artaksatsu the king until month IV of year 13 of Umasu called Artaksatsu the king." (Year 18=386/5 BC).[60]

5. Observations (probably from Nippur) of Jupiter, Venus and Mercury for 363/2 to 362/1 BC: "Year 41 of Artahsatsu, king of the countries." (363/2 BC). "Year 42 of Artahsatsu the king." (362/1 BC).[61]

6. Jupiter observations for 361/0 to 323/2 BC: "[Year 43] of Arsu." (361/0 BC).[62]

155

Artaxerxes III

Jupiter observations for 361/0 to 323/2 BC: "Year 1 of Umasu." (357/6 BC). [63]

8. Jupiter observations for 386/5 to 345/4 BC: "Year 13 of Umasu called Artaksatsu." (345/4 BC). [64]

Darius III

9. Jupiter observations for 361/0 to 323/2 BC: "Year 1 of Artasatu." (334/3 BC). [65]

10. Mercury observations for 362/1: "Year 1 of Daramus." (??) [66] How can the first year (335/4 BC) of Darius III be designated in these Mercury observations if they end in 342/1 BC?

11. Mars observations for 341/0 to 333/2 BC: "l of Da." (335/4 BC). This material is on the Saros Tablet [67]

Number five gives the fullest information: three planets, the king's full name, a complete text, i.e. no bracketed (restored!) words. The other tablets are considerably less specific. Further, Saturn has a sidereal period of thirty years and Jupiter twelve; a given position between them will appear from Earth every sixty years. But in these tablets Jupiter and Saturn are not said to be in combination with each other but rather with planets closer to the sun and thus with a much shorter sidereal period. Therefore a number of date-possibilities would seem to exist for these tablets.

Astronomical Diaries

A third group of tablets Sachs calls *astronomical diaries*. These give an almost day-by-day account of astronomical and weather phenomena for either the first or second half of the Babylonian year. At the end of each month, they give commodity prices, river levels, and noteworthy political and temple events etc. LBAT lists a total of 837 astronomical diaries, but only seventeen are linked to the Persian kings in the period under review. These Sachs dates and assigns in the following manner.

Artaxerxes I

1. "[Year 24 of Ar]su called Artaksatsu the king." [68]

Darius II

2. "[Yea]r 5 of Umasu." Colophon: "Year 5 of Umasu." [69]

CHAPTER 4: FAULTLINES IN THE PERSIAN EVIDENCE

Artaxerxes II

3. "Year 20 of Arsu."[70]

4. "Year 22 of Arsu the king."[71]

5. "[Year 23 of] Arsu called [Arta]satsu the king." Colophon: "Year 23 of Arsu."[72]

6. Colophon: "Year 26 of Arsu [called] Artaks[atsu the king]."[73]

7. Colophon: "29 of Arsu [called] Artaksat[su the king]."[74]

8. "Year 32 Arsu [called] Artaksat[su the king]." Reverse: "Year 32 of Arsu [called] Artaksatsu the king]." (*sic*)[75]

9. "[Year 32 of Arsu] calle[d] [Ar]taksatsu."[76]

10. "[Year 3]8 [of Arsu ca]lled [Artaksatsu the king]." Upper edge: "[Year 3]8 of Arsu called A[rtaksatsu]." Left edge: "Year 38 of Arsu [call]ed Artaksatsu."[77]

11. "[Yea]r [43] of Arsu [called] Artaksatsu the king." Colophons, composite: "Year 43 of Arsu [called] Artaksatsu the king."[78]

Artaxerxes III

12. Composite of five texts on tablet: "Year 12 of Umasu called Artaksatsu the king."[79]

13. "[Year 16 of Umasu] called Arta[ksa]tsu the king."[80]

14. "Year 16 of Umasu the king."[81]

15. Colophon: "[Yea]r 20 of Umasu [called Artaksatsu]."[82]

Darius III

16. "[Year] 3 of Artasata [called] Dar[iyamus the king]." Colophons, composite: "Year[3 of Artasata] ca[ll]ed [Dar]iyamus the king."[83]

By assigning the tablets in this manner, Darius II and Artaxerxes III bear the same name - *Umasu*. And Artaxerxes I and II, who are said to have reigned forty and forty-five years respectively, are both *Arsu called Artaksatsu!*

With this ambiguity in the names as well as the titles, it is difficult to avoid the conclusion that the evidence has been "made to fit". The tablets seem not to have been allowed to stand in their own right, independent of chronological assumptions. And rather than let us know the other date-possibilities they may possess, they have merely been slotted into the Ptolemaic framework. [84]

A key example of this practice is the influential work, *Babylonian Chronology 626 B.C. - A.D. 75*, by R.A. Parker and W.A. Dubberstein. At the outset the authors plainly state:

> The general basis for the chronology of the period here treated is furnished by the Ptolemaic Canon ... [85]

And after stating that there are "no contemporary business documents for the years 17 to 19 of Darius II", they inform us that -

> The lengths of the kings' reigns from here on are established chiefly by use of the well-known Ptolemaic Canon, of the Saros Tablet ... and of the valuable Saros Canon ... [86]

The Use of Intercalary Months

The authors, like Sachs, link the astronomical tablets listed in LBAT to the regnal years of the Persian kings, but their method and the tablets used (in nearly every instance)[87] are different. Except for LBAT 162 they have selected tablet-sets which it turns out *do not* give the king's name. Instead the tablets give notice that an intercalary month is to be added to the Babylonian year, and this in reference to the regnal year of the king, but without actually mentioning his name.

The Babylonians had a lunar year, which would fall about eleven days short of the solar year and agricultural cycle. To compensate they would add an intercalary month every two to three years. This would result in seven months to be added over nineteen years. The months added were either the sixth, Ululu, or the twelfth, Addaru.

Parker and Dubberstein propose that by collecting and tabulating these intercalary notices they can construct a framework which when used with the Ptolemaic Canon will substantiate the chronology of the period. But this involves some "approximation", as acknowledged in the following.

> [S]o that, by a judicious use of the known, the unknown can be approximated with a varying degree of probability from 626 to 367 B.C. [88]

They have found intercalary notices on nine astronomical and two economic tablet sets. When tabulated and assigned with Ptolemy, they come up with a total of twenty-six regnal years for

CHAPTER 4: FAULTLINES IN THE PERSIAN EVIDENCE

Artaxerxes I, Darius II and Artaxerxes II. It will be noted from the following, that in accord with an intercalation being made every two or three years, the regnal years are also two or three years apart.[89]

Unless otherwise noted the regnal year is followed by Sachs' LBAT number for the tablets.

Artaxerxes I

2	1387
5	1422, 23, 24
5	1388
10	1422, 23, 24
13	1422, 23, 24
13	1388
16	1422, 23, 24
19	Economic Tablet
21	1422, 23, 24
21	1388
24	1422, 23, 24
24	162
29	1422, 23, 24
32	1422, 23, 24
35	1422, 23, 24
38	1422, 23, 24
40	1422, 23, 24

Darius II

2	BM 32209, LBAT 1412
5	1422, 23, 24
5	VAT 4924
7	Econ. Text BM 47500
7	1422, 23, 24
7	BM 32209, LBAT 1412
10	1422, 23, 24
10	BM 32209, LBAT 1412
13	BM 32209, LBAT 1412
16	1422, 23, 24
18	BM 32209, LBAT 1412

Artaxerxes II

2	BM 32209, LBAT 1412

BIBLE CHRONOLOGY: THE TWO GREAT DIVIDES

5	1422, 23, 24
7	BM 32209, LBAT 1412
7	1416
10	1422, 23, 24
16	1422, 23, 24
24	1422, 23, 24
26	1415

Except for a total of fifteen unaccounted years between the 5th to 10th and 24th to 29th years of Artaxerxes I and the 10th to 16th years of Artaxerxes II the above tablets are said to cover the reigns of the three kings after Xerxes unto the 26th year of Artaxerxes II.

We find that the primary source for these calculations are three tablets that have been joined together - LBAT 1422, 1423, 1424. These are now at the British Museum under the numbers BM 36910, 36998, 37036. According to Sachs they give the "dates (years and months) of consecutive lunar eclipses, arranged in eighteen year groups." The years 489-379 BC are said to be encompassed. [90] This indicates that they are not immediately contemporary, but have been retroactively calculated afterwards.

LBAT 1422, 23, 24, as they are here presented cover only a small part of the years Ptolemy ascribes to Artaxerxes I, Darius II and Artaxerxes II.

> For <u>Artaxerxes I</u> (41 years): years 5, 10-16, 21-24, 29-35 and 40 are assigned, thus leaving 21 years unaccounted.

> For <u>Darius II</u> (19 years): years 5, 10, 16 and 24 are assigned, thus leaving 12 years unaccounted for.

> For <u>Artaxerxes II</u> (to 24th year): years 5, 10, 16, 24 are assigned, thus leaving 20 years unaccounted for.

To this "primary chain" eight astronomical and two economic tablets have been added to fill the gaps. Most notable are BM 32209 and LBAT 1412 which have been joined together.

Parker and Dubberstein's tabulation is relied upon as a key source for the chronology of the Persian period. Given the above, however, we will have to ask how valid their method is, and to what extent it has been "pieced together" to conform to Ptolemy's Canon. Certainly, the fact that their method utilizes <u>tablets that do not bear the names of Persian kings</u>, places them under a greater burden of demonstration.

CHAPTER 4: FAULTLINES IN THE PERSIAN EVIDENCE

This brings us now to a third kind of Babylonian tablets. These cover a wide range of business, legal and administrative matters, and are known generally as the -

(c) Economic Tablets

Many of the business texts come from the archives of two commercial families - the houses of Egibi and Murashu.

The Murashu Archive

Texts of the Egibi family (Jewish) date from the 1st year of Nebuchadnezzar to the 36th year of Darius Hystaspes [91]. Those of Murashu (perhaps Jewish) are dated from the reigns of Artaxerxes I and Darius II down to his 7th year. [92] Unlike most of the astronomical texts, these bear the king's name as well as the regnal years.

Several reasons are given for believing that the Murushu archive dates to the reigns of Artaxerxes I and Darius II. [93]

1. The kings' names are Artahshaassu and Dariiaamush. The former has twenty-eight texts dated to his 41st year, of which all but one bear his name. [94]

2. Belnaddinshumu, a leading member of the Murashu "firm", appears in tablets dated to both kings. This shows that the two kings reigned successively.

3. Of the sons of Murashu, Belhatin is mentioned in tablets of the first twenty-eight years of Artaxerxes. And his son, Rimul, is seen in the last six years of the same king, and then to the 1st year of Darius. Thus this Darius must have reigned after Artaxerxes.

4. From the count of tablets made (at the turn of the last century) only four were dated in the first twenty years of Artaxerxes (the 1st, 10th, 13th and 20th), while 116 are dated from the 22nd to 41st years of his reign. For Darius II, 326 texts are dated from his accession to 7th years, and a further seven texts are listed down to the 13th year. Nearly all bear the name Dariiaamush. [95] This concentration of a large number of texts in the latter part of Artaxerxes' reign, and an even greater number in the seven years of Darius, points to the conclusion that Darius follows Artaxerxes.

The Murashu archive appears to give clear evidence for the reigns of Artaxerxes I and Darius II, two kings for which we have little contemporary evidence.

As G. van Driel remarks:
> What makes the Murasu archive important out of all proportion to its size is that it comes from a poorly documented period. [96]

But like the other sources we have looked at, with nearly all of the texts ending in the 7th year of Darius II, it does not extend very far into this "poorly documented period." [97]

The situation was much the same with another set of tablets brought out by A.T. Clay. In 1908 he published a volume of Babylonian legal and commercial transactions which assigned one tablet to the 37th year of Artahshatu, and two tablets to the accession and 4th years of Dariamush. [98]

But regarding Darius, he says:

> It will be difficult to determine which of the tablets published in this volme, and in others, that are dated in the reign of the first twenty years of Darius belong to Darius I or Darius II ... Concerning the Murushu documents from Nippur, there can be no question as to which Darius is meant ... [99]

Tablets Compiled by H. Figulla

In 1949 H.H. Figulla brought out a volume of tablet-texts that placed the matter in a considerably different light. These, nearly all from Ur, were dated much further into the Persian period than the ones above from Nippur. Here again, the primary criterion is shown to be Ptolemy.

Twenty-two texts bear the name Darius (but with no fewer than eleven spellings). Based mainly on the names of "businessmen" written on the tablets, and the title *sar Babili sar matati* which is believed to refer exclusively to Darius Hystaspes, fifteen are assigned to Darius I and five to Darius II. Two of these latter do not have a date, the others are dated to the 5th, 7th and 19th years. [100]

Four give the name *Hisiiarsu* (Xerxes), and are dated to his 3rd (twice), 4th(?), and 5th years.

But it is Figulla's assignment of the Artaxerxes tablets that we need to look at more closely. Forty-three, with six spelling variations, bear this title. Three he assigns to Artaxerxes I and

CHAPTER 4: FAULTLINES IN THE PERSIAN EVIDENCE

forty (!) to Artaxerxes II. If he is correct, then after only the barest of evidence for this monarch's reign, we now have strong support indeed for the forty-five years Ptolemy assigns to him (404-359 BC).

How did Figulla come to this conclusion? The minor spelling variations are probably not a factor, and of course Artaxerxes is a title rather than a personal name. The decider is the Canon. Three tablets give the 42nd, 44th and 45th years of Artaxerxes. For this scholar, "as Artaxerxes I reigned only forty-one years", these must refer to "Artaxerxes II whose reign lasted forty-six years." [101]

Further, the tablet bearing the 45th year mentions three men who were parties to the contract described. These are Nidintu-Sin, and two sons of Siniddin. The "sons of Siniddin" are mentioned in tablets for the 9th (twice), 11th, 27th (twice), 33rd, 35th and 45th years. Nidintu-Sin is named in the 4th, 10th and 45th years. Thus Figulla concludes that the tablets for these years must also belong to Artaxerxes II.

Further, as Figulla believes that five of the twenty Darius tablets must refer to Darius II rather than Darius I because they do not bear the full title *sar Babili sar matiti* and as two of these tablets bear the names of two sons of Balatu, and as the "sons of Balatu" are found on tablets of Artaxerxes' 1st, 6th, 36th and 39th years, there is here further evidence that the tablets must refer to Artaxerxes II who followed Darius II.

This line of reasoning is of course only as strong as its starting point, the two-fold proposition that -

> 1. Tablets belonging to Darius Hystaspes will always bear the full title *sar Babili sar matiti*.
>
> 2. Ptolemy is correct in giving forty-one years to Artaxerxes I and forty-five to Artaxerxes II.

Regarding the first, as there is considerable variation in the way Darius is spelled - eleven differences in twenty tablets - can Figulla be certain that variation would not also be likely in the use of *sar Babili sar matiti* for Darius Hystaspes? More recently it has been shown that variation does indeed occur with this king.

> [T]here is not always sufficient internal evidence in texts dated to a Darius to determine which of the three kings of this same name is meant. The criterion of titulary (Darius I is usually entitled "King of Babylon, King of Lands", which is in general replaced by the title "King of Lands" only, in the reign of Xerxes) provides only a rough and possibly

fallacious guide, since certain dates which must be dated to Darius I also sometimes give the shorter title. [102]

The other point, that mention in several tablets of a reign in excess of forty-one years must necessarily rule out Artaxerxes I, needs to be looked at more carefully. For a start, it must be stressed that by this, a large amount of material has been transferred to a king for whom there is very little other near-contemporary evidence. It should also be noted that while Ptolemy says Artaxerxes II reigned forty-five/six years, Diodorus says that his reign was forty-three years (XIII.108.1).

Thucydides in a separate section of his history dealing with Themistocles (I.126-138) alerts us to the possibility that Artaxerxes shared the throne with his father Xerxes in the years after the latter's disastrous defeats in Greece. He relates how Themistocles after falling from favor in Greece fled for refuge to the Persian court. This was a remarkable turnabout, for it was Themistocles who as commander of the Athenian fleet played such a major role in Persia's defeat.

But what is noteworthy, Thucydides says that it is Artaxerxes, rather than Xerxes, who gave Themistocles sanctuary - and this, determined by other events, some considerable years before Artaxerxes is generally reckoned to have come to the throne.

> Themistocles ... sent a letter to Artaxerxes the son of Xerxes, who had recently come to the throne ... "I, Themistocles, have come to you..." (Thucydides 1.137).

According to Thucydides, this occurred at the time the Athenian fleet was blockading the island of Naxos. Indeed, in his attempt to reach Asia Minor, Themistocles' ship was blown off course into the midst of the Athenian fleet.

> After this Naxos left the League and the Athenians made war on the place. After a siege Naxos was forced back into allegiance (I.98).

> There he [Themistocles] found and took passage in a merchant ship which was sailing for Ionia, but was carried by a storm towards the Athenian fleet that was besieging Naxos (I.137).

After mentioning the siege of Naxos, Thucydides goes on to describe the famous Athenian victory at the mouth of the river Eurymedon.

> Next came the battles of the river Eurymedon in Pamphylia, fought on land and sea ... under the command of Cimon (I.100).

CHAPTER 4: FAULTLINES IN THE PERSIAN EVIDENCE

And as Thucydides says that Themistocles fled to Persia at the time of Naxos followed by Eurymedon, Diodorus also places the flight before Cimon's victory at Eurymedon. But here the point is this: Diodorus and other later historians place Eurymedon some six years before the accession of Artaxerxes, and say that the fleeing Themistocles was instead received by Xerxes.

Diodorus chronicles these events as follows:

> But when Themistocles asked that he lead him to Xerxes ... (XI.56, 471 BC).
>
> Thereupon Cimon ... set at once with his entire fleet against the Persian land army, which was then encamped on the bank of the Eurymedon River (XI.61, 470 BC).
>
> And Artabanus, being led at night ... into the king's bed-chamber slew Xerxes and then set out after the king's sons. These were three in number, Darius the eldest and Artaxerxes, who were both living in the palace, and the third, Hystaspes ... Artaxerxes ... slew his brother Darius ... Thus Artaxerxes ... took over the kingship of the Persians (XI.69, 465 BC).

Much has been written concerning this discrepancy, [103] but as Thucydides writes as a near-contemporary, it seems best to follow his account which allows for the possibility that a further six or more years could be added to Artaxerxes' reign.

A very singular piece of evidence for a coregency has been discovered by Floyd Jones in an article by B.W. Savile from the year 1863. [104]

> It is satisfactory to know that the idea entertained by Archbishop Usher of dating the commencement of Artaxerxes' reign nine years earlier than the Canon of Ptolemy allows, grounded upon what Thucydides says of Themistocles' flight to Persia, has been confirmed by hieroglyphic inscriptions in Egypt, showing that Artaxerxes was associated with his father in the twelfth year of Xerxes' reign.

Unfortunately Savile says nothing further about this inscription. A search at the British Library has not turned up anything. I also contacted the director of the Western Asiatic Department at the British Museum, but nothing further turned up.

From all this, it is not unreasonable to suppose that the tablets listed by Figulla should be assigned to Artaxerxes I rather than Artaxerxes II. In fact it seems odd that in his allocation, the Ur archive is divided into two large groups - the tablets of Darius I with the kings before, and the tablets of Artaxerxes II with eight for the Seleucid period after. This means that between Darius I and Artaxerxes II (eighty-two years by Ptolemy) very few tablets are assigned.

Of the forty-three Artaxerxes tablets listed by Figulla, there is one whose identification seems certain beyond all the others. This tablets describes an arrangment of land parcels in the 13th year of Artaxerxes, and refers back to the 21st year of Xerxes when the agreement was first made.[105] This must certainly be Artaxerxes I. And it would probably be better to let this text provide the basis for the identification of the rest, rather than the course followed by Figulla.[106]

To summarize: the evidence of the Babylonian tablets in their three forms - chronicles, astronomical, and economic - lessens substantially after the reign of Artaxerxes I. In this they follow the pattern which we have seen in the other kinds of evidence.

4. TWO FURTHER AREAS OF EVIDENCE

(1) Egyptian Hieroglyphic Inscriptions

The standard catalogue for these is the *Topographical Bibliography of Ancient Egyptian Hieroglyphic Texts, Reliefs and Paintings* by B. Porter and R.L.B. Moss.[107] In going through the indices of ten volumes, I could find only eight inscriptions for a king after Xerxes, and these all in one volume.[108] Each is for "Artaxerxes" without stating which one, but are most likely Artaxerxes I. Three are vases already mentioned above, and the one that is dated is to Artaxerxes' 19th year.

(2) Persian Coins

While Persia had an established coinage system, it has not provided a means of identifying the reigns of the different kings after Darius and Xerxes.

For example A.D.H. Bivar remarks:

> Attempts to distinguish individual portraits have been shown to be unreliable.[109]

CONCLUSION

With this we conclude our investigation into the near-contemporary and later evidence for the Persian kings between Artaxerxes I and Alexander. And while an effort has been made to present the material fully, it must be emphasized that in comparison with the periods before

CHAPTER 4: FAULTLINES IN THE PERSIAN EVIDENCE

and after (i.e. after Alexander), the evidence is very sparse. Thus in the foregoing, the point is not that some material has been gathered, but rather that *much more could not be gathered*. For the mighty Persian empire to have left so few recorded accounts of these years is one of the great puzzles of historical research.

That this is a fact widely acknowledged is demonstrated by the following statements of leading specialists in the Achaemenid history.

ACKNOWLEDGEMENT OF SPARSE EVIDENCE

The accounts of the period from Xerxes to Alexander have been told and retold so often that some may be lulled into thinking that the history is reasonably connected and the gaps are not substantial.

A.L. Oppenheim is emphatic that the opposite is the case.

> To present the Babylonian evidence - cuneiform texts and archaeological remains - for the Achaemenian rule over the satrapy Babairus [i.e. the province of Babylonia] is to write the history of Mesopotamia from 539 BC to 331 BC. This task has not yet been seriously undertaken and seems, at the moment, to be well nigh impossible. There is simply not enough documentation available to erect more than a chronological framework. [110]

As we have seen repeatedly, this "chronological framework" consists of making what evidence does exist conform to Ptolemy.

Oppenheim concludes by saying:

> The encounter between the Achaemenian empire and Babylonia seems to have left a surprisingly insignificant impact on the latter. Much of this impression is patently caused by the inherent sterility of the extant writings and the scarcity of the archaeological evidence. [111]

And Simon Hornblower writes:

> An honest account of the sources for the Persian empire as a whole should, however, stress their poverty, relative to what survives from the Athenian or Roman empires (the hellenistic Seleucids are a better analogy). [112]

In fact the "poverty" of Persian history is such that it must rely to a large extent upon the Greek sources.

[A] history of the Achaemenid period without the Greek sources would be a "history without backbone."[113]

We will show in the final chapter that this "backbone" is none too strong. This is in effect what Hornblower is saying: i.e. that the poverty of Persian history is not so much to be compared with the Athenian, but rather with the Greek period from Alexander onward. For it is only here that the Greek sources become fuller.

THE ARGUMENT THUS FAR

We have seen that the Scriptures may not *specifically* state in so many words that the Seventy Weeks begin with Cyrus. (In fact they probably do!) Nor do they *specifically* give the length of the Persian period. Yet from a substantial range of Scripture considerations we have demonstrated that no other conclusion appears possible than that the Seventy Weeks begin with Cyrus' decree, and that the Persian period is substantially shorter than the years given by Ptolemy.

We have further demonstrated that the best attempts to bridge the conflict between Scripture and Ptolemy and especially that at the heart of the problem, i.e. Nehemiah 10 and 12, have not succeeded.

And finally, we have found the evidence for the outline of the Persian reigns as presented by Ptolemy to be just that - only an outline - with just the barest near-contemporary evidence available.

In our final chapter we will show how Greek history is used to bridge this period. Here, the faultlines are also in evidence.

CHAPTER 4: FAULTLINES IN THE PERSIAN EVIDENCE

NOTES: CHAPTER FOUR

1. Yamauchi, p.278.
2. E.J.Bickerman, *Chronology of the Ancient World*, pp.127, 128.
3. Stanley Mayer Burstein, *The Bablylonica of Berossus*, (Malibu, California: Undena Publications, 1978), p.29.
4. *Ibid.*, p.29, note 117.
5. Manetho, The Loeb Classical Library, trans. by W.E.Waddel, (London: Heinemann, 1940), pp.175-187.
6. Africanus and Eusebius frequently disagree. For Dynasty XXIX Africanus has a year less.
7. Africanus has 38 years.
8. Africanus has 9 years.
9. See Anstey, pp.263-267.
10. See Anstey, pp.18,24.
11. *Ibid.* p.24.
12. *Ibid.* p.290. A further account of the marble, along with its contrary evidence is given in Chapter V.
13. *History of the Peloponnesian War*
14. *A History of My Times* (Hellenica), trans. by Rex Warner, (London: Penguin Books, 1979), p.15.
15. Anstery, pp.99,100.
16. John Gilmore, *The Fragments of the Persika of Ktesias*, (London: Macmillan and Co., 1888), p.2.
17. *Ibid.* pp.5,6.
18. Diodorus has 19 years, Manetho the historian of Egypt (fl. 280 BC) gives him 19 years down to the revolt of Egypt. A Babylonian table of cycles (90 BC) gives 29 years but takes 10 years from the reign of the king following. *Ibid.* p.173, note.
19. Yamauchi, p.339.
20. Josef Wiesehofer, *Ancient Persia from 550 BC to 650 AD*, (London: I.B.Tauris Publishers, 1996), p.8.
21. Yamauchi, pp.131,188.
22. Ilya Gershevitch, preface to *The Evidence of the Persepolis Tablets* by R.T.Hallock, (Cambridge: Middle East Centre, 1971), pp.8,9. Quoted in Yamauchi p.189.
23. Yamauchi, pp.242,243.
24. Roland G.Kent, *Old Persian Grammar Texts Lexicon*, (New Haven, Connecticut: American Oriental Socirty, 1950), pp.113, 153.
25. Yamauchi, p.243; Kent p.115, 157.
26. *Ibid.* p.368. The Persepolis inscription to which Anstey refers is of Darius Hystaspes. Anstey thought that this was likely (p.262).
27. Kent, pp.113,154.
28. Anstey, p.262.
29. Kent, pp.113,114,154,155.
30. *Ibid.* pp.114,155.
31. M.A.Dandamaev, *A Political History of the Achaemenid Empire*, (Leiden: E.J.Brill, 1989), p.307.

32. Anstey, p.262. For a picture see: Richard N.Frye, *The Heritage of Persia*, (New York: Mentor, 1966), number 39.
33. John Curtis, *Ancient Persia*, (London: British Museum Publications, 1989), p.43.
34. Anstery, p.263.
35. Yamauchi, p.369.
36. *Ibid.* p.369.
37. Kent, p.115.
38. A.V.Williams Jackson, *Persia Past and Presnt*, (London: Macmillan, 1906), quoted in Anstey, p.263. Williams' statement is specifically referring to Xerxes and Artaxerxes I in comparison with Darius I, but he seems to imply the same verdict for the latter inscriptions generally.
39. Anstey, pp.261,2.
40. Quoted in Yamauchi, p.92.
41. Yamauchi, p.182.
42. *Ibid.* pp.368-370.
43. Wiesehofer, p.10.
44. See for example, Matthew W.Stolper, "Mesopotamia, 482-330 BC", *The Cambridge Ancient History*, 2nd Edition, Vol.VI, pp.256,257. Compare Wiesehofer, p.10.
45. A.T.Olmstead, *History of the Persian Empire - Achaemenid Period*, (Chicago: Univ. of Chicago Press, 1948), p.480.
46. A.K.Grayson, *Assyrian and Babylonian Chronicles*, (Locust Valley, New York: J.J.Augustin Publ., 1975), p.23.
47. *Ibid.* p.114.
48. See A.J.Sachs, "Achaemenid Royal Names in Babylonian Astronomical Texts", *American Journal of Ancient History*, Vol.2 (1977), pp.131,133.
49. Grayson, p.24.
50. A.J.Sachs, editor, *Late Babylonian Astronomical and Related Texts, Copied by T.G.Pinches and J.M.Strassmaier*, (Providence, Rhode Island: Brown Univ. Press, 1955), p.vi. This work is abbreviated, LBAT, and may be consulted for conversion to British Museum numbers.
51. A.J.Sachs, "Achaemenid Royal Names in Babylonian Astronomical Texts", pp.130-147.
52. See Robert R.Newton, *The Crime of Claudius Ptolemy*, (Baltimore: John Hopkins Univ. Press, 1977), p.53.
53. All reganl dates in this section are one year later than the traditional dating. This Sachs makes an allowance for by giving a dual date.
54. LBAT, p.xxxii.
55. Sachs, *Achaemenid Royal Names*, p.129, LBAT p.xxxii. Sachs' number for this tablet is LBAT 1428, and the British Museum number, BM 34597. I have not seen a reference number for the Saros Tablet.
56. LBAT 1426.
57. LBAT 1411 + 1412.
58. LBAT 1411 + 1412 (obverse of above).
59. LBAT 1387.
60. LBAT 1394 + 1395 + 1399 + 1400.
61. LBAT 1396.
62. LBAT 1397 + 1401 + BM 46031 + LBAT 1398.

CHAPTER 4: FAULTLINES IN THE PERSIAN EVIDENCE

63. LBAT 1397 + 1401 + BM 46031 + LBAT 1398.
64. LBAT 1394 + 1395 + 1399 + 1400.
65. LBAT 1397 + 1401 + BM 46031 + LBAT 1398.
66. LBAT 1368 + 1369 + 1370 + 1371.
67. LBAT 1428 (Saros Canon).
68. LBAT 162.
69. LBAT 163.
70. LBAT 165.
71. LBAT 166.
72. LBAT 167 + 639 + 670.
73. LBAT 171.
74. LBAT 174 + 580 + 731.
75. LBAT 175.
76. LBAT 177 + BM 32511.
77. LBAT 183 + 184 + 185 + BM 32149.
78. LBAT 187.
79. LBAT 189.
80. LBAT 190 + BM 77245.
81. LBAT 191.
82. LBAT 192.
83. LBAT 193 + 194.
84. For a good discussion of what he calls the "Identification Game", see Walter R.Dolen, *The Chronology Papers*, (BeComingOne Papers, http://onelaw.com/beone/cp.3b.htm 1996) Vol.V, pp.1-11.
85. R.A.Parker, W.A.Dubberstein (Providence, Rhode Island: Brown Univ. Press, 1956), p.10.
86. *Ibid*. p.18.
87. Both use LBAT 162 for the twenty-fourth year of Artaxerxes I, and different citations from LBAT 1412.
88. *Ibid*. p.2.
89. Exceptions being the 5th-10th, 24th-29th of Artaxerxes I, and the 10th-16th of Artaxerxes II.
90. LBAT p. xxxii.
91. Anstey, p.258.
92. Several of "what seems to be a foreign body of texts" in the archive, date to the 11th and 13th years of Darius II. G. van Driel, "The Murasus in Context", *Journal of the Economic and Social History of the Orient*, Vol.32 (1989), p.204.
93. H.V.Hilprecht and A.T.Clay, *Business Documents of Murashu sons of Nippur, Dated in the Reign of Artaxerxes I*, (Philadelphia: Univ. of Penn., 1898), pp.15,16.
94. *Ibid*. pp.51 with 86, 87.
95. A.T. Clay, *Business Documents of Murashu Sons of Nippur, Dated in the Reign of Darius II*, (Philadelphia: Univ. of Penn.,1904), pp.48,132; A.T.Clay, *Business Documents of Murashu Sons of Nippur, Dated in the Reign of Darius II, Supplement*, (Philadelphia: Univ.Museums, 1912), pp.18,19,49,50.
96. "The Murasus in context", p.226.

97. A.T.Clay believed that one of the tablets dated to the first year of Artaxerxes I should be assigned to Artaxerxes II. *Business Documents ... Darius II*, p.2. Parker and Dubberstein accepted this, p.19.
98. *Legal and Commercial Transactions Dated in the Assyrian Neo-Babylonian and Persian Periods, chiefly from Nippur*, (Philadelphia: Univ. of Penn., 1908), p.83.
99. *Ibid.* p.19.
100. *Business Documents of the Ne-Babylonian Period*, (London and Philadelphia: Publication of the Two Museums, 1949), pp.3,4.
101. *Ibid.* p.4.
102. Amelie Kuhrt, "Babylonia from Cyrus to Xerxes", *The Cambridge Ancient History*, Second Edition, Vol.IV, p.116. See also pp.134,135.
103. See Floyd Jones, pp.221-223, 229-232.
104. B.W. Savile, "Revelation and Science", *Journal of Sacred Literature and Biblical Record*, Series 4, (London: Williams and Norgate Publ., April 1863) p.156.
105. Figulla, p.4.
106. Parker and Dubberstein (1956) cite Figulla for the beginning of the reign of Artaxerxes II, p.19. However, in recent works, I have not seen Figulla followed in his wholesale allocation of the tablets to this king. Indeed, R.Schmitt, who goes to considerable lengths to cite sources for Artaxerxes II, does not mention Figulla's work. See "Artaxerxes", in *Encyclopedia Iranica*, (London:Routledge and Kegan Paul, 1987), Vol.2, pp.656-658. But see also Matthew W. Stolper, "Some Ghosts from Achaemenid Babylonian Texts", *Journal of Helenic Studies*, 108 (1988).
107. Published by Oxford Univ. Press from 1927-1960.
108. *Bibliography VII...Nubia, The Deserts, and Outside Egypt* pp.336,395,397,398,413.
109. A.D.H. Bivar, "Achaemenid Coins, Weights and Measures", *Cambridge History of Iran*, (Cambridge: Cambridge Univ. Press, 1985), Vol.2, p.618.
110. "The Babylonian Evidence of Achaemenian Rule in Mesopotamis", *The Cambridge History of Iran*, 1985, Vol.2, p.529.
111. *Ibid.* p.585.
112. "Persia", *The Cambridge Ancient History*, Second Edition, Vol.VI, p.46.
113. *Ibid.* p.45, n.2. Quoted from H.Sancisi-Weerdenburg and A.Kuhrt (eds.), "The Greek Sources", *Achaemenid History*, (Leiden, 1987), Vol.2, p.118.

CHAPTER FIVE

FAULTLINES IN THE GREEK EVIDENCE

The depth and scope of Greek history appears impressive, and is thought to more than compensate for the "poverty"[1] of the sources in the concurrent Persian history. The near-contemporary works of Thucydides and Xenophon, the year-by-year account of Diodorus, the many historians Diodorus mentions, the yearly archons of Athens, the reigns of two families of kings in Sparta, the Olympiads, archaeological remains, the consent of later historians, all combine to place the events and timing of Greek history beyond question. In fact it is Greek history which gives substance and credibility to Ptolemy's Canon, and places meat upon the bones of the outline he gives.

The issue we now come to is not so much the events of Greek history but rather their timing, The events are probably quite reasonably presented. But our oft-stated conviction that as the Scriptures cannot be reconciled with Ptolemy for this period[2] it necessary that we pursue the question of the *timing* of Greek history.

First, though, we need to point out:

THE INHERENT WEAKNESS IN GREEK CHRONOLOGY

Unlike what we have seen of Persian history which is structured upon the reigns of kings, Greek history and especially in its most prominent aspect, Athens, had no kings for the period under review,[3] and is instead structured upon *events*. Thus without the events being linked to a king's regnal years, there will be the question as to whether they have been allowed to *float* in reference to each other.

> There was no all-important power center and no dominant rulership before Hellenistic [i.e. before Alexander] and Roman times: thus the geographical scattering of records was extreme, although naturally with some focuses of emphasis such as Athens.[4]

Other, less satisfactory means are used to compensate, but this remains the basic weakness and vulnerability of Greek chronology. And this is the factor we need to keep in mind as we examine its credentials.

In our inquiry we are bound to mention first the historian without whose work there would be no history for much of this period. Herodotus ends with Xerxes' defeat. Our only substantial near-contemporary account is Thucydides' twenty-two year history of the Peloponnesian War. This same historian gives a brief overview of the years before, as does Xenophon for the period after, but it is only Diodorus Siculus who has left us with a connected year-by-year account of the entire period from Xerxes to Alexander.

1. DIODORUS OF SICILY

Before looking at the chronological essence of his history, we note first:

(1) The Sources Diodorus Used

Diodorus by his own account spent thirty years in compiling *The Library of History* (I.4.1). Though his history formally ends with the year 60/59 BC, he does mention a later event in which Caesar intervened in Tauromenium on his native Sicily (XVI.7.1). This is said to have occurred about 36 BC, and is probably near to the time his work was concluded. At least some of Diodorus' history was available and well-known by the mid-first century BC, for Jerome (340-420 AD) in referring to the year 49 BC said, "Diodorus of Sicily, a writer of Greek history, became illustrious." [5]

Diodorus said that he endured much hardship and danger, and visited the most important regions of Europe and Asia (I.4.1). [6] He spent some considerable time in Egypt, and at Rome he says that he was supplied with an abundance of materials necessary for his study (I.4.2).

Given that we are dependent for so much on Diodorus, the great question of course concerns his sources. As Herodotus' work closes in 479 BC, this leaves us for the most part with only Thucydides and Xenophon among near-contemporary historians whose writings now remain.

Thucydides deals with the Peloponnesian War for the years 432-411 BC, and in what is imprecisely called "The Pentecontaetia" (The Fifty Year Period), he briefly digresses to single out important events which occurred before the war.

Xenophon in his *Hellenica* deals with events for the years 411-362 BC. However, as only the first part of his work appears to be a year-by-year account, [7] and as at least ten years are not dealt with, [8] and as a number of key chronological notices "were almost certainly inserted by a

CHAPTER 5: FAULTLINES IN THE GREEK EVIDENCE

later hand",[9] and as Xenophon "is not reliable",[10] and as the *Hellenica* is essentially memoirs rather than history [11], it does not approach being a chronicle for these years.

Therefore from the witness of near-contemporary historians, it is only Thucydides' twenty-two year account of the Peloponnesian War that approaches a "hard chronology" for the proposed 150 years (479-331 BC).

Where then did Diodorus get his material for the other 130 years? Anstey says that he used the approximate computations and conjectures of Eratosthenes (born 276 BC) and Apollodorus (2nd century BC) to fill the gaps. [12] In fact Diodorus mentions a considerable number of historians that were probably accessible to him and thus while much of his history may be reasonably accurate, his timing based on these two men is likely to have gone seriously awry. Before looking at the works of Eratosthenes and Apollodorus and their effect on the recording of secular history, we note first Diodorus' mention of the historians who wrote during this era.

In the annualistic format of *The Library of History*, and with the BC conversion of later editors, Diodorus says the following for the years 479-330 BC.

479	"And of the historians, <u>Herodotus</u> ... brings his narrative to an end with the battle of the Greeks against the Persians at Mycale ..."
432	"<u>Thucydides</u>, the Athenian, commenced his history with this year, giving an account of the war between the Athenians and the Lacedaemonians. This war lasted twenty-seven years, but Thucydides described twenty-two years ..."
431	"Now the causes of the Peloponnesian War were in general what I have described, as <u>Ephorus</u> has recorded them."
424	"Of the historians, <u>Antiochus</u> of Syracuse concluded with this year his history of Sicily, which began with Cocalus the king of the Sicani, and embraced nine Books."
411	Regarding a storm which destroyed Lacedaemonian ships off Mount Athos, Diodorus writes: "These facts are set forth by a dedication, as <u>Ephorus</u> states, which stands in the temple of Coroncia."
	"Of the historians, <u>Thucydides</u> ended his history, having included a period of twenty-two years in eight Books ... Xenophon and Theopompus have begun at

the point where Thucydides left off. Xenophon embraced a period of forty-eight years [411-362 BC], and Theopompus set forth the facts of Greek history for seventeen years" [410-394BC].

409 The Himeraeans with help from Syracuse "slew more than six thousand of them, according to Timaeus, or, as Ephoras states, more than twenty thousand."

406 And Carthage gathering an army of "a little over one hundred and twenty thousand, according to Timaeus, but three hundred thousand, according to Ephorus," they advanced towards Sicily.

Diodorus quotes Timaeus a second time for this year (concerning help that Dexippus of Sparta sent to Sicily). He also mentions Polycleitus, a historian during the time of Alexander.

"And of the historians Philistus ended his first *History* of Sicily with this year ... And Apollodorus [2nd century, covering the years 1184-119 BC] who composed his *Chronology*, states that Euripides also died in the same year."

405 Dionysius came to the aid of Gela with "according to some, fifty thousand soldiers, but Timaeus says it was thirty thousand infantry."

404 Heloris, Polyxenus and Philistus, "who composed his history after these events," gave differing advice as to what Dionysius should do.

Ephorus gave a different reason for the death of Alcibiades (Athenian).

401 Ephorus said that the army that Cyrus was gathering against Artaxerxes was "not less than four hundred thousand."

400 Xenophon was chosen to lead a campaign against the Thracians.

398 "Ctesias the historian ended with this year his History of the Persians, which began with Minus and Semiramis."

396 Ephorus and Timaeus disagree over the size of Carthage's army.

CHAPTER 5: FAULTLINES IN THE GREEK EVIDENCE

395 Theopompus ended his Hellenic history, which, taking up where Thucydides finished his, covered seventeen years.

387 "The historian Callisthenes began his history with the peace of this year between the Greeks and Artaxerxes ... His account embraced a period of thirty years in ten Books and he closed ... with the seizure of the Temple of Delphi..."

376 "Of the historians, Hermeias of Methymne brought to a close with this year his narrative of Sicilian affairs."

370 Ephorus and other historians disagree as to the circumstances of Jason's (of Pherae) death.

"Duris of Samos began his history of the Greeks at this point."

366 "In this period there were men memorable for their culture, Isocrates the orator and those who became his pupils, Aristotle the philosopher, Anaximenes of Lampsacus, Plato of Athens, the last of the Pythagorean philosophers, and Xenophon who composed his histories in extreme old age, for he mentions the death of Epameinondas which occurred a few years later."

363 "Among the historians, Xenophon the Athenian brings the narrative of *Greek Affairs* down to this year, closing it with the death of Epameinondas, while Anaximenes of Lampsacus, who composed the *First Inquiry of Greek Affairs* beginning with the birth of the gods ... closed it ... with the death of Epameinondas. He included practically all the doings of the Greeks and non-Greeks in twelve volumes. And Philistus brought his history of Dionysius the Younger down to this year, narrating the events of five years in two volumes."

361 "The historians Dionysodorus and Anaxis, Boeotians, closed their narrative of Greek history with this year."

360 "Among the writers of history, Theopompus of Chios began his history of Philip at this point and composed fifty-eight books, of which five are lost." [Of this work, the longest history published until then, 217 fragments remain. Diodorus must have relied heavily on this account, Ed.]

357	"Among historians, Demophilus the son of the chronicler Ephorus, who treated in his work the history of what is known as the Sacred War, which ... lasted eleven years ... And Callisthenes wrote the history of the events in the Hellenic world ... Diyllus the Athenian began his history ... in which he included all the events which occurred in this period both in Greece and in Sicily."
343	"Theopompus of Chios, the historian, in his *History of Philip*, included three books dealing with affairs in Sicily. Beginning with the tyranny of Dionysius the Elder, he covered a period of fifty years, closing with the expulsion of the younger Dionysius."
341	"Ephorus of Cyme, the historian, closed his history at this point with the siege of Perinthus, having included in his work the deeds of both the Greeks and the barbarians from the time of the return of the Heracleidae. He covered a period of almost seven hundred and fifty years, writing thirty books and prefacing each with an introduction. [In chapter 14:3 Diodorus referred to its continuation by his son Demophilus. According to Clement of Alexandria (*Stromateis*, I.139.4), Ephorus reckoned 735 years between the Return of the Heracleidae and the archonship of Exaenetus, 335/4 BC, Ed.]. "Diyllus the Athenian began the second section of his history with the close of Ephorus' and made a connected narrative of the history of the Greeks and barbarians from that point to the death of Philip."

This is an impressive list and represents the fullest and earliest account we have of historians who lived from the time of Xerxes to Alexander. It is natural to assume that Diodorus had access to many of these writers, yet as he is composing his history more than three hundred years after they wrote, and as most are not extant, we have no way of knowing to what extent he actually drew from them.

It should also be noted that a number of these are histories of areas outside of mainland Greece. Diodorus' references to those who cover Greece itself are as follows:

479	Herodotus ends history.
432	Thucydides begins history of Peloponnesian War.
431	Ephorus records causes of Peloponnesian War.
411	Ephorus describes a memorial on Mount Athos.
	Thucydides ends history of Peloponnesian War.

CHAPTER 5: FAULTLINES IN THE GREEK EVIDENCE

	Xenophon begins history.
	Theopompus begins history.
404	Ephorus' differing account of Alcibiades' (Athenian) death.
395	Theopompus ends history.
387	Callisthenes begins history.
370	Ephorus' differing account of Jason's (of Pherae) death.
	Duris begins history.
363	Xenophon ends history.
	Anaximenes ends history.
361	Dionysodorus ends history.
	Anaxis ends history.
360	Theopompus of Chios begins history of Philip.
341	Ephorus ends history
	Diyllus begins second stage of history.

Diodorus mentions eleven historians who dealt with Greece during this period: Thucydides, Ephorus, Xenophon, Theopompus, Callisthenes, Duris, Anaximenes, Dionysodorus, Anaxis, Theopompus of Chios and Diyllus. Surprisingly, it is only from Ephorus, and that but four times, that he makes a direct reference. In the other cases he only mentions their works.

Notwithstanding the brevity of his reference to Ephorus, this historian from Cyme on the Asia Minor coast, and who is said to have lived about 405-330 BC, is acknowledged to be Diodorus' primary source.

But all is not straightforward, and the following by Simon Hornblower gives an idea of how historians have wrestled with this question of the sources behind Diodorus:

> For Greece before the fourth century, Ephorus used the obvious sources, Herodotus and Thucydides, supplementing them from authors like Hellanicus ... He is usually thought to have been, together with Timaeus, the direct source ... of Diodorus of Sicily ... But Kenneth Sacks (below, pp.217ff.) shows that the identification of specifically Ephoran material in Diodorus is not straightforward...
>
> For the fourth century, the identification of the traditions lying behind "Diodorus/Ephorus" (if that simple formula is permissible) becomes very much more important because of the absence of any surviving primary source of the reliability of Herodotus or Thucydides: Xenophon is not in the same class as those two. [13]

This supports what was said above, that when the sources are reviewed, the only thing approaching *hard chronology* for this period is Thucydides' twenty-two year history of the Peloponnesian War.

There is however a curious aspect of Ephorus' work, and Diodorus' use of him, which played a major role in the *timing* of Greek events.

But first, as Diodorus is our earliest connected source, it is vital that we get a grasp of what he says happened during those years from Xerxes to Alexander. Only then can we begin to consider questions as to their timing.

(2) A Chronological Table (Mainly of Athens)

Diodorus deals with a number of areas, but his prevailing emphasis is Athens. We will therefore get a better chronological perspective if we focus upon Athens, and to a lesser extent Sparta, and touch upon the others only as they come in contact with these two. It is also important that we give the names of the Athenians and Spartans that Diodorus mentions for each year.

At the beginning of each year's account Diodorus gives notice of Athens' new archon (similar to a magistrate) who was to serve one year. To this annualistic format later editors have added the common BC dates. In addition, Diodorus structured his history according to the Olympiads. Finally, the more familiar "Spartan" is used in this summary rather than Diodorus' "Lacedaemonian".

<u>480-479 Defeat of the Persians</u>

> **480** <u>Calliades archon, 75th Olympiad, Astylus won stadion.</u> Xerxes crosses the Hellespont and wins a costly victory over a Spartan force at Thermopylae. The Spartan king Leonidas is slain. Xerxes goes on to raze Athens, but then suffers a huge naval defeat at the hands of Themistocles and Eurybiades (Athenians) off Salamis.
> *The lyric poet Pindar is in his prime.*

> **479** <u>Xanthippus archon.</u> Themistocles is replaced as general by Xanthippus (not the archon) after accepting gifts. After a further Persian advance into Attica, the Persians are defeated by Aristeides (Athenian) and Pausanias (Spartan) at Platea. Leotychides (Spartan) and Xanthippus win a decisive naval battle at Mycale.
> *Herodotus brings his history to an end.*

CHAPTER 5: FAULTLINES IN THE GREEK EVIDENCE

<u>478-462 The Rise to Dominance of Athens</u>

478 <u>Timosthenes archon.</u> Athens is fortified amid Spartan protests. Themistocles enjoys favor among the Athenians.

477 <u>Adeimantus archon.</u> Themistocles leads a project to enlarge Athens' harbor. Pausanias (Spartan) and Aristeides (Athenian) take Cyprus and Byzantium, but Pausanias is slain after making a secret pact with Xerxes. Aristeides advises the other city-states to form a union and make the island of Delos their common treasury. Athens now enjoyed a leadership which she did not possess before.

476 <u>Phaedon archon, 76th Olympiad, Scamandrius won stadion.</u> Athens not mentioned. Heimon (Syracusan) replaces the inhabitants of Naxos with settlers from the Peloponnesus and Syracuse.
The Spartan king, Leotychides, dies after a reign of twenty-two years, and is succeeded by Archidamus who ruled forty-two years.

475 <u>Dromocleides archon.</u> Sparta decides not to go to war with Athens, after they lose command of the sea.

474 <u>Acestorides archon.</u> Athens and Sparta not mentioned.

473 <u>Menon archon</u> Athens and Sparta not mentioned.

472 <u>Chares archon, 77th Olympiad, Dandes won stadion.</u> Athens and Sparta not mentioned.

471 <u>Praxiergus archon.</u> Sparta tells Athens that Themistocles as well as Pausanias had made a secret pact with Xerxes. Themistocles is forced to flee to Argos and then to Xerxes himself. He died after agreeing to aid Xerxes in another invasion of Greece.

470 <u>Demotion archon.</u> Cimon leads a successful Athenian campaign against the coast and islands off Asia Minor. Further victories were gained off Cyprus and at the River Eurymedon.

469 <u>Phaeon archon.</u> The Spartan king Archidamus defends Sparta against the Helots and Messians. This followed an earthquake in which more than twenty thousand died. Aid was declined from Athens.

468 Theageneides archon, 78th Olympiad, Posidonia won stadion. Athens not mentioned. Sparta does not send aid to the Mycenaeans.

467 Lysistratus archon. Athens and Sparta not mentioned.

466 Lysanias archon. Athens and Sparta not mentioned.

465 Lysitheus archon. Athens and Sparta not mentioned.
Xerxes is slain; Artaxerxes becomes king of Persia.

464 Archedemides archon, 79th Olymiad, Xenophon won stadion. Athens suppresses revolts among the Thasians and Aeginetans. She sends ten thousand colonists into Amphipolis, but an advance into Thrace is repulsed.

463 Tlepolemus archon. Athens supports Egypt in her rebellion against Persia, and prepares for war.

462 Colon archon. Athens in aid of Egypt is victorious in battles with the Persian forces. Artaxerxes fails to get Sparta to attack Athens.

461-431 The Golden Age of Athens

461 Euthippus archon. Athens continues to besiege the Persian forces in Egypt.

460 Phrasicleides archon, 80th Olympiad, Toryllas won stadion. Athens and Egypt come to terms with the Persians. In Athens itself, Sophonides is put to death after inciting a revolt against the customs of the Council of the Areopagus.

459 Philocles archon. Athens defeats the Corinthians and Epidaurians. In another conflict lasting nine months, they defeated the Aeginetans.

458 Bion archon. Athens gains a further victory over the Corinthians. Nicomedes successfully leads the Spartans in aid of the Dorians in their dispute with the Phocians. Athens attacks the Spartans on their return from the battle. The battle is a stalemate.
The Spartan Nicomedes was the guardian of Pleistonax, the king, who was still a child.

CHAPTER 5: FAULTLINES IN THE GREEK EVIDENCE

457 <u>Mnesitheides archon.</u> Myronides (Athenian) defeats a Spartan-Thebian alliance and goes on to defeat the Boeotians. Further successes were gained against the Locrians, Phocians, Thessalians and Pharsalians.

456 <u>Callias archon, 81st Olympiad, Polymnastus won stadion.</u> Tolmides (Athenian) accomplishes at sea what Myronides did on land and ravaged the coast of Laconia which was under the domain of Sparta. Sparta finally overcame the Messians with whom they had long been at war [469].

455 <u>Sosistratus archon.</u> While Tolmides was involved in Boeotia, Athens elects Pericles the son of Xanthippus as their general. He ravaged a large part of the Peloponnesus and sailed on to further successes in Acarnania.

454 <u>Ariston archon.</u> Cimon (Athenian) conducts a truce with the Peloponnesians. This was supposed to last five years.

453 <u>Lysicrates archon.</u> Pericles leads Athenian forces again into the Peloponnesus. Sparta sent aid to the besieged. Pericles sails on to attack and divide a number of areas in Acarnania. Meanwhile Tolmides does the same in Euboea.

452 The year is missing in the manuscripts of Diodorus.

451 <u>Antidotus archon.</u> Athens and Sparta not mentioned.

450 <u>Euthydemus archon.</u> Athens, who had lost many ships in helping Egypt against Persia, resolves again to make war upon Persia. Cimon leads the fleet to victory over Artabazus on Cyprus and Megabazus who was over the Persian land forces in Cilicia.

449 <u>Pedieus archon.</u> Cimon (Athenian) subdues the cities of Cyprus, after which Artaxerxes concluded a treaty with the Greeks. Cimon dies after an illness.

448 <u>Philiscus archon, 83rd Olympiad, Crison won stadion.</u> Athens puts down a revolt in the territory of the Megarians.

447 <u>Timarchides archon.</u> Sparta invades Attica and withdraws after laying siege to a number of Athenian fortresses. Tolmides dies fighting in Boeotia; many Athenians are slain in the huge defeat. The cities of Boeotia regain their autonomy.

446 Callimachus archon. Pericles (Athenian) puts down a revolt in Euboea. A truce was made between Athens and Sparta which was supposed to last for thirty years. Callias and Chares were the negotiators.
Pythagoras gives political advice.

445 Lysimachides archon. Pericles (Athenian) portions out areas in Euboea.

444 Praxiteles archon, 84th Olympiad, Crison won stadion. Athens and Sparta not mentioned.

443 Lysanias archon. Athens and Sparta not mentioned.

442 Diphilus archon. Athens and Sparta with the rest of Greece are at peace.

441 Timocles archon. Pericles (Athenian) sails twice to Samos to put down revolts.

440 Myrichides archon, 85th Olympiad, Crison won stadion. Athens and Sparta not mentioned.

439 Glaucides archon. Athens and Sparta not mentioned.

438 Theodorus archon. Athens and Sparta not mentioned.

437 Euthymenes archon. Athens founds a colony at Amphipolis.

436 Lysimachus archon, 86th Olympiad, Theopompus won stadion. Athens successfully aids Cercyra in their ongoing war with the Corinthians.

435 Antiochides archon. Athens puts down a revolt at Potidaea, where the inhabitants had been incited by Corinth. Athens also founded a city in the Propontis named Astacus.

434 Crates archon. Athens is in dispute with cities of the Peloponnesus as to who founded Thurii in Italy.
Archidamus king of the Spartans dies after reign of forty-two years. Agis succeeds him and reigns twenty-five years.

433 Apseudes archon.

CHAPTER 5: FAULTLINES IN THE GREEK EVIDENCE

Meton (Athenian) presents the nineteen year cycle of adjusting lunar to solar years.

432 <u>Pythodorus archon, 87th Olympiad, Sophron won stadion.</u> Athens dispatches Pharmon in the place of Callias who had fallen in battle. Pharmon continued the ongoing siege of Potidaea.
Thucydides (Athenian) commences his history in which he recounts twenty-two of the twenty-seven years of the Peloponnesian War.

<u>431-405 The Peloponnesian War</u>

431 <u>Euthydemus archon.</u> Pericles is accused of misusing the common fund at Delos. Taking advice from his nephew Alcibiades, he sought to embroil Athens in a great war which would divert attention from this and other questions of corruption. Athens had voted to exclude the Megarians from their markets and harbors. Sparta threatened war if this action was not rescinded. Pericles persuaded Athens to reject the demand and prepare for war. With sides drawn, Archidamus led the Spartans into Attica, and Athens sent a fleet under Corcinus against the Peloponnesian coast.
These were the causes of the Peloponnesian War as recorded by Ephorus.

The war which was eventually won by Sparta, is thoroughly described by Thucydides and appears to be the one solid link in Greek chronology. It will not be necessary to summarize the many battles but only to continue to note Diodorus' yearly mention of the personalities (mainly of Athens and Sparta) and any notes of special significance.

430 <u>Apollodorus archon.</u> Plague breaks out in Athens.
Athens: Cleopompus, Pericles.
Sparta: Brasidas.

429 <u>Epimeinon archon</u>. Phormio (Athenian) leads fleet against the Peloponnesus.
Athens: Pericles dies, Hagnon, Phormio, Xenophon, Phanomachus.
Sparta: King Archidamus, Cnemus.

428 <u>Diotimus archon, 88th Olympiad, Symmachus won stadion.</u> Attica again invaded. Bleak hopes for Athens at year's end.
Sparta: Cnemus.

427 <u>Eucleides archon.</u> Athens launches a first attack upon Sicily.
Athens: Laches, Charocades, Eurymedon, Cleinippides, Paches.

Sparta: Alcidas.

426 <u>Euthynes archon.</u> Athens enjoys some respite from plague. Huge earthquake in Locris thwarts Sparta from again invading Attica.

425 <u>Stratocles archon.</u> Athens gains a notable victory over Brasidas.
Athens: Demosthenes, Cleon.
Sparta: Thrasymedes, Brasidas.
Artaxerxes, king of Persia, dies after a reign of forty years. Xerxes succeeds to the throne and ruled one year.

424 <u>Isarchus archon, 89th Olympiad, Symmachus won stadion.</u> Athens enjoys further successes, but Brasidas counters.
Athens: Nicias, Hipponicus, Hippocrates, Demosthenes.
Sparta: Brasidas.
King Xerxes dies, is succeeded by Sogdianus who ruled seven months. He is slain by Darius who reigned nineteen years. Antiochus of Syracuse concludes his history of Sicily.

423 <u>Ameinas archon.</u> Athens and Sparta agree to one year truce.
Athens: Aristeides, Symmachus, Lamachus.
Sparta: Brasidas.

422 <u>Alcacus archon.</u> War resumes.
Athens: Cleon dies. Sparta: Brasidas dies (fighting each other). A "fifty year truce" is signed between Athens and Sparta.

421 <u>Ariston archon.</u> Despite the truce, Greece remains on the verge of further conflict, with the result that tumults and military movements rumble across the land.

420 <u>Astyphilus archon, 90th Olympiad, Hyperbius won stadion.</u> Athens allows resettlement of Delians. Further splits occur in the truce.

419 <u>Archias archon.</u> War resumes.
Athens: Alcibiades, Laches, Nicostratus.
Sparta: King Agis, Pharax.

418 <u>Antiphon archon.</u> Athens takes three cities.
Athens: Nicias.

CHAPTER 5: FAULTLINES IN THE GREEK EVIDENCE

417 <u>Euphemus archon.</u> Athens aids the Argives.
Athens: Alcibiades.

416 <u>Arimnestus archon, 91st Olympiad, Exaenctus won stadion.</u> Athens proposes a second invasion of Sicily.
Athens: Alcibiades, Nicias, Lamachus.

415 <u>Chabrias archon.</u> Athens launches its attack upon Sicily.
Athens: Alcibiades (flees to the Spartan side).

414 <u>Tisandrus archon.</u> Athens continues the war in Sicily.
Athens: Lamachus slain, Nicias, Eurymedon.
Sparta: Gylippus, Alcibiades.

413 <u>Cleocritus archon.</u> Athens defeated in Sicily.
Athens: Demosthenes, Eurymedon slain, Nicia.
Sparta: Agris, Alcibiades, Gylippus.
Eclipse of moon seen in Syracuse.

412 <u>Callias archon, 92nd Olympiad, Exaenetus won stadion.</u> Athens renounces its democracy, and chooses four hundred men (the oligarchy) to lead. Alcibiades is allowed by Athens to return.

411 <u>Theopompus archon.</u> Athens dissolves the oligarchy.
Athens: Theramenes, Thrasyllus, Thrasybulus, Alcibiades.
Sparta: Mindarus, Doreius, Epicles.
Ephorus gives an account of the temple at Coroncia. Thucydides ends his history with this year. Xenophon and Theopompus begin their histories at this point. Xenophon embraced a period of forty-eight years, and Theopompus seventeen years.

410 <u>Glaucippus archon.</u> Athens gains victories in a huge naval encounter with Sparta.
Athens: Thrasybulus, Thrasyllus, Alcibiades, Conon, Theramenes, Endius, Cleophon.
Sparta: Mindarus slain, King Archelaus.

409 <u>Diocles archon.</u> Athens strengthens her forces near the Hellespont.
Athens: Thrasybulus, Theramenes, Alcibiades, Amytus, Leotrophides, Timarchus, Lampsacus.

Sparta: Hippocratus, Clearcus.
Athens loses Pylos after holding it fifteen years. The historians Ephorus and Timaeus disagree (twice) as to the size of forces in Carthage's invasion of Sicily.

408 <u>Euctemon archon, 93rd Olympiad, Eubatus won stadion.</u> Athens takes the cities near the Hellespont. Sparta again ravages Attica.
Athens: Diodorus, Mantitheus, Alcibiades goes into exile, Adeimantus, Thrasybulus, Antiochus, Conon, Erasindes, Aristocrates, Archestratus, Protomachus, Aristogenes, Diomedes.
Sparta: Lyander, King Agis.
King Pleistonax died after a reign of fifty years and was succeeded by Pausanias who reigned fourteen years.

407 <u>Atigenes archon.</u> The Spartans defeat Athens off Mitylene.
Athens: Conon.
Sparta: Callicratides, Lysander, Dexippus.

406 <u>Callias archon.</u> Athens is victorious off Mitylene, but puts many of her own generals to death.
Athens: Thrasybulus, Pericles son of Pericles, Theramenes, Aristogenes, Protomachus, Thrasyllus, Calliades, Lysias, Aristocrates, Diomedon (many of these put to death).
Sparta: Eteonicus, Callicratidas, Clearchus, Thrasondas, Araeus, Lysander.
Philistus ends his first history of Sicily. Sophocles the writer of tragedies dies at ninety. Apollodorus stated that Euripedes died this year. Timaeus comments on the help the Aeragantini received from Sparta during this year.

405 <u>Alexias archon.</u> After defeats at sea and a blockade of their city, Athens is forced to conclude a treaty, thus ending the Peloponnesian War.
Athens: Philocles executed, Conon, Alcibiades (in Thrace).
Sparta: Lysander, Etconicus, Gylippus, King Agis, Pausanian.
Darius dies after a reign of nineteen years and is succeeded by his eldest son, Artaxerxes, who reigned forty-three years. Apollodorus says that the poet Antimachus flourished at this time.

CHAPTER 5: FAULTLINES IN THE GREEK EVIDENCE

<u>404-372 Spartan Supremacy</u>

404 <u>No archon, 94th Olympiad, Corcinas won stadion.</u> Athens as part of the treaty demolishes her city walls, and under pressure from Sparta chooses thirty men to lead the government. These began to enact a reign of terror.
Athens: Theramenes slain, Critas, Niceratus, Autolycus slain, Alcibiades slain.
Sparta: Lysander, Thorax, Callibuis, Aristus.
Socrates the philosopher seeks to prevent Thoramenes' death. Ephorus gives a different account of Alcibiades' death. Democritus the philosopher died, aged ninety.

403 <u>Eucleides archon.</u> Athens not mentioned. Sparta helps the Byzantines in their war with Thrace. Lysander seeks to remove the Aeracleidae (the two lines of Spartan kings).
Sparta: Clearchus, Panthoedas.

402 <u>Micion archon.</u> Athens not mentioned. King Agis (Spartan) is prevented from offering sacrifices at the Olympic Games in Elis. Pausanias fails in his attack upon Elis.

401 <u>Exaenetus archon.</u> Athens removed the Thirty from power. Sparta aids Cyrus in his unsuccessful attempt to overthrow his brother Artaxerxes. They return with great difficulty to Greece.
Athens: Thrasybulus.
Sparta: Tamos, Cheirisophus, Samos, Clearchus slain, Cheirisophus, Lysander.
Ephorus comments on the size of Artaxerxes' army.

400 <u>Laches archon, 95th Olympiad, Minos won stadion.</u> In Athens, Socrates after accusations by Anytus and Meletus takes his life. Thibron (Spartan) leads a force to help the cities of Asia Minor. Xenophon (Spartan) is chosen to lead an attack upon the Thracians.

399 <u>Aristocrates archon.</u> Athens not mentioned. Conon (Athenian) aids Persia in its battles with Sparta. Sparta is also active against the Thracians.
Sparta: Thibron, Dercylidas.
Astydamas, the writer of tragedies, produced his first play.

398 <u>Ithycles archon.</u> Athens and Sparta not mentioned.
Ctesias ended with this year his "History of the Persians".

397 <u>Lysiades archon.</u> Athens and Sparta not mentioned.
Sophocles (Athenian) began to produce tragedies.

396 <u>Phormion archon, 96th Olympiad, Eupolis wins stadion.</u> Apart from the Athenians, Conon, Hieronymus and Nicodemus being placed in charge of the Persian fleet in their battles with Sparta, Athens is not mentioned. Sparta and Syracuse against Carthage, and Boeotia against the Phocians. An alliance was also struck with Egypt.
Sparta: Pharacidas, King Agesilaus, Pharax, Xenocles, Lysander slain, King Pausanias.
Ephorus and Timaeus disagree as to the size of Carthage's forces in Sicily.

395 <u>Diophantus archon.</u> Athens becomes part of an alliance (the Council of Corinth) to overthrow the Spartan supremacy. Sparta responds by attacking Boeotia; however it loses control of the sea after suffering reverses against the Persians under Conon in Asia Minor.
Sparta: King Agesilaus, Peisander.
Theopompus finished his Hellenic History, covering a period of seventeen years from where Thucydides ended his.

394 <u>Eubulides archon.</u> The Persians imprison Conon. Athens aids others in the Corinthian alliance against Sparta. Known as the Corinthian War, it was to last eight years.
King Pausanias of Sparta goes into exile after a reign of fourteen years, his son Agesipolis succeeded and reigned also fourteen years.

393 <u>Democratus archon.</u> The Corinthian War continues with the Athenian Iphicrates winning battles against Sparta. However, because he had designs on taking Corinth, he was replaced.

392 <u>Philocles archon, 97th Olympiad, Terires won stadion.</u> Thrasybulus (Athenian) is victorious against the Spartan Therimachus (slain) at sea.

391 <u>Nicoteles archon.</u> Athens not mentioned. Sparta increases her grip on Rhodes and pillages Argolis.
Sparta: Eudocimus, Philodocus, Diphilas, King Agesilaus.

390 <u>Demostratus archon.</u> Thrasybulus (Athenian) is slain in his coastal advance against Sparta. He is replaced by Agyrius. Thibron and large numbers of Spartans are slain fighting Artaxerxes in Asia Minor.

CHAPTER 5: FAULTLINES IN THE GREEK EVIDENCE

389 <u>Antipater archon.</u> Athens and Sparta not mentioned.

388 <u>Pyrgion archon, 98th Olympiad, Sosippus won stadion.</u> Athens and Sparta not mentioned.
The Athenian poet, Lysias, in his "Olympiacus" derides the poetry of Dionysius of Syracuse.

387 <u>Theodotus archon.</u> Athens not mentioned. Sparta hard pressed on two fronts sends Antalicides to Artaxerxes to seek peace.
Callisthenes began his history with this peace and embraced a period of thirty years to the seizure of the Temple of Delphi by Philomelus.

386 <u>Mystichides archon.</u> Sparta attacks Mantineia, Athens does not intervene, but with this, wars begin again in Greece.

385 <u>Dexitheus archon.</u> Athens not mentioned. Mantineia falls to Sparta.

384 <u>Diotrephus archon, 99th Olympiad, Dicon won stadion.</u> Athens and Sparta not mentioned.

383 <u>Phanostratus archon.</u> Athens not mentioned. Sparta continues to assert pressure on the Greek cities. Though Agesipolis counselled moderation, Agesilaus pressed for dominance.

382 <u>Euander archon.</u> Athens not mentioned. Sparta takes possession of the Cadmeia in Thebes.
Sparta: Phoebiades, Eudamides, Teleutias slain.

381 <u>Demophilus archon.</u> Athens not mentioned. King Agesipolis is sent against the Olynthians, but no major battle occurred.

380 <u>Pythias archon, 100th Olympiad, Dionysodorus won stadion.</u> Athens not mentioned. Sparta under Polybiades defeats the Olynthians. Sparta reaches her greatest power in Greece as many other cities join her side. King Agesipolis dies after reigning fourteen years, Cleombratus his brother succeeds him and reigns nine years.

379 <u>Nicon archon.</u> Athens and Sparta not mentioned.

378 <u>Nausinious archon.</u> The Spartan garrison in Cadmeia falls to Boeotia and Athens.

377 <u>Calleus archon.</u> Athens successfully urges a number of cities to secede from the Spartan sphere. War breaks out between Athens and Sparta, and between Sparta and Thebes.
Athens: Timotheus, Chabrias, Calistratus, Cedon slain.
Sparta: King Cleombrotus, Sphadriades, King Agesilaus, Phoebides, Pollis.

376 <u>Charisander archon, 101st Olympiad, Damon won stadion.</u> Athens wins a number of notable victories including a naval encounter against Sparta off Leucas. Sparta also suffered a defeat at the hands of the Thebans.
Athens: Chabrias assassinated, Timotheus.
Hermeias closed his history of Sicilian affairs.

375 <u>Hippodamus archon.</u> Artaxerxes hoped to see an end of the Greek conflict so that they might become mercenary soldiers on his side in the impending war with Egypt. All generally wanted peace except Thebes, which was becoming a dominant power.
Athens: Callistratus.
Sparta: King Cleombrotus.
Thebes: Epameinodas, Pelopidas, Georgidas.

374 <u>Socratides archon.</u> Iphicrates (Athenian) led the mercenaries on behalf of Persia in their invasion of Egypt. Confusion and anarchy rage across Greece. Against Thebes' wishes, a city in Boeotia desires to be placed under Athens' control. Athens defeats Sparta at Corcyra.
Athens: Timotheus, Ctesicles, Iphicrates.
Sparta: Aristocrates, Mnasippus slain.

373 <u>Asteius archon.</u> Athens and Sparta not mentioned. A great earthquake strikes the Peloponnesus.

372 <u>Alcisthenes archon, 102nd Olympiad, Thurii won stadion.</u> Athens not mentioned. A "flaming beam" is seen in the sky over many nights. Sparta and Thebes prepare for war.
Thebes: Epameinondas, Geogidas, Pelopidas.

CHAPTER 5: FAULTLINES IN THE GREEK EVIDENCE

371-363 Theban Supremacy

371 <u>Phrasicleides archon.</u> Athens not mentioned. Sparta is defeated by Thebes in the battle of Leactra and irretrievably loses her supremacy.
Sparta: King Cleombrotus slain, King Agesilaus.
Thebes: Epameinandas, Leandrias (Spartan exile).

370 <u>Dysnicetus archon.</u> Athens not mentioned. General chaos ensues across Greece. Jason of Pherae seeks dominance but is assassinated. A great slaughter takes place in Argos. The Arcadian confederacy does not prevent Sparta ravaging the area.
King Agesipolis dies after reigning one year, and is succeeded by his brother Cleomenes who ruled thirty-four years. In Macedonia, King Amyntas dies after a reign of twenty-four years. He left three sons, Alexander, Perdiccas and Philip. The throne passed to Alexander, who ruled one year. Daris of Samos began his history of the Greeks at this point.

369 <u>Lysistratus archon.</u> Sparta invades Arcadia but Thebes intervenes. When Thebes begins a march upon Sparta the Spartans turn to their traditional foe, Athens, for help. Other battles rage at this time.
Sparta: Polytropus slain, Ischolas slain.
Thebes: Epameinondas.
In Macedonia, Philip, one of the sons of the former king, is taken hostage to Thebes.

368 <u>Nausigenes archon, 103rd Olympiad, Pythatratus won stadion.</u> Autocles (Athenian) goes to the aid of Alexander of Pherae. Sparta gains a huge victory in Arcadia in what was known as the "Tearless Battle".
Thebes: Epameinondas.
In Macedonia, Ptolemy assassinates Alexander and reigns three years.

367 <u>Polyzelus archon.</u> Chares (Athenian) goes to the aid of the Phlisians in their war with the Argives. Epameinondas (Theban) takes a number of cities in the Peloponnese.

366 <u>Cephisodorus archon.</u> Athens loses Oropus to Thebes. The Sparta Boeotian conflict ends having lasted five years since the battle of Leuctra.
Isocrates the orator, Plato of Athens, the last of the Pythagorean philosophers, and Aristotle flourished at this time. Xenophon was at this time writing his history in extreme old age, for he mentions the death of Epameinondas a few years later.

365 Chion archon. Athens aids the Arcadians in recapturing Triphylia. In Macedon Ptolemy is assassinated by his brother-in-law Perdiccas, who ruled five years.

364 Timocratus archon, 104th Olympiad, Phocidas won stadion. Laches (Athenian) backs down from the newly formed Theban fleet. Pelopidas (Theban) helps Thessaly to a crushing victory over Alexander of Pherae. Timotheus (Athenian) takes Torane and Potidaea.
An eclipse of the sun took place during the Thessalian conflict.

363 Charieleides archon. In a battle which arose over the question of the site of the Olympic Games, Epameinondas (Theban) supported the Tegeans against the Mantineians in their desire to see the games returned to Elis. With the Spartans drawn into the conflict, Epameinondas proposed the master-stroke of marching on Sparta itself. King Agis, with the help of Athens and others, was waiting. Epameinondas was slain and with him the supremacy of Thebes.
With this event Xenophon and Anaximenes of Lampsacus brought their Greek histories to a close. And Philistus concluded his five year account of Sicilian events with this year.

362-336 BC The Rise of Philip of Macedon

362 Molon archon. Chabrias (Athenian) and Agesilaeus (Spartan) help Egypt in her war with Persia. Agesilaus dies on the way back to Sparta. Thebes sends Pammanes to the aid of Megalopolis.
Artaxerxes dies having reigned forty-three years. Ochus, who assumed the title "Artaxerxes", succeeded to the throne and reigned twenty-three years. Athanas of Syracuse writes his books of Sicilian affairs.

361 Nicophemus archon. Leosthenes (Athenian) is defeated by Alexander of Pherae. Athens puts him to death.
Two Boeotian historians, Dionysodorus and Anaxis, close their narrative of Greek history.

360 Callimedes archon, 105th Olympiad, Porus won stadion. Athens attempts to recover Amphipolis. Philip, the son of Amyntas and father of Alexander the Great, having escaped his detention in Thebes, comes to the throne of Macedonia.
Theopompus begins his history of Philip.

CHAPTER 5: FAULTLINES IN THE GREEK EVIDENCE

359 <u>Eucharistus archon.</u> Athens and Sparta not mentioned. Philip defeats the Illyrians.

358 <u>Cephisodotus archon.</u> Philip not mentioned. War in Euboea involves Athens. Athens sends Chares and Chabrias to recover Chios, Rhodes, Cos and Byzantium. Chabrias loses his life in what became known as the Social War.

357 <u>Agathocles archon.</u> Athens, Sparta and Philip not mentioned. *Demophilus son of Ephorus, Callisthenes and Diyllus wrote historical accounts of Greece in this period.*

356 <u>Elpines archon, 106th Olympiad, Malian won stadion.</u> Chares, Iphicrates and Timotheus are recalled to Athens, thus bringing the Social War to an end. Philip defeats the Thracians, Paeonians and Illyrians.

355 <u>Callistratus archon.</u> Athens and Philip not mentioned. Philomelus the Phocian seizes the shrine at Delphi in collusion with Archidamus King of Sparta. This began the "Sacred War" and lasted nine years.

354 <u>Diotimus archon.</u> Philip not mentioned. Athens and Sparta side with the Phocians in the Sacred War. In the ensuing battles, the Boeotians defeated the Phocians, and Philomelus fearing capture hurls himself off a cliff.

353 <u>Thudemus archon.</u> Thebes defeats the Phocians. Chares who had aided the rebel Persian Artabazus is recalled to Athens and then sent to the Hellespont where he takes Sestus. Sparta takes Orneae. Philip is victorious at Methone (but loses an eye) and also eventually wins a battle against the Phocians.

352 <u>Aristodemus archon, 107th Olympiad, Micrinas won stadion.</u> Philip not mentioned. The Phocians regroup and with the help of Athens and Sparta embark upon further battles. Sparta led by King Archidamus experiences victory and defeat in encounters with Thebes and the inhabitants of Megalopolis.

351 <u>Theellus archon.</u> Persia sends financial aid to Thebes in their war with the Phocians. Athens and Sparta though friendly with Artaxerxes did not send him help for his invasion of Egypt.

350 <u>Apollodorus archon.</u> Athens, Sparta and Philip not mentioned.

349 Callimachus archon. Athens and Sparta not mentioned. Philip marches against the cities of Chalcidice, and against Pherae.

348 Theophilus archon, 108th Olympiad, Polycles won stadion. Philip subdues cities on the Hellespont. The orator Demosthenes urges Athens to make all-out war on Philip.

347 Themistocles archon. Athens, Sparta and Philip not mentioned.

346 Archias archon. Athens not mentioned. Despite the support of King Archidamus (Spartan) on the Phocian side, the Phocians surrender to Philip, thus ending the Sacred War. After this Archidamas died having reigned twenty-three years. His son Agis succeeded and ruled fifteen years [but see year 338].

345 Eubulus archon. Athens, Sparta and Philip not mentioned.

344 Lyciscus archon, 109th Olympiad, Aristolochus won stadion. Philip wins further victories over Illyria, Thessaly and the neighboring Greeks.

343 Pythodotus archon. Athens and Sparta not mentioned. Philip moves into Thrace and defeats their king.
Theopompus in his History of Philip included three chapters dealing with affairs in Sicily over a period of fifty years.

342 Sosigenes archon. Athens, Sparta and Philip not mentioned.

341 Nicomachus archon. Phocion (Athenian) expels Cleitarchus, the tyrant of Eretria, who had been installed by Philip. Philip attacks Perinthus, and when the Byzantines send aid to the besieged, Philip places a siege around Byzantium.
Ephorus of Cyme closed his history at this point having covered nearly 750 years. Diyllus the Athenian began the second section of his history with the close of Ephorus.

340 Theophrastus archon, 110th Olympiad, Anticles won stadion. Chares (Athenian) forces Philip to lift his siege of Byzantium.

339 Lysimachides archon. Athens, Sparta and Philip not mentioned.

CHAPTER 5: FAULTLINES IN THE GREEK EVIDENCE

338 <u>Charondes archon.</u> Philip, having won much of Greece to his side, turns his attention towards Athens. Demosthenes directs the Athenians to enter an alliance with Boeotia and sends Chares and Lysicles to await Philip's arrival. With Alexander, Philip's son, at the head of one of the wings, the Macedonians won a crushing victory. Afterwards Philip entered a pact of friendship with his vanquished foes.
King Archidamus died fighting in Italy, his son Agis followed him in a rule which lasted nine years [see year 346].

337 <u>Phrynichus archon.</u> At Corinth, Philip is made plenipotentiary of all Greece. Preparations are made for war upon Persia.

336 <u>Pythodorus archon, 111th Olympiad, Cleomantis won stadion.</u> Philip begins the war on Persia by sending an advance party to liberate Greek cities in Asia Minor. But, before he himself can set out, Philip is assassinated by one of his body-guards, thus ending a rule of twenty-four years.

<u>335-330 BC, Alexander Defeats Persia</u>

335 <u>Euaenetus archon.</u> Alexander succeeds to the throne, punishes his father's murderers, and removes any rivals. Athens (with the involvement of Demosthenes) is forced into further submission. Darius after the brief reign of Arses is made king in Persia. Preparations are made for the looming war.

334 <u>Ctesicles archon.</u> Alexander crosses the Hellespont and defeats the Persians at the river Granicus. He gains a second victory over the regrouped Persian forces in the Halicarnassus.

333 <u>Nicocratus archon.</u> Alexander gains a third victory at Issus in Syria. Darius flees to Babylon where he seeks to gather an even larger force to thwart the invader.

332 <u>Niceratus archon, 112th Olympiad, Grylus won stadion.</u> Leaving Syria, Alexander marches towards Egypt and takes Tyre with its island fortress. In Greece, the Spartan king Agis was openly aiding the Persian side.

331 <u>Aristophanes archon.</u> Alexander marches into Egypt and gains its submission without a battle. After giving instructions for the building of a new city to be named Alexandria, he leads his army back to Persia. After crossing the Tigris the two armies meet near Arbella, with again a crushing victory going to Alexander.

> **330** <u>Aristophon archon.</u> In Greece revolts against Alexander were put down in Thrace, and also in the Peloponnesus where King Agis lost his life. Alexander next brought his army to Babylon and was received gladly. Crossing the Tigris he came to Persepolis where his soldiers plundered and burnt the city as an act of vengeance for what Xerxes had done to the Acropolis at Athens. Before Alexander could engage Darius, news came that he had been assassinated in Bactria.

This, then, from our earliest connected source, is the essence of Greek history centered upon Athens. There seems to be no reason to question the basic validity of Diodorus' presentation. These events did indeed happen. There are, however, grounds for questioning their *timing*, and it is here that the faultlines appear.

Two immediate observations need to be made:

1. As the archon which Diodorus mentions at the beginning of each year is never clearly seen to be active in the events of the time - indeed it is doubtful if he is ever mentioned outside of the heading - there is no way of being certain that Diodorus placed these events in the correct annual "slot".

2. Despite Diodorus' emphasis on Athens and the apparent abundance of his sources, nearly one-third of the above years make no mention of Athens at all. Many other years mention only one or two Athenian events of apparently short duration.

It is here that the faultlines begin to appear. But before pursuing the matter further, we need to look at the persons and structures which did much to shape the chronology that Diodorus and Ptolemy followed.

2. KEY ARCHITECTS OF GREEK CHRONOLOGY

In Diodorus we see our first full and formal presentation of the chronology Ptolemy was later to follow. However to determine how it came about we need to look especially at the work of three men - Ephorus, Eratosthenes and Apollodorus. Others played a role, but these are the three key names that we need to look at.

CHAPTER 5: FAULTLINES IN THE GREEK EVIDENCE

(1) Ephorus

As noted above, Ephorus, who seems to have lived unto the time of Alexander[14], is acknowledged to be Diodorus' primary source.

Of him Diodorus writes:

> Ephorus ... in the universal history which he composed has achieved success, not alone in the style of his composition, but also as regards the arrangement of his work: for one of his Books is so constructed as to embrace events which fell under a single topic. Consequently we also have given our preference to this method... (V.1.4).

From this and other considerations it is gathered that Ephorus would write on a given topic down to a certain point and then take up another subject. He did not generally use an annalistic format.[15] Three hundred years later, Diodorus drew upon this material and divided it into a year-by-year sequence which we now have.

Further, when Ephorus' timeframe (see Diodorus XVI.76.5) is compared with the Spartan king lists it has been concluded that he used a generational chronology for much of his *Universal History*. That is, he would date persons and events according to a generation lasting probably thirty-five years [16].

This is of course an "educated guess approach"!

As Donald Prakken says:

> Obviously a chronology based on generations would be better suited to mythical history than to contemporary events. As Ephorus proceeded to write a history of the fifth and fourth centuries, he would have had less and less recourse to such an unsatisfactory method; and since some of the later books covered a period of ten years or less, such a system would not have been of much value here.[17]

Notice that Prakken does not say that Ephorus' use of generational chronology *ceased* with the 5th and 4th centuries BC, but rather that it became *less and less*. This would indicate that in writing his history from Xerxes down to his own time (not long before the rise of Alexander), Ephorus had to rely at least in part upon the same artificial system that he had used extensively before Xerxes.

With this in mind, we come now to the primary formulator of the kind of chronology Diodorus and Ptolemy used.

(2) Eratosthenes

Here we have the most influential name in early chronology.

Prakken again remarks:

> Ephorus' *Histories* undoubtedly added to the general interest in historical chronology, and interest which was soon to give rise to the studies of Eratosthenes and Apollodorus in this field.[18]

Eratosthenes of Cyrene (c.275-194 BC), after spending time at Athens, and under the influence of Arcesilaus and Ariston, was summoned to Alexandria by Ptolemy III. There he was to become tutor to the royal family, and succeed Apollonius Rhodius as head of the famous Alexandrian Library. He wrote extensively in the fields of literature, mathematics, geography and chronology, and was considered the most versatile scholar of his time.[19] His *Chronographiai,* or *Chronological Tables* we know only in outline, and these from fragments, and the writings of early historians. [20]

P.M.Fraser explains that Eratosthenes had a definite reason for writing on the subject.

> Eratosthenes set out to replace the multifarious local systems of chronology by a universal chronology of Greek history embracing the period from the sack of Troy to the death of Alexander the Great. [21]

This is a most important statement, as it reveals the low view that the scholarly elite of that day had of the chronology before Alexander. Writing perhaps one hundred years after Alexander's death Eratosthenes showed the same disdain as the later Talmudic rabbis who reached back to the pre-Alexander days to alter their own national chronology in the Sedar Olam.

Concerning the *multifarious local systems* to which Fraser refers, one especially is noted.

> [W]e need only compare his system with the slightly earlier, rather amateurish scheme, or lack of scheme, represented in the Persian Marble ... in which all dates are calculated by intervals from the date of compilation, 264/3, reckoned by Athenian kings [i.e. in the very early period] and archons, without reference to any general scheme of chronology such as Olympiads. [22]

As Fraser notes, Eratosthenes relied upon the Olympiads for his chronology. Indeed, Rudolf Pfeiffer stresses -

CHAPTER 5: FAULTLINES IN THE GREEK EVIDENCE

> The most reliable authentic documents on which Eratosthenes could base the dates of historical events were the lists of the winners in the Olympic games. [23]

According to the historian Polybius (c.200-118 BC; XII.II.1), it was the Sicilian historian Timaeus (c.356-260 BC) who first used the list of Olympic victors as a tool for his historical chronology. [24] This Eratosthenes followed and developed into a "chronological ladder" upon which Graecian and other events were placed. It became a standard of historical reckoning, and along with the yearly archons, the quadrennial Olympiads were adopted by Diodorus.

But as Aldnen Mosshammer explains, all was by no means plain sailing for his "new standard".

> [T]he Olympic era provided a convenient numerical scale for chronological references. The influence of this innovation was enormous. Still, the mass of synchronisms, intervals, hypotheses of doxological succession, and other data with chronological implications that had been produced by the literature of the preceding two centuries could neither be entirely accommodated to the Eratosthenic system nor completely supplanted by it. The earlier authors continued to exert an influence of their own, and they are frequently cited in chronological contexts by authors like Pausanias, Strabo, Plutarch, Diogenes, Laertius, and Clement of Alexandria. [25]

And then there is the fundamental question as to whether on this "chronological ladder" the events have been placed on the correct "rungs".

Alan Samuel acknowledges a vulnerability here:

> By Hellenic times the list of victors was complete and reasonably consistent and the framework for chronology was established and accepted. Whether all this was right, or whether events were assigned to years correctly, is another matter. [26]

The "Hellenic times" when these things were "established and accepted" can only refer to the time of and shortly before Eratosthenes. And while Samuel goes on to say that we should be "very dubious" about using Olympiad dating before 450 BC, [27] the confusion out of which Eratosthenes' system arose shows that we should also have some doubts about the period after 450 BC.

According to Anstey, the result of Eratosthenes' landmark work was a chronology that "greatly exaggerated the antiquity of the events of Greek history." [28]

There is an irony connected with this *Founder of Critical Chronology,* [29] in that his work largely disappeared from view. [30] We see the effect and the influence - for it is without doubt the essence of Diodorus and Ptolemy - but very little of the work itself. In fact Diodorus does not even mention Eratosthenes. Instead he seems to have received Eratosthenes' work second-hand through Apollodorus - and, as we will see shortly, with a considerable twist!

Of this transfer from Eratosthenes to Apollodorus, Mosshammer writes:

> As is well known, he adopted the Chronographic system of Eratosthenes, a systematic redaction of the most fundamental annalistic standards - the Spartan king lists, the Athenian archon list, and the list of Olympic victors now converted into a numbered system ... [31]

But as we leave Eratosthenes, it cannot be put too strongly that he would not have been so widely acclaimed as the *father* of chronology, were it not that both fundamental and influential changes took place through him. This, we think, moved toward an expansion of Greek history.

The following example illustrates this.

> Eratosthenes (FGrHist 241 F 11) identified the philosopher Pythagoras with the Olympic victor of 588, but Aristoxenus ... [born c.370 BC] synchronized Pythagoras with Polycrates 530. [32]

A difference of nearly sixty years!

(3) Apollodorus

While Eratosthenes may have been the "father", it was the *Chronicle* which Apollodorus (born c.180 BC) dedicated to Attalus II of Pergamum that became the "vulgate" of Greek chronology.[33] Trained at Alexandria, Apollodorus was to spend most of the latter part of his life in Athens. His *Chronicle* was written in metrical verse (!) and dealt in considerable detail with the important events of Greek history from the fall of Troy (1184 BC) down to 144 BC *(FGrH ii B.244)*.

Diodorus states his dependence on this work:

> As for the periods included in this work ... we follow Apollodorus of Athens (I.5.1).

The chronology that Diodorus received from Apollodorus had undergone a still further revision from that which Eratosthenes left. Apollodorus, as all acknowledge, "followed the lines laid down by Eratosthenes," [34] but he added a novelty which could only lead itself toward a further expansion of Greek history.

CHAPTER 5: FAULTLINES IN THE GREEK EVIDENCE

We have already seen that Ephorus, in the periods before Xerxes, based his chronology on generations of about thirty-five years. This approach after Xerxes did not cease, but as Prakken says, only became "less and less." [35]

The same seems generally to apply to the device introduced by Apollodorus.

In a theory borrowed from Pythagoras, Apollodorus' system was based on a man reaching his "acme" (bloom) of intellectual maturity at the age of forty, and a theoretically perfect life at eighty (!!).

Alden Mosshammer explains:

> This Pythagorean teaching provided the model for Apollodorus' chronological constructions using the interval of 40 years ... He accordingly considered a person whose dates were not otherwise known to have been forty years old at the time of some appropriate event ... Thales, for example, was assigned the theoretical age of 40 at the time of the great solar eclipse he had supposedly *predicted (FGrHist 244 F 28)*, while Thucydides reached his acme at the beginning of the great war that he both witnessed and recorded for all posterity *(FGrHist 244 F 7)*. Apollodorus dated the events by tying the chronological implications of the material to his general structure of annalistic chronology. Then he computed a birthdate for the person the 40th year earlier. If the date of death was known, Apollodorus computed the total life span directly. If the date was not known, Apollodorus either assigned the person a theoretically perfect life of eighty years or, more frequently, he used synchronisms to establish what he considered an appropriate date ...
>
> Apollodorus applied the doctrine even when he was able to establish actual dates of birth and death by actual dates ... The date of one's acme was important, quite apart from its significance for the person at issue. It also served as a starting point for further chronological computations.
>
> A second fundamental principle ... was the establishment of a 40-years interval between the acme of master and pupil or between the acmes of successive sets of practitioners in the same field. [36]

Those who feel that their Greek chronology is on a firm footing need to consider carefully the implications of the foregoing. The chronological footings, despite the imposing superstructure of Greek history, are anything but secure.

Nor does further explanation become any more assuring.

> The acme method and its corollary were used in conjunction with the kinds of synchronistic treatment typical of Greek chronography and in combination with certain epochal dates considered appropriate starting points for computation ... Some of these

epochal dates were part of the chronographic system inherited from Eratosthenes. In addition, Apollodorus established new chronographic epochs in the context of his own computations. [37]

Thus the epochs upon which Apollodorus pinned these forty year periods came from others, from Eratosthenes, and from *himself*.

Mosshammer details yet another example of this shifting, uncertain foundation.

> The interval of 40 years is well attested for Apollodorus, and well documented in Jacoby's study. Problems arise when we ask if that was the only interval that Apollodorus used. If so, distortions in the chronology may be suspected, since intervals of 40 years were sometimes too long ... There is, however, evidence to suggest that Apollodorus used theoretical ages of 25 and 64 as well as 40. This larger set of intervals permitted more flexibility in the method, accomodating a variety of traditional relationships. [38]

And seeing where such procedures must inevitably lead, Mosshammer cautions -

> We must not press too hard and try to show that a theory of proportionals underlies the entire Apollodoran system, much less the entire chronolographic tradition ... Nevertheless, it is important to recognize that Apollodorus' model was rooted in a philosophical model, not a strictly historiographic practice. The acme at age 40 was a philosophical ideal. [39]

Therefore, if not "entire", this system based so much on subjectivity, certainly did play a major role. Nor is this a scheme that is relegated only to the earlier periods of Greek history, for Mosshammer gives as many examples of it being applied after Xerxes as before.

Apollodorus' work was the *vulgate* and virtual *final word* of the kind of chronology Diodorus and Ptolemy were to preserve for posterity. He probably died about sixty years before Diodorus began his *Library of History*. And in this work, as we have seen, Diodorus acknowledged that he "followed Apollodorus of Athens" (I.5.1).

Our inquiry into these three shapers of Greek chronology - Ephorus, Eratosthenes and Apollodorus - has shown how shifting and tenuous the chronology was that Diodorus and Ptolemy "set in stone".

We now come to three structures that were used to give "backbone" to this fluid state of Greek chronology.

CHAPTER 5: FAULTLINES IN THE GREEK EVIDENCE

3. THE PRIMARY TIMESCALES

Greek history in its most prominent aspect - Athens - is not based upon the reigns of kings, but rather on events. This raises the question as to whether they have been correctly timed or have perhaps drifted with reference to each other. Early chronologists have sought to address this problem by linking the events of Athenian history to several different timescales, the main ones being the Spartan king lists, the Olympiads, and the list of Athenian archons. But given that these linkages were formulated a considerable time after the events took place, the question must be asked whether the events were placed at the correct points on these timescales.

The first and least significant of the three are -

(1) The Spartan King Lists

There were two kingly lines at Sparta: the Agiads and the Eurypontids. The origin for this perhaps lay in the union of two tribes to form the one large city-state. In the period we are looking at, the powers of these kings were curtailed, with each acting as a check upon the other in governing matters. Agis (930-900 BC) and Eurypon (890-860 BC) are traditionally said to head the two lines. [40]

According to Plutarch (c.50-120 AD) in *Lycurgus* (I.3), and Diodorus (I.5.1), the succession of Spartan kings played an important role in the chronologies of Eratosthenes and Apollodorus.[41] But this only after the lists had undergone a "chronographic construction based on a genealogical count." [42]

From Diodorus' annalistic account, the following shows the years that Spartan kings are supposed to have reigned, and the years in which they are active in some event. * signifies an unusually long reign.

    The Agiads

(Pleistarchus)		Diodorus does not mention.
* Pleistoanax	458-408	No events.
Pausanias	408-394	405 (with Agis), 401,396,exile...
Agesipolis I	394-380	383(with Agesilaus),381
Cleombrotus I	380-371	377
Agesipolis II	371-370	No events.

205

BIBLE CHRONOLOGY: THE TWO GREAT DIVIDES

    Cleomenes II   370-336   No events.

The Eurypontids

Leotychides II	498-476	479
* Archidamus II	476-434	469 (active in 429, after death!)
Agis II	434-409	Reigns 25 years, but active after (!), 419,08,05(with Pausanias),02
Agesilaus II?	-362	Length of reign not given. 396,95,91,83 (with Agesipolis),77,70,63(with Agis,62.).
Archidamus III	362-338	355,52(death also mentioned in 346).
Agis III	338-330	332

Notwithstanding the length of years Diodorus gives to these kings, very little is said about any activity they were involved in. From the defeat of Xerxes (480 BC), for the next seventy-five years no activity is ascribed to the Agiad line and very little to the Eurypontid. For the entire period, 480-330 BC, the Agiads have only six years in which a king is mentioned, while the Eurypontids have seventeen. But of this latter, nearly half belong to Agesilaus.

Furthermore, the regnal year in which an activity is supposed to have occurred is not stated. Thus the reigns are not chronologically tied to events.

Notice that the "quiet" first and last sections, and the relatively busy middle sections of the two lists parallel each other. And note too, the repetition of names in the Eurypontid line.

The Spartan king lists lack substance. There is a contrived look. Clearly they cannot provide a credible "backbone" for Greek history.

Mention should also be made, that like Athens with her archons, Sparta had yearly magistrates called ephors, who gave their names to the year. Polybias (c.200-after 118 BC) alludes to Timaeus (c.356-260 BC), the historian of Sicily, making a comparison of Spartan ephors and kings, Athenian archons, and Olympic victors, for chronological purposes (XII.II.1).[43] However, ephor-reckoning is not used in Diodorus, and its effect upon chronology does not appear to be significant. [44]

The second major timescale, and one of which we have already spoken, is –

CHAPTER 5: FAULTLINES IN THE GREEK EVIDENCE

(2) The Olympiads

According to Plutarch (died after 120 AD, *Numa* I.4), Hippias of Elis (died c.415 BC) drew up the first list of Olympic victors. Later, two writers of Sicilian history, Philistus (died c.356 BC) and Timaeus (died c.260 BC) are said to be the first to use such a list for chronological purposes. It was not, however, until Eratosthenes (died c.194 BC) that we find a full integration of Greek history with the Olympiad list.

Mosshammer, in his survey of the sources, expresses doubt that Olympiad-reckoning began as early as Philistus.

> The earliest evidence for the existence of a numbered system of Olympiads appears in a fragment of Philistus (*FGrHist 556 F 2*) ... Since the fragment derives from a late author (Stephanus of Byzantium ca. 500 AD) to whom the system of numbered Olympiads was a commonplace, and because the numeral in the fragment is in fact a conjectural emendation, we cannot be sure that the attribution of numbered Olympiads to an authority as early as Philistus is correct. According to Polybius (XII.II.1), it was the early third-century Sicilian historian Timaeus who first used the list of Olympic victors as a synchronistic tool for historical chronology (*FGrHist 566 T 10*) ... By the end of the third century, the Alexandrian scholar Eratosthenes *(FGrHist 241)* had made Olympiad reckoning the basis of a consistent chronological system that was subsequently widely developed. [45]

The fact that the Marmor Parium (264 BC) does not mention the Olympiads is an indication that this means of reckoning was not in significant use before Eratosthenes. [46]

Thus we do not have here a chronicler, in for example the year 400 BC, placing contemporary events upon this Olympic timescale. But for the most part it comes much later with Eratosthenes and Apollodorus (died after 144 BC) timing and ascribing these events.

Given the confusion that existed before them, given their dependence on hand-written and perishing sources, and given the difficulty in accessing records across a considerable geographic area, we should not underestimate the daunting task this was, and how vulnerable it was to serious and even fundamental error.

This same applies to the third timescale.

(3) The Archons of Athens

A main problem with using the list of Olympic victors to help determine chronology is, of course, that this is a list of *athletes* rather than public figures. They are not mentioned by Diodorus as taking part in the yearly events of Greece. [47] There is therefore no proven link between the Olympic list and the years they are supposed to represent.

The case is virtually the same with the list of Athenian archons (magistrates). These served for one year, and as they gave their name to the year, they are known as the *archons eponymous.*

Diodorus uses the archon list to designate the years from 480 BC (the crossing of Xerxes into Europe) to 302 BC. His is our fullest extant list, but others used this kind of dating before him. The Marmor Parium (264 BC) used it, as did also Demetrius of Phalerum, who became librarian at Alexandria in 297 BC (Plutarch, *Aristides* I.2; V.9).

The list as presented by Diodorus is thought to be reasonably sound.

> The extant list of Diodorus, Books 11-20, along with supplements and confirmations from the Marmor Parium and the anonymous Olympiad Chronicle, *P.Oxy.12*, produce a full list of archons from 480/79 to 302/1. That these three sources, along with others, are in agreement, demonstrates that the list from the fifth century on was well known as a single tradition. [48]

Nevertheless it is from Diodorus that we have this "full list". And in much of it he stands alone! This is especially the case for the years 480-353 BC, where Samuel lists collateral support for only twenty-eight years. [49] Further, before and after 480-302 the list is marked by much greater uncertainty. [50] This perhaps explains why Diodorus did not use archon dating in these periods.

Neither do the three great historians of the era - Herodotus, Thucydides and Xenophon - rely on archon dating.

Regarding Herodotus and Thucydides, Samuel writes:

> Herodotus dates by an archon only once, to assign the battle of Salamis to the archonship of Kalliades (VIII.51.1), and with Herodotus' obvious and continuous concern for detailed chronology we might expect him to date by archons more frequently were there a convenient list to refer to. And although Thucydides' strictures against archon reckoning in V.20 were directed more against the lack of precision in that form of chronology, it is noteworthy that in II.2, in marking the outbreak of hostilities, he did not seem to be confident of either the general cognizance or the future memory of the Attic archon, and so added other time notes. [51]

CHAPTER 5: FAULTLINES IN THE GREEK EVIDENCE

Coming to Xenophon's *A History of My Times*, we read for example in I.2.1 -

> The following years was that of the ninety-third Olympiad ... Euarchippus was ephor at Sparta and Euctemon archon of Athens.

Samuel, however, in giving evidence for Diodorus' list, does not cite any of the notices in Xenophon. The editor of *A History of My Times* gives the likely reason:

> Such chronological notices (cf.I.3.1, 6.1; II.1.10, 3.1 and 9f.) were almost certainly inserted in the text of Xenophon by a later hand. [52]

Therefore given that the archon list has been set forth as the primary means of determining Greek chronology, it is strange that these three historians seem to have made so little use of it. It is also strange, and this brings us back to the basic weakness of the system, that the archons themselves are not seen to be active in or near the years they represent. Realizing, that in order to be appointed, an archon had to be a person with considerable property holdings, income and influence, and given that the office brought great prestige, we would expect to see them active during at least some of these years. But the general consensus for the period under review is that -

> No influential politician held the office ... [53]

Comparing the archon list with the 189 individuals (my count) Diodorus mentions for 480-330 BC, some possibilities, however, should be considered from among Athenians of the same name.

> 1. Xanthippus is archon in 479 BC. Xanthippus, the son of Ariphron, is put in command of the Athenian fleet (479) in the place of Themistocles, and is thus engaged throughout the year.

> 2. Chares is archon in 472 BC. Callias and Chares (of Sparta?) arrange a treaty between Athens and Sparta in 446. Chares the Athenian admiral, 367-338.

> 3. Conon is archon in 462 BC. Conon the Athenian admiral, 410-394.

> 4. Callias is archon in 456 BC. Callias of Athens the negotiator 446, also 449-432.

> 5. Chabrias is archon in 415 BC. Chabrias the Athenian general 393-358.

6. Phormion is archon in 396 BC. Phormion the Athenian admiral, 432-429, (probably died in 428 [54]).

Therefore only six of the 189 men mentioned by Diodorus could even remotely be considered as a possible archon. But as the biographical accounts for each in *The Oxford Classical Dictionary* do not entertain this possibility, the conclusion must remain that "no influential politician held the office".

However, two names, Themistocles (493) and Aristeides (489), appear in the earlier and less certain part of the archon list. Except for some reservations about Aristeides, both are thought to be the personalities well-known to history after 480 BC.

According to Samuel [55] the only source indicating that a Themistocles was an archon is this following quotation from the early historian of Rome, Dionysius of Halicarnassus (died c.6 BC).

> After this ... when Themistocles was archon at Athens ... and the year before the seventy-second Olympiad (VI.34.1)...[56]

This very likely is the kind of "formula" - chronological note - Diodorus would have received from Eratosthenes and Apollodorus! Plutarch, however, in his biography on Themistocles, not only fails to mention him being an archon, but states that his "family was too obscure to further his reputation" (*Themistocles* I.1), and that "he was still a young man at Marathon (490 BC; III.3.4). And Herodotus says that at the time of Salamis (480 BC), Themistocles "had lately made his way into the first rank of citizens" (VII.143). These factors weigh heavily against him being identified with the archon of 493 BC.

Regarding Aristeides, the Marmor Parium is the only source for an archon with this name (489 BC). Diodorus says that Aristeides led the Athenian navy to victory at Plataea in 479 BC, but lost out to Themistocles in a bid to enlarge the harbor in Athens (477 BC). Aristeides is also seen leading Athens' forces in 423 BC (!).

Aristotle (died 322 BC), in commenting on the new law of ostracism, said that it was enacted two years after Marathon (490 BC) in 488 BC. This would make it one year after the archonship of Aristeides.

> [A]fterwards came their victory in the battle of Marathon; and in the archonship of Phaenippus, two years after the victory ... they put in force for the first time the law about ostracism (*Athenian Constitution* XXII.3).

CHAPTER 5: FAULTLINES IN THE GREEK EVIDENCE

After mentioning some examples of Athenians being ostracized over the next several years, Aristotle goes on to say -

> And it was during this period that Aristeides son of Lysimachus was ostracized. Three years later in the archonship of Hypechides they allowed all the persons ostracized to return because of the expedition of Xerxes (XXII.7,8).

Aristotle mentions four of the archons who served during these ten years. He also describes a major change in the way an archon was appointed. And as the office of archon along with the new law of ostracism are the main points of his discussion here, it is odd that he omits any mention of the archonship of Aristeides, or that the Aristeides that was ostracized had not long before been an archon.

But the confusion about Aristeides being an archon is best illustrated in the following statement from Plutarch.

> Aristeides at once received the office of Archon *Eponymous*. And yet Demetrius of Phalerum says that it was a little while before his death, and after the battle of Plataea, that the man held this office. But in the official records, after Xanthippides, in whose year of office Mardonius was defeated at Plataea, you cannot find, long as the list is, so much as the name Aristides; whereas immediately after Phaenippus, in whose year of office the victory at Marathon was won, an Aristides is recorded as archon (*Aristides,* V.7).

The Athenian archon list is the key touchstone in Greek chronology. It, beyond any of the other chronological tools, is claimed to be the timescale upon which the events of Greek history can be placed. But as it cannot clearly be demonstrated that even a few of the 150 archons are active in the years near to the ones they are supposed to represent, it must be suspected that it is a *sliding* scale upon which events have been placed by subjective judgements.

An early example of this practice appears to be -

(4) The Marmor Parium

Martin Anstey in his *Romance of Bible Chronology* generated a great deal of interest in this marble stele. He pointed out that it mentioned only two Persian kings between Xerxes and Alexander, and, with some other considerations, he concluded that it gave some support to the shorter chronology. [57] The evidence as we will see is contradictory.

The Parian Chronicle, or as it is more generally called, *the Marmor Parium (MP),* was brought to London in 1627 and placed in the gardens of Arundel House in the Strand. It, along with a number of other items, had been purchased by William Petty in Asia Minor (probably Smyrna). Originally, tough, it had come from the Aegean island of Paros.

The chronicle is written on coarse marble, five inches thick. At the time of its initial inspection in London, it was said to be 2'7" wide, and with part of the lower right hand corner broken off, 3'7" on the left side and 2'11" on the right side. It contained ninety-three lines. After considerable work, its Greek text with a Latin translation was published by John Selden in 1628. [58]

During the English Civil War the marble was broken, resulting in the loss of lines 1-45. For this we must rely on Selden's "not always accurate" transcript.[59] In 1667, this remaining part was presented to Oxford University, and is now on display in the Ashmolean Museum in that city. I viewed the marble in 1997, and certainly to my untrained eye, little if any of the text was discernible. A second part of the Marmor Parium, containing lines 101-132, was found in 1897 on Paros and is now in a museum there.[60]

The standard Greek text is that of F. Jacoby (*FGrHist* 239), and a new Greek transcription is at present being undertaken by A. Athanassakis of the University of California, Santa Barbara. [61] The 1789 volume by John Hewlett contains an English translation of lines 1-79. [62] Beyond this I have only seen excerpts in English.

The chronicle lists events of Greek history from the mythical period down to the writer's own time: the archonship of Diognetus in 264 BC. For each event he gives the number of years calculated back to this point. Beginning with the archonship of Creon, which he says was 420 years before the time of the inscription (264+420=684 BC), he links events to the archons.

MP A breaks off about twenty years before Alexander's advance against Persia. From Xerxes' defeat down to this break off, twenty-eight years of selected events are chronicled. *MP B* starts with year 336 BC and breaks off at 299 BC. From 313 to 299 BC, each year is chronicled.

For the period from Xerxes to Alexander, it is clear that the chronicler gives the same number of years as that which would later be ascribed by Diodorus and Ptolemy. From the archonship of Diognetus in 264 BC he says there were 227 years back to Darius' defeat at Marathon (264+227=491 BC). And, for Xerxes' defeat at Thermopylae, he gives 217 years (264+217=481 BC).

CHAPTER 5: FAULTLINES IN THE GREEK EVIDENCE

However, the chronicler's selection of events for this period is odd to say the least. Others have called it "capricious".[63] For the twenty-eight years chronicled in *MP A* from 481 to the break off in 354 BC, [64] the following entries demonstrate this strange choice of events:

1. Fully twelve of the years deal solely [65] with actors, poets and philosophers. More frequently it is their successes rather than births or deaths that are mentioned.

2. Eight of the years deal solely with the accessions or deaths of rulers in Syracuse or Macedonia. No events in either place are mentioned.

3. Only eight of the years are taken up with events of history:

    481 Xerxes' victory at Thermopylae.
    480 Xerxes' defeat at Plataea.
    406 Cyrus rebels against his brother, Artaxerxes.
    400 Return of Greeks who aided Cyrus.
    373 Thebes defeats Sparta at Leuctra.
    371 Megalopolis is built.
    358 The Phocians plunder the temple at Delphi.
    357 Artaxerxes dies and is succeeded by Ochus.

The *Marmor Parium A* lists historical events *in only six years* after Xerxes to 358 BC! No mention is made of the *major* event of these years, the Peloponnesian War. And what is especially strange, apart from the listing of the archons, not a single historical event in Athens is mentioned. There is not here even the beginnings of a historical summary!

The fact that the chronicler is as interested in Syracuse as he is in Athens, makes it a reasonable probability that his time-reckoning from Xerxes to Alexander was based upon the chronology of Timaeus of Sicily. Timaeus' influential *History*, primarily of Sicily, was finished not long before the Marmor Parium. And as we have seen, chronologically, Timaeus was a leading influence in the work of Eratosthenes (c.275-194 BC).

The *MP* chronicler went to a great deal of trouble to inscribe so little of historical substance for these long years. But given that this is the *oldest* [66] continuous chronological record that we have of Greek history (everything else is "copies of copies"), here we seem to have an example, that in the setting of these years they appear to have had more than a little trouble filling the gaps.

Despite its impressive appearances, the fore-going has shown the extent to which Greek chronology is characterized by uncertainty and vagueness. It has long held the mantle of "orthodox", but the materials and methods used by its founders - Eratosthenes and Apollodorus - demonstrate a fundamental instability.

We close by examining -

4. THREE NOTABLE FAULTLINES

The Biblical evidence points to the standard chronology being too long for the period from Xerxes to Alexander. If this is true, then the secular evidence should show clear signs of disruption and dislocation. That it does, is seen in the following:

(1) Men who were Too Long in the "Limelight"

A head of state, military leader, renowned writer, or other notable figure will seldom be shown by history to have *flourished* in the public eye for much more than forty years. This period of *recognized* activity and productivity is called a "floreat".

The material in Diodorus indicates that the following had unusually long floreats. If the name, place, and activity are the same, these examples should not be too quickly dismissed as referring to two persons.

The following demonstration would perhaps have been easier were it not that Greek history for this period was one of nearly constant warfare. Many of the famous were eventually slain. But some lived through it all. And the following, apparently, for a very long time!

> Aristeides of Athens [67]
>
> 479   Leads the Athenians to victory at Plataea.
> 477   Loses out to Themistocles in a bid to build the harbor at Athens.
> 423   With Symmachus leads the Athenians in retaking Antandrus.
>
> Artabazus of Persia
>
> 479   Takes over command of the retreating Persian forces from the slain Mardonius.
> 477   Acts as a go-between in a secret pact between Pausanias and Xerxes.

CHAPTER 5: FAULTLINES IN THE GREEK EVIDENCE

462 Sent by Artaxerxes with Megabyzus to take control of the Persian forces in Egypt.
450 Defeated on Cyprus by the Athenian Cimon.
362 Sent by Artaxerxes against Cappadocia.
356 Revolts against Artaxerxes with the aid of the Athenian, Chares.
353 Continues his revolt.
344 Resides at the court of Philip in Macedonia.

Euagorus of Cyprus

405 Gives refuge to the Athenian, Canon.
399 Gives Canon leave to return.
391 Thwarted by Artaxerxes in his attempt to gain control of all of Cyprus.
387 Prepares for an attack from Artaxerxes.
386 Makes an alliance with Alcoris of Egypt.
385 Enters into terms with the Persians.
374 Is assassinated!
351 Artaxerxes in seeking to put down revolts on Cyprus, gains the aid of Euagorus who "in a former period had been king on the island."
350 Euagorus' hopes of regaining the kingship of Cyprus do not materialize.

Laches of Athens

427 With Charocades leads an Athenian force to Sicily.
419 With Nicostratus and Alcibiades leads an Athenian force into Arcadia.
364 As general of the Athenian fleet, Laches is forced to withdraw in the encounter with Epameninondas.

Leptines of Syracuse

397 Is admiral of Dionysius' fleet.
396 Keeps watch off Moyte.
390 Sent to aid the Leucanians in their attacks upon the Greek cities.
386 Driven into exile by Dionysius (his brother).
383 Loses his life in war with Carthage!
351 As commander of the Syracusans with Callipus, Leptines drives Dionysius the younger from Rhegium.
342 Forced into exile, after an attack by Timoleon.

Two of the above, Euagorus and Leptines, seem to have gotten a new lease of life after "coming back from the dead"! But in both cases, after the mention of their deaths, the narrative in Diodorus picks up again with the individual having the same name, location and activity.

Martin Anstey lists a number of men from this era who are shown from historical writings to have had very long lives and floreats. [68]

Long Lives

Xenophanes	141 yrs.	*Timaeus, Plutarch*
Pythagoras	99 yrs.	*Aristogenus, Jamblicus*
Aeschylus	(69 or) 154 yrs.	Author of *Life of Aeschylus*
Isocrates	99 yrs.	*Corsini*
Cratinus	97 yrs.	*Lucian*
Sophocles	95 yrs.	*Lucian*
Democritus	(104 or) 109 yrs.	*Lucian, Laertius*
Hippocrates	109 yrs.	*Suidas*
Timotheus	97 yrs.	*Suidas*

Long Floreats

Plato (comic poet)	63 yrs.	*Scholiast* with *Plutarch*
Parmenides	68 yrs.	*Laertius*
Gorgias (ambassador)	79 yrs.	*Suidas* with *Pausanias*
Antiphanes (comic poet)	71 yrs.	*Suidas* with *Athenaeus*
Aristophanes (comic poet)	53 yrs.	Internal evidence
Aristophon (ambassador)	63 yrs.	*Demosthenes*

The unusually long lives and floreats of so many distinguished men point strongly to the conclusion that the years from Xerxes to Alexander had been lengthened.

A second major faultline is to be found at Great Russell Street in London.

(2) An Artifact Gap in the British Museum

The British Museum is the world's largest repository of antiquities. Here in some one hundred huge galleries are displayed the remains and treasures of Daniel's four kingdoms: Babylon, Persia, Greece, Rome. Here also are ancient Assyria and Egypt. This is certainly the place to see

CHAPTER 5: FAULTLINES IN THE GREEK EVIDENCE

the Ancient World. And as regards our inquiry, it is here that a very interesting phenomenon is revealed.

By an actual count I was able to establish that the numbers of artifacts dated to the years 475-350 BC are considerably fewer than those dated to 600-475 BC or 350-225 BC.

A survey of the artifact galleries [69] reveals the following numbers of items (or at times groups of items if described by one card):

600-475   475-350   350-225

Gallery 3, Archaic Greece
    Sparta, Boeotia and Europa
    24   0   0
    Archaic Greek Coins
    61   0   0
    Ephesus
    13   0   0
    The Greeks in the East
    29   0   0
    The Greeks in Egypt
    30   1   1
    Athens
    53   0   0
    Corinth
    <u>34</u>   <u>0</u>   <u>0</u>
    244   1   1

Gallery 3A, Greek Vases
    392   18   0

Gallery 4, Andokidos, Techniques in Vase Painting
    12   1   0

Gallery 5, Greece 500-430
    Items along wall
    13   0   0

        Various
    20   0   0

BIBLE CHRONOLOGY: THE TWO GREAT DIVIDES

    Large Vases
    4   0   0
    Vases, flasks, figures
    22   61   0
    Large Items
    <u>2   3   0</u>
    61   64   0

<u>Gallery 14, The Hellenistic World, Art and Culture</u>
    Sanctuary of Demeter, Mainly Images
    0   0   21
    Coins
    0   0   10
    Seal Stones
    0   0   2
    Figures
    0   0   10
    Gold and Jewelry
    0   0   38
    Bowls
    0   0   2
    Portrait, Column, Figures
    <u>0   0   3</u>
    0   0   86

<u>Gallery 54, Ancient Anatolia</u>
    2   0   0

<u>Gallery 65, Egypt and Africa</u>
    Meroe
    0   1   1
    Nubia
    <u>11   3   0</u>
    11   4   1

<u>Gallery 71, Italy before The Roman Empire</u>
    The Faliscans
    0   1   2
    Northern and Eastern People
    15   1   1
    Sannites and Other Oscan People
    0   2   10

CHAPTER 5: FAULTLINES IN THE GREEK EVIDENCE

Arms and Armor		
4	4	4
Peoples of Apulia		
6	6	8
Canosa, City of Apulia		
0	0	14
Etruscan Colonization in Campania		
29	3	0
Tombs		
0	0	1
Etruscan Life		
16	17	9
Limestone Panels, Coins		
3	6	8
Orientalizing Period		
1	0	0
Bucchero Ware		
2	0	0
Urn and Statue		
2	0	0
Isis Tomb and Various Items		
19	0	0
Etruscan Sculpture and Jewelry		
60	1	0
Cerviti, Etruscan Tombs		
9	0	0
Etruscan Temple Architecture		
4	8	0
Etruscan Bronzes		
2	15	0
Etruscan Sanctuary and Jewelry		
1	35	0
Etruscan Jewelry		
0	15	37
Etruscan Mirrors		
1	3	9
Sanctuary of Diana, Jewelry		
0	0	32
Bronzes from Palestrina		
1	1	21
175	118	157

BIBLE CHRONOLOGY: THE TWO GREAT DIVIDES

Gallery 72, Cyprus
    Weaponry
    1   0   1
    Writing
    3   5   5
    Sanctuary Remains
    12   3   2
    Religion, Heroes
    7   3   6
    Jewelry
    20   30   14
    Coins
    6   28   10
    Trade and Manufacture
    19   6   3
    Images, Sculpture
    2   2   4
    The Human Form
    19   4   4
    Art: Flora, Fauna, Plants and Animals
    20   1   1
    Bronze Tripods
    <u>3   0   1</u>
    112   82   51

Gallery 73, The Greeks in Southern Italy
    Corinthian Potters in Camparia
    8   2   0
    Vases and Pottery
    0   53   126
    Armor
    4   9   17
    Tombs
    0   13   33
    The Bronze Rider of Taranto
    0   7   0
    Syracuse and Sicily
    12   5   0
    Gela
    9   3   0
    Locri
    6   12   0
    Bronzes

CHAPTER 5: FAULTLINES IN THE GREEK EVIDENCE

	600-475	475-350	350-225
Chalcidian Vases	9	7	0
Campania	7	0	0
Coins	9	21	0
Large Vases	12	35	23
Jewelry	0	0	11
Various Items	24	15	13
	0	0	18
	100	183	233

Gallery 77, Greek and Roman Architecture
    1   6   5

Gallery 79, Sculptures from Asia Minor
    1   2   0

Gallery 80, Greek Sculptures
    16   16   12

Gallery 81, Greek Sculptures
    0   0   50

Gallery 82, Rhodes, Asia Minor, The Greeks in Egypt
    35   1   0

Gallery 88, Items from Western Asia Minor
    1   3   0

Totals

	600-475	475-350	350-225
Gallery 3	244	1	1
Gallery 3A	392	18	0
Gallery 4	12	1	0
Gallery 5	13	0	0
Gallery 14	0	0	86
Gallery 54	2	0	0

Gallery 65	11	4	1
Gallery 71	175	118	159
Gallery 72	112	82	53
Gallery 73	100	183	235
Gallery 77	1	6	5
Gallery 79	1	2	0
Gallery 80	16	16	12
Gallery 81	0	0	50
Gallery 82	35	1	0
Gallery 88	1	3	0
	1115	435	602

The years 475-350 BC represent the most illustrious era of ancient Greece. Yet in this count, the period before has more than double the number of artifacts, and the period after, nearly a third again as many.

Surely it is reasonable to assume that this "most illustrious" period would be able to show as many and likely greater numbers of artifacts than those before and after. But from this very considerable sampling, it cannot!

For our final illustration of a faultline, we leave the shores and isles of Greece and cross over to the land of Israel. Here we are faced with the question as to how a "full" chronology in Greece can exist side-by-side with one that is virtually non-existent in Israel!

(3) Judaea - A One Hundred Year Blank

If, as according to the Ptolemaic reckoning, the Old Testament history of Judaea ends with the twelve year plus governorship of Nehemiah (445-432 BC), what are we to make of the remaining one hundred years down to Alexander? Indeed what do the Jews who follow this reckoning say about these years? Certainly they would have kept careful and substantial records if these years do in fact exist.

However, there is a nearly total historical blank! Their historians after discussing Ezra and Nehemiah can point to very little that is supposed to have happened in Israel during these remaining one hundred years to Alexander.

Encyclopedia Judaica is typical:

CHAPTER 5: FAULTLINES IN THE GREEK EVIDENCE

> With one or two notable exceptions, our information for the remaining 100 years of Persian rule dries up. [70]

The exceptions are the conflicts among the priests described by Josephus, and the Jewish settlement of Elephantine on the Nile. These we discussed in the section dealing with the priests.

Encyclopedia Judaica makes the same point in its entry on "Persia".

> Again, almost nothing is known about contacts between the Persians and the Jews. [71]

And again, in the entry dealing with "Greece", there is no mention of any contacts between Greece and Israel during these years. [72]

How could it be that so little is known about events in Israel, or of her contacts with foreign powers during these one hundred years? Why do the Jews themselves not have a record of these years? Why this blank?!

As the prestigious *Cambridge Ancient History* admits:

> We have as yet very meagre sources for fourth-century historical developments at Samaria and Jerusalem ... [73]

And it was precisely because of this void that the Sedar Olam, in setting out a traditional Jewish chronology, could reduce the Persian period nearly "out of sight". Of course the drafters of this chronology went too far. But the fact that it was done to such an extent demonstrates strongly that Jews of the time believed Greek chronology for the Persian period was unstable.

"O Lord, hear; O Lord, forgive; <u>O Lord, hearken and do; defer not</u>, for thine own sake, O my God: for thy city and thy people are called by thy name."

(Daniel 9:19)

CONCLUSION

With this we close our inquiry into a considerable range of historical material that bears upon the question of the number of years from Xerxes to Alexander. Sources from Babylon, Persia, Greece, Egypt and Judaea have been examined. While the *events* of these times have been presented with reasonable accuracy, the evidence is either too meagre or has too many gaps, for a convincing case to be made for the Ptolemaic *timing*.

Nor can eclipse dating be relied upon for the simple reason that *too many* eclipses occur on a yearly basis to make an identification possible with the *too few* recorded eclipses during this period. One writer refers to attempts at eclipse dating as an "identification game".

> All this above, especially since the ancient so-called eclipses are vague as to type or magnitude (partial or total), vague as to exact location, and vague as to time period makes it extremely difficult to identify the year of their occurrence. This enables chronologists (Ptolemy included) to play the identification game.[74]

Or as Anstey puts it:

> [S]ince there are never less than 2 eclipses in any year, usually 4, and sometimes as many as 7, and since an eclipse repeats itself more or less completely every 18 years and a few days, and much more completely every 54 years and a month, there will always be an eclipse available within a reasonable number of years with which to identify any recorded event, the date of which we desire to fix.[75]

Only the Sixty-nine Weeks of Daniel can provide a certain bridge across these long years. Without a secular interregnum, the Weeks link directly from the decree of Cyrus and the end of the seventy-year captivity unto the crucifixion of Christ. Thus as the Scriptures provide a complete *genealogy* from Adam to Christ (Luke 3), they also provide a complete *chronology*. And this without any appeal or reliance upon secular considerations.

Briefly stated the Scriptural demonstration of this and of the fact that the time from Cyrus to Alexander must be considerably less than that posited by Ptolemy is as follows:

1. The Seventy Weeks seem certain to begin with the Cyrus Decree (Dan.9:25).

> (1) It was prophesied that Cyrus would indeed build Jerusalem (Isa. 45:13).

(2) It is likely that God "stirred" the heart of Cyrus by acquainting him with the prophecy of Isa. 44:28-45:13.

(3) Even if we allow for exaggeration, the Jews' enemies are quite adamant that the returnees had begun to rebuild the city. This was the basis of their accusation to the king of Persia (Ezra 4:12).

(4) There is a repetition of the phrase the *commandment going forth* in Dan.9:23,25. This likely ties Cyrus' decree to the commencement of the weeks.

(5) The decree of Cyrus was the basis and precedent for actions of subsequent Persian kings (Ezra 5:9-6:8).

(6) As the revelation of the Seventy *Weeks* was God's answer to Daniel's prayer concerning seventy years (Dan. 9:2), there is therefore a link between the two time periods. And, as the decree forms the *conclusion* to the seventy years, there is every likelihood that it is the *commencement* to the Seventy Weeks.

(7) The start of the Seventy Weeks was something Daniel could actually see and "know" in an experiential way (Dan. 9:25).

(8) Given the minor nature of the so-called decree of Artaxerxes, the Jews would have difficulty knowing that they must then start counting the weeks. Whereas the decree of Cyrus was a world-wide proclamation (cp. Neh.2:4-16 with Ezra 2:1,2).

(9) The wise men would have been far more likely to count the years to Christ from Cyrus' decree than from the other "decrees".

(10) Jerusalem's desolation was to be limited to *seventy years* (Dan.9:2)., not seventy years plus a further ninety-one years (536-445 BC). Daniel in his prayer (9:16-19) besought the Lord that He "defer not" this reconstruction work (9:19).

(11) If the seven weeks (forty-nine years) of restoration begin with Cyrus' decree, then Scripture points to their logical conclusion in the reforms on Nehemiah (Neh. 13). But if they only begin ninety-one years later then the events which mark their conclusion are unknown to us.

CONCLUSION

(12) How is it that Nehemiah could be shocked and sorrowful over the report of Jerusalem's broken walls if ninety-one years had passed since the return from Babylon (Neh. 1:3,4). And, if as some say there had been a partial restoration followed by a further destruction of the walls, then their basic premise is contradicted that the decree of Cyrus did not address the reconstruction of the city.

(13) Josephus who wrote before Ptolemy clearly shows that Cyrus' decree mandated the city at large (*Antiquities* XI:1).

2. The Scripture lists show that the 586/536/445 BC chronology is untenable.

(1) Seventeen priests and Levites who returned with Zerubbabel (Neh. 12:1-8) also sealed the covenant with Nehemiah (Neh. 10:1-10). This is the great conundrum for the Ptolemaic Chronology.

(2) Sixteen of the wall-builders (Neh. 3:1-32) were also covenant-signers (Neh. 10:1-27). As many of the covenant-signers returned with Zerubbabel (only the priests and Levites are listed in Neh. 12:1-8), this implies that the wall-builders themselves were not far removed from that event. This also refutes a proposed solution to the Nehemiah Ten and Twelve "problem" which says that Neh. 7:5-12:26 is a "flash-back" from 445 BC to 536 BC.

(3) Fifteen chiefs of the people who returned with Zerubbabel (Ezra 2, Neh. 7) are also listed among the covenant-signers with Nehemiah (Neh. 10:14-18).

(4) Thirteen "first inhabitants" of Jerusalem after the exile are listed in both I Chr. 9 (cp.9:2) and Neh. 11. Five of those listed are specifically associated with Nehemiah (Neh. 12:25,26).

(5) Two Levites, Jeshua and Kadmiel, are linked together from the time of the return, and unto the building of the walls (Ezra 2:40; Ezra 3:8,9; Neh. 9:4,5; Neh. 10:9; Neh. 12:1,8).

3. Mordecai and Ezra were living at the time of Jerusalem's destruction.

(1) Seraiah, Ezra's father, was the high priest slain by Nebuchadnezzar (Ezra 7:1; II Kings 25:18-21).

(2) Mordecai was carried into captivity with Jeconiah, eleven years before Jerusalem's fall (Est. 2:5-7). It is in accord with English and Hebrew grammar that the "who" of verse six refers to the chief person in the sentence immediately preceding, i.e. Mordecai.

4. Ezra, Nehemiah and Mordecai are listed among the returnees from Babylon (Ezra 2:2; Neh. 12:1). Given the rarity of their names in Scripture, it is not likely that we would have two trios of the same names, one active in 536 BC and the other eighty to ninety years later.

5. There does not appear to be a long interval between the governorships of Zerubbabel and Nehemiah (Neh. 12:47).

6. The line of the high priests shows that the Traditional Chronology from Cyrus to Alexander is too long. Josephus follows the Scripture's list of six post-exilic priests (Neh. 12:10,11) and says that the sixth, Jaddua, went out to meet Alexander the Great (331 BC). Support for this is seen in Neh. 13:28, where Nehemiah is shown at that time to be contemporaneous with the third, fourth and fifth generations of this priestly line. The Elephantine papyri give further insight and support for this shortened view, as does a "single" Sanballat spanning the period from Nehemiah to Alexander.

7. Daniel 10:20-11:4 limits the times and numbers of the Persian kings.

(1) Xerxes rather than Artaxerxes Longimanus appears to be the last Persian king mentioned in Scripture (Ezra 4:4-7; 6:14).

(2) The prominent king of Ezra, Nehemiah and Esther is the same, and is Darius rather than Xerxes. All the regnal years in these books refer to Darius.

(3) Nehemiah's reforms at the end of Darius' reign complete the first seven of the Seventy Weeks.

Thus we have seen that it is not only Nehemiah 10 and 12 that point to the shorter chronology - this is but the tip of the iceberg - an entire range of Scriptural considerations point in the same direction. And while a number of writers on the subject have either not been aware of or have ignored these implications, for chronologists generally, if there is going to be any bending of the evidence it will usually be on the Bible side. To them, Ptolemy's Canon and the outlines of Greek history are set in stone.

CONCLUSION

The research into this question by Isaac Newton, followed notably by Floyd Jones, has been different. Here there is a serious attempt to grapple with the issues, and bring the two systems together in a way which honors Scripture and yet acknowledges Ptolemy's Canon. However, their best efforts have probably demonstrated that this cannot be done.

The two chronological "divides" presented in this book have an obvious bearing upon the counting of the years from Adam. And the second has implications for the Times of the Gentiles (Luke 21:24). See the end of Chapter One.

The *First Divide*, the *Crux Chronologorum,* brings to light a redemptive chronological structure that underlies the events of Scripture. Out of what appeared to be an impossible contradiction, Sir Edward Denny discovered a solution that wonderfully illustrates God's forgiveness of the sinner. [76]

The *Second Divide* demonstrates the epic struggle to dislodge the Seventy Weeks of Daniel from its place as the cornerstone of history, chronology and prophecy.

Martin Anstey best sums up this epic dispute:

> Here as everywhere else it is "thy sons O Zion against thy sons, O Greece" (Zech. 9:13). It is Nehemiah and Daniel against Ptolemy and Eratosthenes. It is Hebraic Chronology against Hellenic chronology. [77]

Even so, come, Lord Jesus. (Revelation 22:20).

NOTES: CHAPTER FIVE AND CONCLUSION

1. Simon Hornblower, "Persia", *The Cambridge Ancient History*, Second Edition, Vol.VI.,p.46.
2. The best effort at such a reconciliation is Floyd Jones' adaptation of Isaac Newton's "flash-back" proposal. But for the reasons given, this does not appear to be workable.
3. The two lines of Spartan kings listed by Ptolemy are mentioned infrequently as playing an important role in the evnts which shaped Greece at this time. Nor are events linked to their regnal years.
4. "History", *Encyclopedia Britannica*, 20th edn., p.600.
5. *The Library of History*, Introduction p.vii.
6. The editor's contention - that as Diodorus does not mention the Acropolis, he is unlikely to have visited Athens (p.xiii) - is refuted by the fact that he *does* mention the Acropolis (XVII.72.6).
7. *A History Of My Times* (Hellenica), trans. by Rex Warner, (London:Penguin Books, 1979), p.30.
8. *Ibid.* i.e. 408,03,02,00,383,81,80,74,64,63.
9. *Ibid.* p.61, note.
10. *Ibid.* p.16.
11. *Ibid.* p.28.
12. *The Romance of Bible Chronology*, p.291.
13. *Greek Historiography*, Simon Hornblower editor, (Oxford: Clarendon Press, 1994), pp.36,37.
14. Donald W. Prakken, *Studies in Greek Genealogical Chronology*, (Lancaster, Pennsylvania: Lancaster Press, 1943), pp.74,75.
15. *Ibid.* p.79. See also: G.L.Barber, *The Historian Ephorus*, (London: Cambridge Univ. Press, 1935), pp.47,48.
16. Prakken, p.102.
17. *Ibid.* pp.77-78.
18. *Ibid.* p.102.
19. *The Oxford Classical Dictionary*, Second Edition, (Oxford: The Clarendon Press, 1970), p.405. See also: Rudolf Pfeiffer, *History of Classical Scholarship*, (Oxford: Clarendon Press, 1968), pp. 152-154.
20. The standard compendim containing this and other Greek fragments and texts is: Felix Jacoby, *Die Fragmente Der Griechischen Historiker, FGrHist*, Berlin and Leiden, 1923-58). A full translation is apparently not available in English.
21. P.M.Fraser, Eratosthenes of Cyrene, (London: Oxford Univ. Press, 1970), p.26.
22. *Ibid.* p.28.
23. *History of Classical Scholarship*, p.163.
24. Alden A. Mosshammer, *The Chronicle of Eusebius and Greek Chronographic Tradition*, (London: Associated University Presses, 1979), p.187.
25. *Ibid.* p.99.

CONCLUSION

26. Alan E. Samuel, *Greek and Roman Chronology*, (Munich: Oscar Beck, 1972), p.190.
27. *Ibid.* p.190.
28. *The Romance of Bible Chronology*, p.36. Anstey however, in describing this exaggeration, at times "lumped together" the earlier and later periods of Greek history.
29. Pfeiffer, *History of Classical Scholarship*, p.163.
30. Fraser, *Eratosthenes of Cyrene*, p.26.
31. *The Chronicle of Eusebius and Greek Chronographic Tradition*, p.117.
32. *Ibid.* p.117.
33. *Ibid.* p.278.
34. Anstey, p.36.
35. *Studies in Greek Genealogical Chronology*, pp.77,78.
36. *Ibid.* pp.120,121. Mosshammer's research is based on *Apollodors Chronik* by F. Jacoby.
37. *Ibid.* p.121.
38. *Ibid.* p.122.
39. *Ibid.* p.124.
40. *The Oxford Classical Dictionary*, Second Edition, p.1007.
41. Mosshammer, p.100.
42. *Ibid.* p.95.
43. Samuel, *Greek and Roman Chronology*, p.189, n.4.
44. Mosshammer, pp.89-91.
45. *Ibid.* pp.86,87.
46. Anstey, p.105.
47. With but one exception, none of the 189 persons (my count, excluding archons) Diodorus mentions for the years 480-330 BC are those of the Olympic victors. The exception is a Xenophon of Corinth who was Olympic victor in 464 BC, and a Xenophon who led Athens' armies in 429 BC. They are not likely to be the same. Xenophon, the famous historian, is said to have been born about 430 BC.
48. Samuel, p.206.
49. *Ibid.* pp.206-209.
50. *Ibid.* pp.196,197,210-214.
51. *Ibid.* pp.196,197.
52. *A History of My Times,* Penguin Books, 1979, p.61.
53. *The Oxford Classical Dictionary,* Second Edition, p.101.
54. *Ibid.* p.827.
55. Samuel, p.205.
56. *Roman Antiquities*, The Loeb Classical Library.
57. Anstey, pp. 289-291.
58. John Hewlett, *A Vindication of the Authenticity of the Parian Chronicle*, (London, 1789), pp.35,135-143.
59. Nancy Thomson de Grammond, Ed., *An Encyclopedia of the History of Classical Archaeology*, (Chicago: Fitzroy Dearhorn Publ., 1996), Vol. II, pp.727,728.
60. *Ibid.* p.728.

61. Letter of reply from Michael Vickers, Curator of Greek and Roman Antiquities, Ashmolean Museum, Oxford.
62. *A Vindication of the Authenticity of the Parian Chronicle,* pp.23-34. One or two other titles by the same author contain this same translation.
63. *An Encyclopedia of the History of Classical Archaeology,* Vol.II, p.728.
64. These dates and material are from the translation in Hewlett's volume. The dates are one year earlier than that presented by Jacoby.
65. During two of those years, "a stone fell into the river" and "a great light blazed across the sky".
66. Mosshammer, p.97.
67. Plutarch (died after 120 AD) is uncertain as to the circumstances of Aristeides' death and gives several differing accounts (*Aristides* XXVI, XXVII).
68. Anstey, p.288.
69. Several galleries were closed for refurbishing when this count was made in early 1997.
70. "History", Vol. VII, p.624.
71. "Persia", Vol. XIII, p.306.
72. "Greece", Vol. VI. p.868.
73. Hayim Tadmor, "Judah", *The Cambridge Ancient History,* Second Edition, 1994, Vol. VI, p.289.
74. Walter R. Dolen, *Chronology Papers,* (http://onelaw.com/beone/cp.3b.htm), Vol. V.p.1.
75. *The Romance of Bible Chronology,* p.286.
76. Denny's book, *Forgiveness Seventy and Seven Fold* (1849), is at the British Library. Its shelfmark is 3185.d.41.
77. Anstey, p.31.

INDEX OF WORDS AND PHRASES

0 years, 23, 61, 139
1005 BC, 13, 20
12th year of Xerxes' reign, 18
135 AD, 30, 145
2nd century AD, 15, 16, 29, 69
2nd year of Darius, 97, 98
3000th anniversary, 13, 20
32 AD, 18, 70
33 AD, 14, 23, 37, 40, 41
33 years, 76
345 years, 20
3761, 25, 40
4 BC, 18, 117, 155, 156, 178
4004 BC date for Creation, 17
445 BC, 13, 14, 15, 17, 18, 22, 34, 37, 42, 76, 80, 81, 82, 84, 91, 95, 99, 108, 226, 227
480 years, 14, 17, 20, 26, 36, 42, 47, 51, 58, 60, 62, 64, 65, 66
483 years, 14, 18, 29, 31, 33, 36, 37, 40, 41, 70, 76, 117, 130
490, 21, 22, 23, 31, 37, 38, 39, 40, 42, 45, 61, 71, 210
490-year cycles, 22, 39
50th year, 21
53 years, 14, 16, 27
536 BC, 13, 15, 17, 18, 19, 23, 40, 81, 82, 83, 84, 94, 96, 103, 133, 227, 228
536/445 BC chronology, 77, 78, 79, 82, 86, 91, 227
611 years, 32, 36, 47, 51, 52
6th Millennium, 29
70th week, 23, 24, 70
747 BC, 15
7x7 Sabbatic years, 21
Absalom, 62
Adam, 5, 6, 15, 16, 24, 36, 37, 39, 44, 52, 66, 69, 81, 225, 229
Addaru, 158
Aegean, 120, 212
Africanus, 143, 144, 169

Agiads, 205, 206
agricultural cycle, 158
Ahasuerus, 27, 33, 37, 43, 44, 69, 92, 93, 115, 116, 118, 119, 120, 121, 123, 124, 125, 126, 127, 129
Akiva, 30, 31, 43
Akkadian, 148, 153
alabaster vase, 149
Alcoris of Egypt, 215
Alexander, 14, 16, 24, 27, 28, 37, 38, 39, 69, 70, 96, 107, 108, 109, 110, 111, 112, 113, 114, 129, 130, 131, 133, 137, 138, 139, 142, 143, 144, 145, 146, 148, 166, 167, 168, 173, 174, 176, 178, 180, 193, 194, 197, 198, 199, 200, 211, 212, 213, 214, 216, 222, 225, 228
Alexander the Great, 16, 28, 37, 38, 39, 70, 96, 109, 114, 137, 194, 200, 228
all points, 5, 94
Anaximenes of Lampsacus, 177, 194
ancient Florida, 16
Anderson, 18, 24, 45, 70
Annals, 17, 18
annular, 16
Anstey, 3, 17, 22, 35, 36, 37, 39, 40, 41, 43, 44, 45, 48, 52, 55, 56, 58, 60, 61, 66, 67, 119, 132, 135, 150, 151, 169, 170, 171, 175, 201, 225, 231, 232
Antiochus of Syracuse, 175, 186
Antiquities, 112, 132, 133, 134, 135, 144, 227, 231, 232
apocryphal books, 121
Apollodorus, 143, 175, 176, 185, 188, 195, 198, 200, 202, 203, 204, 205, 207, 210, 214

Aramaic letters, 105
Archbishop of Armagh, 17
Archon, 211
Aristotle, 177, 193, 210, 211
Arrian, 151

Artaxerxes, 15, 17, 18, 19, 22, 23, 27, 32, 33, 34, 37, 38, 43, 44, 69, 70, 71, 74, 75, 77, 80, 82, 84, 93, 94, 100, 101, 105, 113, 114, 115, 116, 117, 118, 119, 121, 122, 123, 124, 125, 126, 127, 128, 129, 130, 135, 137, 138, 139, 140, 141, 142, 143, 144, 145, 146, 맴147, 148, 149, 150, 151, 152, 153, 154, 155, 156, 157, 159, 160, 161, 162, 163, 164, 165, 166, 170, 171, 172, 176, 177, 182, 183, 186, 188, 189, 190, 191, 192, 194, 195, 213, 215, 226, 228
Artaxerxes I Longimanus, 139
Artaxerxes II, 70, 130, 138, 140, 141, 143, 147, 148, 150, 152, 153, 154, 155, 156, 157, 159, 160, 163, 164, 165, 171, 172
Artaxerxes III, 70, 130, 138, 141, 150, 152, 153, 154, 155, 156, 157
Artaxerxes Longimanus, 18, 38, 69, 70, 75, 77, 113, 114, 116, 121, 122, 128, 146, 228
Asaph, 53, 83
Ashmolean Museum, 146, 212, 232
Ashtaroth, 59
Assyrian chronological scheme, 20
astronomical diaries, 156
astronomical tablets, 153, 158
Aswan in Egypt, 105
Athens, 139, 140, 141, 146, 173, 177, 180, 181, 182, 183, 184, 185, 186, 187, 188, 189, 190, 191, 192, 193, 194, 195, 196, 197, 198, 200, 202, 204, 205, 206, 208, 209, 210, 213, 214, 217, 230, 231
Authorized Version, 5, 13, 17, 39, 57, 63, 66, 70
Baal, 59
Babylonian, 15, 32, 33, 35, 36, 43, 71, 112, 134, 152, 153, 154, 156, 158, 161, 162, 166, 167, 169, 170, 172
Babylonian Chronology, 158

Babylonian year, 156, 158
Bagoas, 142
Bagohi, the governor of Judah, 105
Bar Kokhba, 24, 29, 30, 31, 43, 145
Bar Kokhba revolt, 24

Barag, 105, 133
Belhatin, 161
Belnaddinshumu, 161
Berossus, 143, 169
Bessus, 142
Binnui, 82, 84, 85, 88
Birth of Abraham to the Exodus, 22, 25
Bivar, 166, 172
BM 36910, 36998, 37036, 160
British Library, 5, 165, 232
British Museum, 5, 35, 153, 160, 165, 170, 216
build the walls, 15, 17, 18, 32, 70, 73, 82
Bullinger, 17, 22, 32, 33, 34, 35, 36, 40, 43, 44, 52, 55, 56, 58, 60, 61, 66, 121
C. I.Scofield's, 35
Caleb, 59
Callisthenes, 177, 178, 179, 191, 195
Cambyses, 27, 33, 37, 38, 44, 69, 77, 97, 98, 113, 115, 116, 118, 119, 120, 123, 128, 129, 137, 143, 144, 151
Canon, 15, 16, 17, 20, 37, 38, 69, 70, 71, 92, 95, 99, 112, 137, 154, 158, 160, 163, 165, 171, 173, 215, 228, 229
captivity, 15, 17, 22, 23, 33, 34, 37, 71, 78, 84, 91, 93, 131, 133, 225, 228
champion of the Hebrew Scriptures, 20
Charocades, 185, 215
Christ, 5, 6, 15, 17, 18, 23, 24, 29, 31, 36, 37, 42, 52, 66, 69, 71, 75, 76, 81, 97, 107, 117, 130, 132, 145, 225, 226
Christian era, 15
Chronica, 143
chronology, 3, 5, 13, 14, 16, 17, 19, 20, 21, 22, 24, 25, 26, 27, 28, 29, 30, 31, 32, 36, 37, 39, 41, 51, 52, 54, 56, 57, 61, 63, 66, 69, 76, 85, 96, 97, 101, 112, 128, 130, 131, 143, 145, 146, 148, 152, 154, 155, 158, 160, 173, 175, 180, 185, 198, 199, 200, 201, 202, 203, 204,

206, 207, 208, 209, 211, 213, 214, 222, 223, 225, 228, 229
Cimon lays siege to a Persian garrison, 140
Claudius Ptolemaeus, 15
Clay, 152, 162, 171, 172

INDEX OF WORDS AND PHRASES

Clive Spencer-Bentley, 5
Colophon, 156, 157
commencement to the Seventy Weeks, 74, 226
Companion Bible, 32, 36, 43, 48, 56, 67, 134
Conquest of Heshbon, 57, 58
consecutive-eclipse tablets, 154
conventional wisdom, 5
Covenant Signers, 81
Creation of Adam to the Birth of Abraham, 22, 25
Cross, 5, 23, 36, 40, 69, 108, 109, 111, 130, 133
Crux Chronologorum, 3, 5, 14, 21, 47, 65, 229
Ctesias, 147, 148, 176, 189
current year (2010) is 5771, 14
Cushan, 56, 58, 59, 60, 64
Cycle, 48, 49, 50
Cyrus, 13, 14, 16, 17, 24, 27, 28, 32, 33, 34, 36, 37, 38, 39, 43, 44, 68, 69, 70, 71, 72, 73, 74, 75, 76, 77, 79, 80, 97, 98, 112, 113, 114, 115, 116, 118, 128, 129, 130, 135, 137, 138, 140, 143, 144, 147, 151, 168, 172, 176, 189, 213, 225, 226, 227, 228
Cyrus to Christ, 17, 32
Dakes Bible, 48
Dan Barag, 105
Daniel, 3, 5, 13, 15, 23, 27, 28, 29, 32, 33, 36, 38, 39, 69, 71, 72, 73, 74, 75, 76, 77, 103, 110, 111, 112, 113, 116, 118, 122, 128, 129, 130, 132, 136, 138, 216, 224, 225, 226, 228, 229
Dareius, 138, 142
Dariiaamush, 161
Darius, 16, 18, 27, 28, 33, 34, 36, 37, 38, 43, 44, 69, 70, 71, 74, 77, 93, 97, 98, 100, 103, 104, 106, 107, 109, 111, 113, 114, 115, 116, 117, 118, 119, 120, 121, 122, 123, 124, 125, 126, 127, 128, 129, 130, 135, 137, 138, 139, 140, 142, 143, 144, 145, 146, 147, 148, 149, 150, 151, 152, 153, 154, 155, 156, 157, 158,

159, 160, 161, 162, 163, 165, 166, 169, 170, 171, 172, 186, 188, 197, 198, 212, 228
Darius Hystaspes, 16, 18, 27, 28, 33, 34, 37, 38, 44, 69, 77, 93, 97, 100, 113, 115, 118, 120, 121, 122, 125, 126, 127, 128, 145, 146, 148, 150, 152, 161, 162, 163, 169
Darius Hystaspes (522-486 BC), 18
Darius II, 27, 70, 111, 130, 138, 140, 142, 143, 144, 147, 148, 149, 150, 151, 152, 154, 155, 156, 157, 158, 159, 160, 161, 162, 163, 171, 172
Darius III, 27, 70, 111, 130, 138, 142, 144, 148, 150, 151, 152, 154, 155, 156, 157
Darius III Codomanus, 142
Darius the Mede, 27, 36, 113, 118, 119
dating of events, 13
David, 13, 14, 46, 47, 51, 52, 53, 54, 60, 62, 92, 101
Day of Atonement, 21
days of Joiakim, 87, 98, 99
days of Nehemiah, 87, 95, 98
Deborah and Barak, 58
decree, 14, 29, 31, 33, 36, 37, 69, 70, 71, 73, 74, 75, 76, 77, 79, 80, 81, 98, 122, 127, 128, 130, 131, 168, 225, 226, 227
decree of Cyrus, 31, 33, 37, 69, 70, 71, 73, 74, 75, 131, 225, 226, 227
decrees, 71, 72, 74, 75, 79, 226
Dedication of the Temple, 22
Delaiah, 105, 108
Demetrius of Phalerum, 208, 211
Denny, 3, 20, 21, 22, 23, 24, 32, 36, 39, 40, 42, 45, 51, 52, 66, 67, 232
Diodorus, 70, 115, 117, 120, 122, 127, 134, 135, 138, 142, 143, 145, 147, 148, 154, 164, 165, 169, 173, 174, 175, 176, 177, 178, 179, 180, 183, 185, 188, 198, 199, 201, 202, 204, 205, 206, 208, 209, 210, 212, 214, 216, 230, 231
Diodorus Siculus, 115, 134, 174
divided monarchy, 14, 19, 20, 22, 26, 41
Diyllus the Athenian, 178, 196
Dubberstein, 158, 160, 171, 172
Duris of Samos, 177

Ecbatana, 127, 150
eclipses, 16, 38, 154, 160, 225
Edward Denny, 47, 62, 66
Edwin Thiele's, 13

Edwin Yamauchi, 137
Egibi and Murashu, 161
Egibi family, 161
Eglon, 48, 58, 63, 64, 67
Egyptian, 15, 18, 135, 144, 149, 166
Ehud, 48, 50, 58, 64
Elamite, 148, 152
Elephantine, 100, 105, 106, 107, 108, 109, 223, 228
Elephantine Papyri, 100
Eliashib, 77, 96, 97, 98, 99, 100, 101, 102, 103, 104, 105, 106, 107, 108, 112, 129, 130
Encyclopaedia Britannica, 92
Encyclopedia Judaica, 42, 43, 133, 134, 222, 223
Ephorus, 175, 176, 177, 178, 179, 180, 185, 187, 188, 189, 190, 195, 196, 198, 199, 200, 203, 204, 230
Ephraim, 20, 56
epic poem of Firdusi, 146
Eratosthenes, 38, 39, 175, 198, 200, 201, 202, 204, 205, 207, 210, 213, 214, 229, 230, 231
Esther, 27, 32, 33, 36, 37, 43, 69, 91, 92, 93, 94, 115, 116, 118, 119, 120, 121, 123, 124, 125, 126, 127, 132, 135, 145, 228
Ethan, 53
Ethiopia, 35, 44, 115, 118, 119, 120, 123, 124
Euagorus of Cyprus, 215
Eurypontids, 205, 206
Eusebius, 38, 143, 144, 169, 230, 231
Ezra, 13, 18, 19, 27, 28, 32, 33, 34, 36, 37, 39, 42, 44, 53, 69, 70, 71, 72, 73, 74, 75, 76, 77, 82, 84, 85, 86, 87, 88, 89, 90, 91, 93, 94, 95, 96, 97, 98, 99, 100, 102, 104, 105, 106, 107, 114, 115, 116, 117, 118, 121, 122, 123, 125, 126, 127, 128, 129, 132, 133, 134, 145, 222, 226, 227, 228
Figulla, 162, 163, 165, 166, 172
Firdusi, 16, 146
First Adam, 5

first inhabitants, 86, 87, 90, 227
first is the ACTUAL TIME, 21

Floyd Jones, 17, 19, 42, 45, 48, 51, 57, 62, 63, 64, 71, 82, 84, 92, 93, 117, 165, 172, 229, 230
forty-nine years, 76, 77, 116, 128, 131, 226
Frank Cross Jr, 108
G. Campbell Morgan, 3, 35
Gabriel, 73, 74
Gallery, 217, 218, 220, 221, 222
Gedeliah, 95
GENEALOGY OF DAVID, 51
generations, 5, 29, 31, 37, 39, 51, 52, 53, 54, 90, 103, 105, 131, 199, 203, 228
Gershevitch, 149, 151
Gill, 133
Goliath, 62
Grayson, 153, 170
Great (Arta) Xerxes, 116
great dilemma in reconciling Nehemiah 10 and 12 with the Ptolemaic dating., 18
Grecian, 15, 26, 137
Greek island of Paros, 146
Greek physician, 147
Hadassah, 91, 92
Hamadan, 150
Haman, 69, 126, 129
Hananiah governor of Samaria, 108
Hasmonean (Maccabean) family, 26
Hellenica, 169, 174, 230
Heloris, Polyxenus and Philistus, 176
Heman, 53, 54
Henadad, 84, 88
Henry, 132
Herodian, 26
Herodotus, 34, 43, 114, 117, 118, 119, 120, 122, 134, 138, 147, 174, 175, 178, 179, 180, 208, 210
Hieroglyphic Texts, 166
Hilkiah, 89, 90
Hisiarsu, 154
Hisiiarsu, 162
Hornblower, 167, 168, 179, 230
I Esdras, 95, 120, 121, 123, 124, 125, 135

Ilya Gershevitch, 149, 169
India, 35, 44, 115, 118, 119, 120, 123, 124

INDEX OF WORDS AND PHRASES

intercalary month, 158
intercalary notices, 158
Inter-Testamental Period, 16
Ish-bosheth, 64
Ivan Panin, 64, 67
Jaddua, 96, 97, 99, 103, 104, 106, 107, 108, 109, 110, 111, 112, 130, 133, 144, 145, 228
Jephthah, 49, 50, 56, 57, 58, 61, 64, 65
Jerusalem, 13, 14, 15, 18, 20, 26, 27, 29, 32, 33, 34, 37, 41, 42, 43, 44, 70, 71, 72, 73, 74, 75, 76, 77, 78, 79, 80, 81, 82, 84, 86, 87, 88, 90, 91, 93, 94, 96, 97, 98, 99, 100, 101, 104, 106, 110, 112, 115, 116, 121, 123, 124, 126, 130, 131, 134, 136, 223, 225, 226, 227, 228
Jesus Christ, 29, 31
Jews, 13, 16, 20, 24, 25, 27, 30, 31, 32, 33, 34, 36, 38, 39, 42, 43, 45, 69, 70, 71, 72, 73, 75, 79, 80, 93, 94, 97, 102, 105, 106, 107, 108, 109, 110, 111, 112, 116, 125, 126, 132, 144, 145, 146, 222, 223, 226
Johan(an), 105
Johanan, 89, 97, 100, 101, 102, 103, 104, 105, 106, 107, 108, 129, 130, 133
John Gill, 94, 95, 123
Joiada, 96, 97, 103, 104, 106, 107, 112, 129, 130
Joiakim, 91, 96, 98, 99, 100, 112, 129
Jones, 17, 18, 19, 20, 22, 24, 32, 40, 42, 44, 55, 58, 59, 61, 62, 63, 64, 65, 112, 117, 118, 119, 132, 134, 135
Josephus, 16, 38, 70, 72, 74, 78, 79, 80, 94, 95, 96, 99, 100, 103, 105, 106, 107, 108, 109, 111, 112, 116, 117, 130, 132, 133, 134, 135, 143, 144, 145, 146, 223, 227, 228
Joshua and Caleb, 59
Joshua-Judges chasm, 56, 57, 58
Jozadak, 87, 91, 97, 98, 133
Jubilee Cycle, 21
Judah ha-Nasi, 30
Jupiter, 155, 156
Keil, 92, 132, 133

Kent, 151, 169, 170
Kidner, 106, 133
King David, 13

King
Nabonassar, 15
King of Israel, 24
king of kings, 127
king of Persia, 72, 73, 75, 97, 102, 111, 115, 116, 182, 186, 226
Kingdom of Persia, 13
Kish, 91, 92, 121
Kuh-i-Rahmat, 152
Lacedaemonians, 140, 141, 175
Laches of Athens, 215
Last Adam, 5
LBAT, 153, 155, 156, 158, 159, 160, 170, 171
LBAT 1422, 23, 24, 160
Leptines of Syracuse, 215
Levites, 15, 17, 80, 81, 82, 83, 85, 87, 88, 94, 96, 97, 98, 99, 103, 104, 106, 107, 130, 132, 227
London, 5, 6, 13, 32, 35, 42, 132, 134, 135, 146, 169, 170, 172, 211, 212, 216, 230, 231
Long Floreats, 216
Longimanus, 116, 117, 121, 122, 124, 127, 128, 130, 134
lunar, 15, 16, 24, 39, 40, 42, 45, 153, 154, 158, 160, 185
Lysander, the admiral of the Lacedaemonians, 140
Maccabean, 26
Manetho, 39, 144, 169
Marmor Parium, 146, 207, 208, 210, 211, 212, 213
Martin Anstey, 3, 42, 211, 216, 229
Matthew Henry, 93, 94, 122, 132, 135
McClintock and Strong Cyclopedia, 90
Mentor, 142, 170
Mercury, 155, 156
Merrill Unger's, 78
Messiah, 18, 23, 29, 30, 31, 33, 42, 43, 70, 73, 75, 77, 136
Mishnah, 30, 111
Mizpeh, 42, 47, 50, 54, 55, 60, 61, 64, 65
Moorman, 1, 6

Mordecai, 33, 69, 88, 91, 92, 93, 94, 95, 98, 121, 124, 125, 126, 227, 228

Mosshammer, 201, 202, 203, 204, 207, 230, 231, 232
Mount Athos, 175, 178
Murushu archive, 161
Naxos, 164, 165, 181
Nebuchadnezzar, 13, 24, 32, 33, 34, 35, 36, 37, 41, 42, 43, 44, 78, 89, 90, 91, 93, 94, 97, 131, 133, 161, 227
Nehemiah, 13, 15, 17, 18, 19, 22, 23, 27, 28, 32, 33, 34, 35, 36, 37, 39, 43, 44, 70, 73, 75, 77, 78, 79, 80, 81, 82, 83, 84, 85, 86, 87, 88, 91, 93, 94, 95, 96, 98, 99, 100, 101, 102, 103, 104, 106, 107, 108, 109, 111, 114, 116, 117, 118, 121, 122, 125, 126, 127, 맴128, 129, 131, 132, 133, 134, 145, 168, 222, 226, 227, 228, 229
Newton, 18, 19, 83, 84, 85, 112, 134, 170, 229, 230
Nidintu-Sin, 163
Nippur, 155, 162, 171, 172
Olmstead, 152, 170
Olympiad, 180, 181, 182, 183, 184, 185, 186, 187, 188, 189, 190, 191, 192, 193, 194, 195, 196, 197, 201, 207, 208, 209, 210
Oppenheim, 167
orthodox rabbis, 13, 27
Othniel, 48, 50, 58, 59, 64
Panin, 64
Parker, 158, 160, 171, 172
Paros, 212
Pasargadae, 151
Peloponnesian War, 135, 147, 169, 174, 175, 178, 180, 185, 188, 213
Perinthians, 142
Persepolis, 44, 118, 119, 131, 135, 148, 149, 150, 151, 152, 169, 198
Persepolis Fortification Tablets, 152
Persepolis Treasury Tablets, 152
Persian, 15, 16, 24, 26, 27, 28, 31, 32, 33, 35, 36, 37, 38, 39, 43, 70, 71, 74, 75, 93, 97, 100, 103, 104, 106, 108, 112, 113, 114, 115, 116, 117, 118, 119, 120, 121, 130, 131, 134, 135, 137, 138, 139, 140, 141, 142, 143, 144, 145, 146, 147, 148, 149, 151, 152, 153, 154, 155, 156, 158, 160, 162, 164, 165, 166, 167, 168, 169, 170, 172, 173, 180, 182, 183, 190, 195, 197, 200, 211, 214, 215, 223, 226, 228
Pharez, 51, 52
Philip of Macedon, 142, 194
planetary and lunar observations, 155
Plataea, 120, 210, 211, 213, 214
Plutarch, 201, 205, 207, 208, 210, 211, 216, 232
Pre-Millennial, 23
Pre-Tribulational, 23
priest of Bel, 143
Pseudo-Smerdis, 38, 113, 114, 115
Ptolemy, 15, 16, 17, 18, 19, 20, 26, 27, 28, 37, 38, 39, 69, 70, 71, 80, 86, 93, 95, 99, 106, 112, 131, 137, 138, 143, 144, 145, 147, 148, 150, 158, 160, 162, 163, 164, 165, 167, 168, 170, 173, 193, 194, 198, 199, 200, 201, 204, 212, 225, 227, 228, 229, 230
Ptolemy II Philadelphus, 144
Pythagorean teaching, 203
Rabbi Akiva, 30
Rabbi Simon Schwab, 28
REDEMPTION TIME, 21
registers, 82, 83, 86
Returnees, 99
Roman, 15, 167, 173, 218, 221, 231, 232
royal genealogy, 52
Sachs, 153, 154, 155, 156, 158, 159, 160, 170
Salamis, 114, 120, 127, 139, 140, 180, 208, 210
Sanballat, 103, 104, 105, 106, 107, 108, 109, 111, 129, 130, 133, 145, 228
Sanballat governor of Samaria, 105
Sanballat II, 108
Saros Tablet, 153, 154, 156, 158, 170
Savile, 165, 172
Schwab, 29, 30, 43
Scofield Bible, 35
Second Coming, 24, 66
Sedar Olam, 14, 16, 22, 24, 25, 26, 27, 28, 29, 30, 31, 40, 41, 42, 145, 146, 200, 223

Sedar Olam Rabbah, 24, 145
Seder Olam Zuta, 95

INDEX OF WORDS AND PHRASES

Septuagint, 42, 119, 125
Seraiah, 13, 42, 81, 87, 89, 90, 91, 93, 94, 227
Servers, 99
Sestos on the Hellespont, 120
seven plenteous years, 23
seven years of dearth, 23
Seventy Week, 3, 5, 13, 14, 15, 16, 22, 28, 29, 31, 32, 33, 36, 42, 44, 66, 69, 71, 74, 75, 76, 80, 103, 116, 117, 128, 145, 168, 225, 226, 228, 229
Seventy Weeks of Daniel, 5, 15, 28, 31, 66, 229
seventy-one years after the Temple dedication, 79
siege of Naxos, 164
Simon the Just, 112, 134
Siniddin, 163
Sir Edward Denny, 3, 20, 229
Sir Isaac Newton, 18, 82
Sir Robert Anderson's, 14, 82
slaying of Seraiah, 89
solar, 16, 18, 24, 39, 40, 42, 45, 70, 158, 185, 203
solar year, 18, 42, 45, 70, 158, 185
Solomon, 12, 14, 30, 40, 47, 52, 54, 61
Sparta, 137, 173, 176, 180, 181, 182, 183, 184, 185, 186, 187, 188, 189, 190, 191, 192, 193, 194, 195, 196, 205, 206, 209, 213, 217
St Paul, 36
standard chronology, 5, 26, 65, 214
Susa, 79, 124, 137, 147, 148, 149, 150, 153
Talcht-i-Rustam, 151
Talmudic authority, 30
Talmudic rabbis, 29, 146, 200
Temple, 3, 5, 14, 16, 18, 20, 21, 23, 24, 26, 27, 30, 32, 33, 34, 36, 37, 39, 40, 44, 47, 51, 54, 55, 60, 61, 62, 69, 70, 71, 73, 77, 78, 79, 80, 82, 83, 84, 86, 88, 94, 95, 97, 98, 99, 100, 101, 102, 103, 111, 122, 123, 125, 126, 129, 133, 145, 177, 191, 219
tested, 5
Themistocles, 38, 122, 135, 139, 164, 165, 180, 181, 196, 209, 210, 214

Theopompus, 175, 177, 178, 179, 184, 187, 190, 194, 196
Theopompus of Chios, 177, 178, 179
Thiele, 13, 14, 19, 20, 22, 40
three great time spans, 58
three periods, 22, 26, 27, 58
three periods (*), 22, 58
threefold cord, 86
Thucydides, 117, 120, 135, 147, 148, 164, 165, 173, 174, 175, 177, 178, 179, 180, 185, 187, 190, 203, 208
Timaeus, 176, 179, 188, 190, 201, 206, 207, 213, 216
Times of the Gentiles, 36, 37, 41, 131, 229
Tiribazus, 141
Tissapherus, 140
Tobiah, 77, 101, 102, 103
Traditional Chronology, 70, 81, 82, 85, 88, 90, 92, 95, 98, 100, 112, 228
Trinitarian Bible Society, 32
Ululu, 158
Umasu, 153, 154, 155, 156, 157
Unger, 77, 79, 82, 114, 118, 119, 132, 134
Uruk, 153
Ussher, 13, 17, 18, 19, 20, 22, 24, 25, 26, 31, 32, 35, 36, 39, 40, 41, 55, 61, 65
Venus, 155
Westcott and Hort text, 32
William Lloyd, 17
Xenophon, 117, 147, 148, 173, 174, 175, 176, 177, 179, 182, 185, 187, 189, 193, 194, 208, 209, 231
Xerxes, 18, 44, 69, 70, 79, 92, 93, 94, 100, 113, 114, 115, 116, 117, 118, 119, 120, 121, 122, 127, 129, 134, 135, 137, 138, 139, 140, 142, 143, 144, 145, 146, 147, 148, 149, 150, 151, 152, 153, 154, 160, 162, 163, 164, 165, 166, 167, 170, 172, 174, 178, 180, 181, 182, 186, 198, 199, 203, 204, 206, 208, 211, 212, 213, 214, 216, 225, 228
Xerxes cannot be the Artaxerxes of Ezra and Nehemiah, 122
Xerxes was co-regent, 18
Yamauchi, 134, 135, 137, 150, 169, 170
Yeb, 105
Yoma 69a of the Babylonian Talmud, 111
Yose (Josi) ben Halafta, 30

Youngs Concordance, 86
Zechariah, 24, 28, 33, 43, 44, 69, 97, 98, 116, 125
Zerubbabel, 13, 15, 18, 23, 28, 33, 34, 73, 81, 82, 83, 85, 88, 89, 93, 94, 95, 96, 97, 102, 125, 227, 228

BIBLIOGRAPHICAL SOURCES

ENCYCLOPEDIA AND DICTIONARY ENTRIES

"Akiva", *Encyclopedia Judaica.*
"Archontes", The Oxford Classical Dictionary, Second Edition. "Artaxerxes", *Encyclopedia Iranica.* "Bar Kokhba", *Encyclopedia Judaica.*
"Eratosthenes", *The Oxford Classical Dictionary,* Second Editioa
"Ezra", *Cyclopedia of Biblical, Theological, and Ecclesiastical Literature.*
"Greece", *Encyclopedia Judaica.*
"History", *Encyclopedia Britannica,* 20th Edition.
"History", *Encyclopedia Judaica*
"Marmor Parium", *An Encyclopedia of the History of Classical Archaeology,* 1996.
"Messiah", *Encyclopedia Judaica.*
"Mishna", *Encyclopedia Judaica.*
"Persia", *Encyclopedia Judaica.*
"Sanballat", *Encyclopedia Judaica.*
"Seder Olam", *Encyclopedia Judaica.*
"Simeon the Just", *Encyclopedia Judaica.*
"Sparta", *The Oxford Classical Dictionary,* Second Edition.
"Yose ben Halafta", *Encyclopedia Judaica.*

GENERAL

Anstey, Martin. *The Romance of Bible Chronology.* London: Marshall Brothers Ltd., 1913.

The Apocrypha, (Authorized Version). Cambridge: Cambridge Univ. Press. Aristotle.

Athenian Constitution. The Loeb Classical Library.

Barag, Dan P. "Some Notes on a Silver Coin of Johanan the High Priest", *Biblical Archaeologist,* Sept. 1985.

Barber G.L. *The Historian Ephorus,* London: Cambridge Univ. Press, 1935.

Beecher, Willis J. *The Dated Events of the Old Testament.* Philadelphia: Sunday School Times, 1907.

Bickerman, E. J. *Chronology of the Ancient World,* Revised Edition. London: Thames and Hudson, 1980.

Bivar, A.D.H. "Achaemenid Coins, Weights and Measures", *The Cambridge History of Iran*. Vol. II, 1985.

Bullinger, E. W. *The Companion Bible*. Grand Rapids: Zondervan Bible Publishers, 1979.

Burstein, Stanley M *The Babylonica of Berossus*. Malibu, California: Udona Publications, 1978.

Clay, A.T. *Legal and Commercial Transactions Dated in the Assyrian, Neo-Babylonian and Persian Periods, Chiefly from Nippur*. Philadelphia: Univ. of Penn., 1903.

Clay, A.T. *Business Documents of Murashu Sons of Nippur, Dated in the Reign of Darius 11*. Philadelphia: Univ. of Penn., 1904.

Clay, A.T. *Business Documents of Murashu Sons of Nippur, Dated in the Reign of Darius 11, Supplement*. Philadelphia: Univ. Museums, 1912.

Cowley, A.E. *Aramaic Papyri of the Fifth Century B. C.* Oxford: Oxford Univ. Press, 1923.

Cross Jr., Frank M. "The Discovery of the Samaria Papyri", *Biblical Archaeologist,* 4, 1963.

Cross Jr., Frank M "Aspects of Samaritan and Jewish History in Late Persian Times", *Harvard Theological Review,* 59, July 1966.

Curtis, John. *Ancient Persia* London: British Museum Publications, 1989.

Dandamaev, MA. *A Political History of the Achaemenid Empire*. Leiden: E.J. Brill, 1989.

Denny, Edward B. *Forgiveness Seventy and Sevenfold*. London: James Nisbet and Co., 1849.

Diodorus Siculus. *The Library of History*. The Loeb Classical Library.

Dionysius of Halicarnassus. *Roman Antiquities*. The Loeb Classical Library.

Dolen, Walter R. *The Chronology Papers*. BeComingOne Papers, httpy/onelaw.comAjeone/cp.3b.htm, 1996.

Epstein, I; editor. *The Babylonian Talmud,* London: Soncino Press, 1938.

Ewan, G. *Chronology*. Unpublished booklet, n.d.

Fendel, Zechariah. *Charting the Mesorah: Creation through Geonim*. New York: Haskafah Publ., 1994.

Fensham, Charles. *The Books of Ezra and Nehemiah*. Grand Rapids: Eerdmans Publ. Co., 1982.

BIOGRAPHICAL SOURCES

Figulla, H.H. *Business Documents of the New-Babylonian Period*. London and Philadelphia: Publications of the Two Museums, 1949.

Fraser, P.M *Eratosthenes ofCyrene*. London: Oxford Univ. Press, 1970.

Frye, Richard N. *The Heritage of Persia*. New York: Mentor, 1966.

Gill, John. *Gills Commentary,* Grand Rapids: Baker Book House, 1980.

Gilmore, John. *The Fragments of the Persika ofKtesias*. London: Macmillan and Co., 1988.

Grayson A.K. *Assyrian and Babylonian Chronicles*. Locust Valley, New York: J.J. Augustin Publ., 1975.

Hallock, R.T. *The Evidence of the Persepolis Tablets*. Cambridge: Middle East Centre, 1971.

Hayes, C.J. and Hanscom, J.H. *Ancient Civilizations*. New York: Macmillan, 1968.

Henry, Matthew. *Matthew Henry's Commentary,* 6 Volumes. New York: Fleming H. Revell Co., n.d.

Herodotus, *The Histories,* Translated by George Rawlinson. London: Everyman Library, 1996.

Hewlett, John. *A Vindication of the Authenticity of the Parian Chronicle*. London, 1789.

Hilprecht, H.V. and Clay A.T. *Business Documents ofMurashu sons of Nippur, Dated in the Reign of Artaxerxes I*. Philadelphia: Univ. of Perm., 1898.

Hornblower, Simoa "Persia", *The Cambridge Ancient History,* Second Edition, Vol. VI, 1994.

Hornblower, Simon; editor. *Greek Historiography*. Oxford: Clarendon Press, 1994.

Jackson, A. V.Williams. *Persia Past and Present*. London: Macmillan, 1906.

Jacoby, Felix. *Die Fragmente Der Griechischen Historiker*. Berlin and Leiden, 1923-58.

Jamison, Robert. *JFB Commentary,* 6 Volumes. London: Collins Sons Ltd., n.d.

Jones, Floyd N. *Chronology of the Old Testament,* 2nd Edition. Houston: F.J.Ministries, 1993.

Josephus, Flavius. *The Works ofJosephus, Antiquities of the Jews*. Translated by William Whiston. Peabody, Massachusetts: Hendrickson Publ., 1957.

Keil, C.F. *Ezra Nehemiah Esther*. Grand Rapids: Eerdmans Publishing Co., n.d

Kent, Roland G. *Old Persian Grammar Texts Lexicon.* New Haven, Connecticut: American Oriental Society, 1950.

Kidner, Derek. *Ezra and Nehemiah,* Leicester, England: Inter-Varsity Press, 1979.

Kuhrt, Amelie. "Babylonia from Cyrus to Xerxes", *The Cambridge Ancient History,* Second Edition, Vol.IV, 1988.

Lindsay, Gordon. *God's Plan of the Ages,* 4th Edition. Dallas: Christ For All Nations Inc., 1971.

Lumen. *The Prince of the House of Judah.* London: Elliot Stock, 1905.

Manetho. *The LoebClassical Library.*

McFall, Leslie. "A Translation Guide to the Chronological Data in Kings and Chronicles", *Bibliotheca Sacra.* Jaa-Mch. 1991.

Mosshammer, Alden A. *The Chronicle ofEusebius and Greek Chronographic Tradition.* London: Associated University Presses, 1979.

Newton, Isaac. *The Chronology of Ancient Kingdoms Amended.* London: Histories and Mysteries of Man Ltd., 1988.

Newton, Robert R. *The Crime of Claudius Ptolemy.* Baltimore: John Hopkins Univ. Press, 1977.

Olmstead, AT. *History of the Persian Empire - Achaemenid Period* Chicago: Univ. of Chicago Press, 1948.

Oppenheim, A. L. "The Babylonian Evidence of Achaemenian Rule in Mesopotamia", *The Cambridge History of Iran,* Vol. II 1985.

Paine, Frank L. *The Miracle of Time.* Somerset, England: Shiloah Ministries, 1994.

Parker, R.A. and Dubberstein, W.A. *Babylonian Chronology 626B.C.-A.D.75.* Providence, Rhode Island: Brown Univ. Press, 1956.

Panin, Ivan. *Bible Chronology.* Burnaby B.C.: The Association of the Covenant People, 1950.

Pentecost, Dwight. *Things to Come.* Grand Rapids: Dunham Publ. Co., 1958.

Pfeiffer, Rudolf. *History of Classical Scholarship.* Oxford: Clarendon Press, 1968.

Plutarch. *Aristides.* The Loeb Classical Library.

BIOGRAPHICAL SOURCES

Plutarch. *Lycurgus*. The Loeb Classical Library.

Plutarch. *Numa*. The Loeb Classical Library.

Plutarch. *Themistoctes*. The Loeb Classical Library.

Porter, B. and Moss, R.L.B. *Topographical Bibliography of Ancient Egyptian Hieroglyphic Texts, Reliefs and Paintings*. Oxford: Oxford Univ. Press, 1927-1960, Vol. VII.

Praakcn, Donald W. *Studies in Greek Genealogical Chronology*. Lancaster, Pennsylvania: Lancaster Press, 1943.

Prideaux, Humphrey. *The Old and New Testament Connected to the History of the Jews*. Oxford: Oxford Univ. Press, 1851.

Sachs, A.J. "A Classification of the Babylonian Astronomical Tablets of the Seleucid Period", *Journal of Cuneiform Studies, 2,* 1948.

Sachs, A.J.; editor, *Late Babylonian Astronomical and Related Texts Copied by T.G.Pinches and J.W.Strassmaier*. Providence, Rhode Island: Brown Univ. Press, 1955.

Sachs, A. J. "Achaemenid Royal Names in Babylonian Astronomical Texts'", *American Journal of Ancient History,* 2,1977.

Samuel, AlanE. *Greek and Roman Chronology*. Munich: Oscar Beck, 1972.

Sancisi-Weerdenburg, H. and Kuhrt, A.; editors. "The Greek Sources", *Achaemenid History*. Leiden: E.J.Brill, Voi.H, 1987.

Savile, B.W. "Revelation and Science", *Journal of Sacred Literature and Biblical Record,* Series 4, April 1863.

Schwab, Simon. "Comparative Jewish Chronology", *Dr. Joseph Breuer Jubilee Volume*. New York: Philipp Felheim Inc. 1962.

Stolper, D. "Mesopotamia, 482-330 BC", *The Cambridge Ancient History,* Second Edition, Vol. VI, 1994.

Stolper, Matthew W. "Some Ghosts from Achaemenid Babylonian Texts". *Journal of Hellenic Studies,* 108,1988.

Tadmor, Hayim. "Judah", *The Cambridge Ancient History,* Second Edition, Vol. VI, 1994.

Thucydides. *History of the Peloponnesian War,* Translated by Rex Warner. London: Penguin Books, 1972.

Unger, MerrilL *Unger's Commentary on the Old Testament*. Chicago: Moody Press, 1981.

Van Driel, G. "The Murashus in Context", *Journal of the Economic and Social History of the Orient*, 32, 1989.

Ware, A. E. *The World in Liquidation*. London: Simpkin Marshall Ltd., 1953.

Wiesehofer, Josef. *Ancient Persia from 550BC to 650AD*. London: LB.Tauris Publ., 1996.

Williamson, H.G.M. "The Historical Value of Josephus *Jewish Antiquities* XI297-301", *The Journal of Theological Studies*, 28, 1977.

Williamson, H.G.M. *Ezra andNehemiah*. Waco Texas: Word Books Publ., 1985.

Xenophon *A History of My Times* (Hellenica), translated by Rex Warner. London: Penguin Books, 1979.

Yamauchi, Edwin H. *Persia and the Bible*. Grand Rapids: Baker Book House, 1990.

ABOUT THE AUTHOR

Dr. J. A. Moorman studied for a while at the Indianapolis campus of Purdue University, attended briefly Indiana Bible College, and graduated from Tennessee Temple Bible School. Since his graduation, he has been involved in church planting, Bible Institute teaching, and extensive distribution of Scriptures and gospel tracts in Johannesburg, South Africa from 1968—1988, and in England and London since 1988. More recently he has been seeking to get Scripture portions into Latin Europe. He married his wife, Dot, on November 22, 1963.

Dr. Moorman has written the following scholarly books defending the King James Bible and the Hebrew, Aramaic and Greek Words that underlie it:

1. *When the King James Bible Departs from the So-Called "Majority Text"*.
2. *Early Manuscripts, Church Fathers, and the Authorized Version.*
3. *Forever Settled.*
4. *Missing in Modern Bibles—The Old Heresy Revived.*
5. *The Doctrinal Heart of the Bible—Removed from Modern Versions.*
6. *Samuel P. Tregelles—The Man Who Made the Critical Text Acceptable to Bible Believers.*
7. *8,000 Difference Between the Textus Receptus and the Critical Text.*

All of these scholarly and well-documented works by Dr. Moorman are replete with manuscript and other evidence which he has gleaned from his own vast resources as well as references found in the British Museum and other libraries in the London area.

Pray for this humble friend of this vital cause as he continues his evangelistic, research, and preaching ministries.

Dr. Moorman is currently pastor of Bethel Baptist Church in London, England and is serving as a missionary to England and Europe. He is known for standing on street-corners many hours handing out gospel tracts throughout England and Europe. May God bless his unfailing service to the Lord Jesus Christ.

www.ingramcontent.com/pod-product-compliance
Lightning Source LLC
Chambersburg PA
CBHW081220170426
43198CB00017B/2667